A CASEBOOK ON **Roman**

AMERICAN PHILOLOGICAL ASSOCIATION

CLASSICAL RESOURCES SERIES

Sander M. Goldberg, Series Editor

A CASEBOOK ON
Roman Property Law

Herbert Hausmaninger and Richard Gamauf

TRANSLATED WITH INTRODUCTION,
SUPPLEMENTARY NOTES, AND GLOSSARY BY

George A. Sheets

OXFORD
UNIVERSITY PRESS

OXFORD
UNIVERSITY PRESS

Oxford University Press, Inc., publishes works that further
Oxford University's objective of excellence
in research, scholarship, and education.

Oxford New York
Auckland   Cape Town   Dar es Salaam   Hong Kong   Karachi
Kuala Lumpur   Madrid   Melbourne   Mexico City   Nairobi
New Delhi   Shanghai   Taipei   Toronto

With offices in
Argentina   Austria   Brazil   Chile   Czech Republic   France   Greece
Guatemala   Hungary   Italy   Japan   Poland   Portugal   Singapore
South Korea   Switzerland   Thailand   Turkey   Ukraine   Vietnam

Published by Oxford University Press, Inc.
198 Madison Avenue, New York, New York 10016

www.oup.com

Oxford is a registered trademark of Oxford University Press

Originally published as Casebook zum römischen Sachenrecht,
MANZ Studienbuch, 10. Auflage, MANZ'sche Verlags- und
Universitätsbuchhandlung, Wien 2003.

© 2003 MANZ'sche Verlags- und Universitätsbuchhandlung GmbH, Wien

Library of Congress Cataloging-in-Publication Data
Digesta. English & Latin. Selections.
A casebook on roman property law / Herbert Hausmaninger and Richard Gamauf ;
    Translated with Introduction and Supplementary Notes by George A. Sheets.
    p. cm.
    Translation of: Casebook zumr?mischenSachenrechtt.
        ISBN 978-0-19-979111-8—ISBN 978-0-19-979113-2   1. Property (Roman law)—
Examinations, questions, etc.   I. Gamauf, Richard, 1964-   II. Hausmaninger, Herbert.
Casebook zum römischenSachenrecht.   III. Title.
    KJA2436.A2D54 2011
    346.45'63204—dc22   2011004598

9 8 7 6 5 4 3 2 1
Printed in the United States of America
on acid-free paper

Contents

Chapter II: Keeping Possession and Losing Possession

Appendix *321*

Case Analysis of Gai. D 41.1.5.1 (Case 8) *321*
Case Analysis of Ulp. D 41.2.13 pr. (Case 47) *324*

Index of Sources *326*

Translator's Glossary of Latin Terms and Phrases *333*

Translator's Preface

In recent years the study and teaching of Roman law has found an increasing presence in U.S. colleges and universities. Two textbooks that have helped to stimulate and sustain this interest are Professor Bruce W. Frier's *A Casebook on the Roman Law of Delict* (Scholars Press, 1989) and *A Casebook on Roman Family Law* (APA Classical Resources series, no. 5: Oxford University Press, 2004), the latter co-authored with Professor Thomas A. J. McGinn. Both of these texts are modeled after the German-language casebooks by Professor Herbert Hausmaninger (University of Vienna) on the Roman law of contracts and Roman property law, respectively. The latter, entitled *Casebook zum römischen Sachenrecht*, is currently in its 10th edition (MANZ Verlag, 2003), now co-authored with Professor Richard Gamauf (University of Vienna). The book before you is an authorized translation of that edition.

I originally prepared this translation for use in a Roman Law course that I teach in the Law School and in the Department of Classical and Near Eastern Studies at the University of Minnesota. Subsequently, it seemed that the book might be of use in a wider range of instructional settings. To make that more practical, I have added a Translator's Introduction that provides an overview of the history of Roman law and the complex nature of its relationship to the Anglo-American legal tradition. Supplementary notes and translations have also been introduced throughout the text in order to clarify terminology and concepts that might be unfamiliar to readers not trained in the civil law tradition. Longer supplements are footnoted as "Translator's notes." Shorter glosses are simply embedded in the text and set off with square brackets.[1] All glosses in parentheses originally appeared in parentheses in the German source-text. Finally, for easier reference, a "Translator's Glossary" of Latin Terms and Phrases has been added at the end of the book.

I am grateful to the American Philological Association and Professor Sander Goldberg, editor of the APA Textbook Series, for supporting this project. I also thank Professor Boudewijn Sirks, Regius Professor of Civil Law at Oxford University, for serving as one of the manuscript referees and making excellent suggestions for improvements to it. He is not, of course, responsible for any errors that remain.

George A. Sheets

Minneapolis, July 2011

---

[1] In the Latin case-texts and their translations square brackets have a different signification: see fn. 38 to Case 57 for an explanation.

Translator's Introduction

Definition of Roman Law

The term "Roman law" is commonly used in a variety of senses. Most literally, it refers simply to the law that regulated aspects of the lives of the citizens of ancient Rome. In this historical sense, Roman law was of course not something that remained always the same over time and place. It was an evolving tradition of substantive rules, legal procedure, and implicit or explicit policy goals. Two sets of events are commonly, even if somewhat arbitrarily, taken to mark the historical bookends of this tradition in antiquity. At the beginning of the tradition is the publication in written form of a body of customary rules and procedures that collectively constitute the "Law of the Twelve Tables" ("tables" being a translation of Latin *tabulae*, referring to large panels upon which the laws were said to have been inscribed originally). According to tradition, this publication (actually a two-step process involving first ten tables and then two more) took place in 450 BCE, a time when Rome itself was scarcely more than a moderately sized town with a river port and surrounding agricultural land. Jumping ahead nearly 1,000 years, we come to the other bookend: the summative revision and restatement of Roman law that was promulgated between 529 and 534 CE in Constantinople at the command of the emperor Justinian. The intervening millennium witnessed the growth and decline of an empire that, at its apogee in the early second century CE, encompassed a territory of over 2 million square miles, within which there lived a population of perhaps 60 millions. In terms of legal development, the same millennium was marked by (1) the passage of thousands of legislative enactments—initially and quite sparingly by the assemblies of the Roman Republic, later and more frequently by a long line of Roman emperors; (2) the emergence and refinement of a body of procedural law within the competence of judicial magistrates—especially the Urban and Peregrine Praetors of the later Roman Republic and early Empire; and (3) the production of a professional legal literature in the forms of learned commentary to statutory and edictal law, *responsa* to particular cases (both actual and hypothetical), and pedagogical treatises. Notwithstanding this rich history, the essential unity of the Roman legal tradition can be documented by the fact that various provisions of the Twelve Tables could still be cited as valid law in the Justinianic restatement.

Our knowledge of ancient Roman law is drawn from numerous sources that survive from antiquity, but by far the most important of them are the Justinianic enactments referred to in the previous paragraph. In the European middle ages, this Justinianic legislation came to be called collectively the *Corpus Juris Civilis*, or *Body of (Roman) Civil Law*. The *Corpus Juris* is important not only because of what it contains, but even more because of the profound influence of that content on the legal and political traditions of Europe and of those states around the globe that have inherited, adopted, or otherwise developed legal and political systems that are rooted in those same traditions. The influence of the *Corpus Juris* accounts for a second sense in which the term "Roman law" is commonly used: i.e., to refer to the direct and/or indirect legacy of Roman legal thought in modern legal systems and their historical precursors. Many of the national legal systems in the world today, including the modern regime of public international law, have been built on the Roman legacy. Modern systems that are generically called "civilian" or "civil law" systems ultimately take that epithet from their historical indebtedness to the Roman civil law in this second sense. Beginning in the high middle ages and gathering momentum through the early modern period, Roman law in this second sense came to constitute the *ius commune* ("common law") of continental Europe. In some areas the *ius commune* served to provide a rich source of rules and procedures where local customary law was deemed to be deficient or silent. In others it provided the foundation and framework for productive new streams of positive law. In still other jurisdictions, the *ius commune* was adopted wholesale as the operative system of law. As Barry Nicholas observed: "[This] astonishing second life of Roman law gave to almost the whole of Europe a common stock of legal ideas, a common grammar of legal thought, and, to a varying but considerable extent, a common mass of legal rules."[1]

Over the past two centuries, the enactment of national legal codes in most civil law countries has mostly brought to an end the continuing influence of the *Corpus Juris* as a living source of law. However, since these national codes were themselves drafted within the tradition of the *ius commune*, Roman concepts and doctrines are still very much alive in derivative forms. The European civil codes, in turn, have provided models for national codes in many other parts of the globe. Indeed to a significant degree the modern codes can be seen as the current embodiments of a "third life" for Roman law.

Apart from the civil law systems, the largest family of legal systems in the world today is comprised of those based on the "English common law," a term not to be confused with the continental *ius commune*. Members of this family include, of course, the common law of the United States and of each of its member states except Louisiana. Historically, the English common law first takes recognizable shape with the establishment of crown courts and their distinctive writ procedure in the reign of Henry II (1154–1189). This was the very period when formal study of, and training in, texts of the *Corpus Juris* had begun in earnest in Bologna and elsewhere, including the emerging university of Oxford. Parallel developments were also occurring in the context of canon law, which in conceptual structure and procedure was cognate with the Roman civil law. Both the Romano-canon law and Roman civil law stood in marked contrast to the distinctive common law system of writ procedure and royal courts; yet despite their differences, the influence of the new (Roman) learning is readily detectable even in the earliest

---

[1] Nicholas, B. *An Introduction to Roman Law*, 3rd ed. Clarendon Law series. Oxford: Clarendon Press, 1962, 2.

treatises of the English common law.[2] By the Tudor period (1485–1603), however, the continental *ius commune* had come to be seen by English common lawyers as an alien legal tradition,[3] a view that hardened into orthodoxy in the 16th and 17th centuries, when the putative purity of the common law was identified with belief in a customary English constitution of immemorial antiquity.[4] Especially through the influential writings of Sir Edward Coke (d. 1634), belief in English exceptionalism and arguments based upon it would come to play an important role in the growing political and legal struggle between parliament and crown. This then gives us a third connotation that "Roman law" sometimes carries: i.e., a legal tradition that is presumptively alien to the Anglo-American common law. The reality, however, is more nuanced.

There can be no denying that the *ius commune* and continental jurisprudence have played substantial roles in the development of English and American law. Historically, the common law was primarily a law of procedure, and from an early period the continental *ius commune* often played a supplementary role in shaping the common law's substantive content. It is well known, for example, that English equity jurisprudence from its inception was heavily indebted both procedurally and doctrinally to the *ius commune*. The common law of wills and probate was largely derived from canon law. The law of admiralty is a civil law importation. The common law of tort and contract has borrowed fundamental distinctions and concepts from the Roman law of obligations, and in numerous judicial decisions over the centuries a civilian rule or doctrine has been used as a foil to sharpen or articulate a corresponding common law principle. As stated by Justice Blackburn in the celebrated case of *Taylor v. Caldwell*, 122 E. R. 309 (Q.B. 1863) at 314: "Although the Civil law is not of itself authority in an English Court, it affords great assistance in investigating the principles on which the law is grounded."

Turning more specifically to the law of property, one can readily see, despite the common law's still recognizable origin in feudal tenures, the massive influence of Roman law. For example, the law of easements and equitable servitudes is largely derived from Roman doctrine. So too are the concepts of prescription through adverse possession, of original and derivative possession, indeed of possession versus ownership, of real property versus chattel, of

---

[2] The first such treatise, known as "Glanvil" and bearing the title *Tractatus de legibus et consuetudinibus regni Angliae* ("Treatise on the Laws and Customs of the Kingdom of England"), published c. 1188, shows in its Prolog the unmistakable influence of Justinian's *Institutes*, while the treatise itself makes use of numerous terms borrowed from the Roman law. Bracton's *De Legibus et Consuetudinibus Angliae* ("On the Laws and Customs of England"), published c. 1235, is even more indebted to the *Institutes* in its organization and presentation of the English law.

[3] See Sir John Fortescue's *De laudibus legum Angliae* ("In Praise of the Laws of England") published *c.* 1470.

[4] Pocock, J. G. A. *The Ancient Constitution and the Feudal Law: A Study of English Historical Thought in the Seventeenth Century*. Cambridge: Cambridge University Press, 1957, 30–55.

accession, specification, confusion, first occupation, abandonment, treasure trove, and many others.

Quite apart from the continuing presence of Roman concepts and rules in both the civilian and common law traditions today, Roman property law is a subject of particular historical interest because of the role that Roman ideas about property have played in the political and intellectual history of the West. Justinian stated that the precepts of law in general were three: "to live honorably and honestly; to cause no harm to the other, and to give each person his or her due."[5] Broadly speaking, however, the first two of these propositions can be subsumed in the third, and at the heart of the third is the Roman notion of strong personal rights in private property. Arguably the legacy of that notion has defined much of the agenda and shaped much of the discourse of Western political philosophy since Roman times.

Content of the *Corpus Juris Civilis*

Leaving aside the later legislation of Justinian and his successors, three works constitute the definitive restatement of Roman law that Justinian promulgated. For the study of Roman property law the least important of the three is the "Code" (*Codex*), a collection of approximately 5,000 imperial "constitutions"—meaning the product of an emperor's legislative, judicial, or administrative enactments—from the reign of Hadrian (114–138 CE) to the date of the Code's promulgation (initially 529 CE, subsequently updated and reissued in 534 CE in the form that now survives).

The second Justinianic compilation, which is far more important for an understanding of Roman juristic reasoning and doctrine covering the entire range of Roman private law, is the *Digesta* or "Digest," a collection of excerpts from the most important and influential juristic literature of the Roman legal tradition. The task of compiling the Digest was formally begun in December of 530 CE, and the finished compilation was promulgated as positive law by Justinian exactly three years later (December 16, 533). As the act of promulgation states, "nearly 2000 books and more than 3 million lines" of juristic writing were reviewed and excerpted by the compilers for incorporation into a work of 50 books containing 150,000 lines of text. That work is the Digest. Since the source of every excerpt in the Digest is explicitly cited, we know that the excerpts are drawn from a total of 39 authors and 203 different works that range in size from a single "book" (manuscript scroll) to treatises of 80 and more "books." The great preponderance of the 39 authors lived and wrote in the first two and one half centuries of the Common Era, a period that

---

[5] Inst. Iust. 1.3: *iuris praecepta sunt haec: honeste vivere, alterum non laedere, suum cuique tribuere.*

modern scholars accordingly call the "classical period" of Roman jurisprudence. The Digest is therefore our chief witness to Roman legal science in its most productive era. The "post-classical" jurisprudence that has survived is, generally speaking, more prone to dogmatism and reliance on established authority rather than independent legal reasoning. Of the pre-classical jurists, called the "elders" (*veteres*) in later texts, undoubtedly the most important was Q. Mucius Scaevola "Pontifex" (d. 82 BCE), whose 18 books of *Commentary on the Civil Law* might fairly be considered to have marked the beginning of Roman juristic literature.

A third Justinianic compilation was published at the same time as the Digest and has been equally influential. This is the *Institutiones* ("Institutes") of Justinian, a textbook that was intended to serve as the authoritative introduction to and synopsis of the totality of Roman law. The four books of the Institutes follow an arrangement and program that was apparently created by the jurist Gaius nearly three centuries before. They present Roman law as a logically coherent and comprehensive system of doctrines. Justinian's framework has been immensely influential on how law, as an object of study and body of doctrine, came to be thought of in both civil and common law jurisdictions.[6] One can still detect its vestiges in the structure of modern civil codes in the Roman tradition.

---

[6] One will recall that this was the plan adopted by Bracton. Essentially the same plan would later be re-adopted by William Blackstone for his *Commentaries on the Laws of England* (first edition 1765–69, with many subsequent editions and reprintings). Blackstone served through much of the 19th century as the chief authority for academic training in law in both England and the United States.

Plan of this Casebook

Rather than expounding the subject of Roman property law as a collection of doctrines and rules, this casebook presents the reader with excerpts of Roman legal argument to illustrate the articulation and application of law to specific fact-situations. "Cases," consisting of brief excerpts from Roman juristic sources, are selected and grouped with a view to providing both an overview of the particular topic and an opportunity to explore its elements. The authors attach to each case a set of questions that invite the reader to, e.g., justify an argument, reconcile one holding with another, supply missing but necessary facts to account for a holding, and/or engage in other analytical activities. For the initial cases and occasionally thereafter, model answers are provided for the questions that have been posed. The goal behind all the questions, however, is to stimulate critical examination of rules and policies and to invite consideration of how such rules and policies might operate under other plausible circumstances.

In addition to covering the substance of Roman property law, this casebook aims to illustrate the survival and adaptation of elements of that law in selected modern European civil codes. This is accomplished by the authors' quotation of excerpts from, principally, three of the most important of those codes: the General Civil Code of Austria (*Allgemeines Bürgerliches Gesetzbuch,* abbreviated as *ABGB*), the German Civil Code (*Bürgerliches Gesetzbuch*, abbreviated as *BGB*), and the Civil Code of Switzerland (*Zivilgesetzbuch*, abbreviated as *ZGB*). The *ABGB* was adopted in 1812 and is, among the codes currently in force, second in date of adoption only to the French Civil Code enacted under Napoleon in 1804. In origin, however, it was the product of a much longer period of development than the French Civil Code and was more thoroughly rooted than the latter in the spirit of the Enlightenment. In his book on the Austrian legal system, Hausmaninger notes that "the ABGB reflects the ideology of rationalist Natural law in its latest phase, and contains much Roman law substance. It is a brief, clear, and flexible code containing general principles that permit later adaptation by scholars and judges."[7] He contrasts the Austrian Code with the later German and Swiss civil codes. Both of the latter reflect the influence of 19th-century German legal scholarship. "The defining characteristics of the *BGB*," writes Hausmaninger (p. 312), "are scholarly logic, abstraction, and systematization." He goes on to note that these characteristics have led to criticism of the *BGB*'s extreme conceptualism and complexity, and to judicial resistance to its limited scope for equitable interpretation according to circumstances. By contrast, the Swiss Code, was "draft[ed] in popular and clear language, in an easily accessible structure and with deliberately incomplete rules, permitting the judge to decide what is appropriate, reasonable, and equitable" (p. 316 ff., footnotes omitted).

---

[7] Hausmaninger, H. *The Austrian Legal System*, 3rd ed. Wien: Manz, 2003, 310.

By comparing and contrasting how the code excerpts in this book have adopted, adapted, or rejected a Roman rule or concept, it is possible for the reader to see the dynamic character of the Roman legal tradition in action. In order to facilitate comparison with corresponding rules and concepts in the common law tradition, additional texts and questions prepared by the translator have been mounted on a website that accompanies this translation: **www.oup.com/us/ romanpropertylaw.**

Further Reading

There are many excellent introductions to Roman law. An accessible overview of the entire subject with chapters devoted to each of the various substantive areas of Roman law is Andrew Borkowski and Paul du Plessis, *Textbook on Roman Law*, 4th ed. Oxford: Oxford University Press, 2010. The same text can serve as a sourcebook of representative texts and is accompanied by a website at http:// www.oup.com/uk/orc/bin/9780199276073. David Johnston's *Roman Law in Context*, Cambridge: Cambridge University Press, 1999, is a concise introduction to the social and economic setting of Roman law in the classical period. For the institutional and political history of Roman law in antiquity, see H. F. Jolowicz, *Historical Introduction to the Study of Roman Law,* 3rd ed. by B. Nicholas, Cambridge: Cambridge University Press, 1972. The sources of Roman law in three different senses—the legal, the historical, and the published—are helpfully identified and described by O. F. Robinson, *The Sources of Roman Law: Problems and Methods for Ancient Historians*. London: Routledge, 1997. For the subsequent history of the Roman legal tradition, see R. C. van Caenegem, *An Historical Introduction to Private Law*, Cambridge: Cambridge University Press, 1992; P. Stein, *Roman Law in European History*, Cambridge: Cambridge University Press, 1999. Corrections to the English translation of *The Digest of Justinian*, ed. A. Watson, rev. English-language edition. Philadelphia: University of Pennsylvania Press, 1998, continue to be posted on the *ius civile* website maintained by Professor Ernest Metzger at http:// iuscivile.com/materials/digest. A useful translation of Justinian's *Institutes* is P. Birks and G. McLeod, *Justinian's Institutes*, Ithaca, NY: Cornell University Press, 1987.

Abbreviations

ABGB	Allgemeines bürgerliches Gesetzbuch (Austrian Civil Code)
ANRW	*Aufstieg und Niedergang der römischen Welt*
BGB	Bürgerliches Gesetzbuch (German Civil Code)
BIDR	*Bulletino dell'Istituto di Diritto Romano*
C	*Codex Iustinianus*
D	*Digesta*
Inst. Iust.	*Institutiones Iustiniani*
JAP	*Juristische Ausbildung und Praxisvorbereitung*
OR	Obligationenrecht (Swiss Law of Obligations)
PS	*Pauli Sententiae*
RIDA	*Revue internationale des droits de l'antiquité*
SDHI	*Studia et documenta historiae et iuris*
TR	*Tijdschrift voor rechtsgeschiedenis*
WEX	Wahlfach Examinatorium
ZGB	Zivilgesetzbuch (Swiss Civil Code)
ZPO	Zivilprozeßordnung (Austrian Code of Civil Procedure)
ZRG	= ZSS
ZSS	*Zeitschrift der Savigny-Stiftung für Rechtsgeschichte, romanistische Abteilung*

Foreword on Textual Transmission and Text Criticism

The texts of classical Roman jurists contained in this book were composed between the first and third centuries CE but they have not been preserved for us in their original form. Because of the limited durability of papyrus as writing material, new copies of the texts had to be made on a regular basis. The copying process was prone to error and could produce various unintended alterations to the text if the copier miswrote a word, omitted part of the text, or erroneously introduced into the text an earlier reader's marginal or interlinear note. Additionally, there were intentional intrusions, as when a frequently used classical work (such as Ulpian's *Commentary on the Praetor's Edict*) was updated and re-published in the post-classical period—i.e., was changed to reflect innovations in the law since earlier publication of the same work.

Our modern knowledge of Roman legal thought largely rests on the form in which excerpts of juristic works were taken into the Digest of Justinian. The Emperor Justinian charged a commission of scholars with the task of excerpting, abbreviating, and adapting the classical jurists' writings with a view to removing what was obsolete and contradictory, so as to allow for a new Justinianic law. Without doubt, very substantial alterations were made to the juristic texts when the Digest was compiled from 530 to 533 CE.

Justinianic legal innovations are generally called "interpolations," even though they primarily consist not of additions to but omissions from the earlier texts. The Digest commission essentially limited itself to a task of abbreviation, by omitting case examples and citations of supporting or opposing opinions of other jurists. The haste of their work occasionally left evidence of disturbances to the text. These are recognizable by gaps in the argument or logical contradictions and for the most part can be explained as evidence of careless abbreviation or combination. Sometimes, indeed, such disturbances to the text had already appeared in pre-Justinianic times and were simply taken over by the compilers without correction.

Older literature on Roman law (from the end of the 19th to the middle of the 20th century) adopted an attitude to the texts of the Digest that suspected the compilers not only of formal alterations but also of substantive ones. The consensus of more recent scholarship is that the Digest for the most part preserves the thought of the classical jurists without alteration.

Acquiring Possession

Introduction

The Roman jurists drew a distinction between possession (*possessio*), meaning *actual control* over a thing, and ownership (*dominium, proprietas*) as the legal right to the thing: "Ownership and possession have nothing in common" (Ulpian);[1] "[Possession] is properly a factual, not a legal, issue" (Ofilius and Nerva the son).[2] Legal consequences, however, did attach even to mere possession, especially in its most significant manifestations: possession protected by "interdict" and possession leading to "prescription." These forms of possession could sometimes prevail even over the claims of a non-possessing owner, as in the following situations: (1) In order to preserve societal peace, the legal order must restrict the use of self-help in pursuing a legal right. That means that even wrongful possessors were given temporary protection (by the process of "interdict") against intrusion by third parties or even by the rightful owner himself.[3] (2) In order to settle disputed or uncertain legal claims, the legal order allows good-faith, undisturbed possession over a prescribed period of time to ripen into ownership (by "prescription").[4]

---

[1] *Nihil commune habet proprietas cum possessione* (Ulpian D 41.2.12.1).

[2] *Eam* (i.e., *possessionem*) *enim rem facti, non iuris esse* (Ofilius and Nerva filius D 41.2.1.3).

[3] Example: Smith steals from Jones a book that belongs to Brown. The thief, Smith, has a right of possession that is protected by interdict against Brown, the owner. The latter [Brown] may not recover the property by self-help but must bring a suit against Smith for surrender of the property.

[4] Example: Smith buys from Jones in good faith a piece of land that actually belongs to Brown. After Smith has occupied the land for two years, he has become the owner by prescription.

Moreover, whoever wishes to transfer ownership to a *res nec mancipi*[5] must provide *possessio* of the thing to the acquirer by means of *traditio ex iusta causa* (delivery pursuant to a recognized basis for acquisition, such as sale, gift, etc.). If the owner has lost possession of his property, he can sue to have the *possessor* surrender the property.

Because of the important legal consequences that attach to possession, the Roman jurists gave special attention to the processes of acquiring possession and losing possession.

The doctrine of the classical Roman jurists regarding acquisition and loss of possession is to be found chiefly in Title 41.2 of the Digest, entitled "Concerning the Acquisition and Loss of Possession."[6] As a guide to the creation of this title Justinian's compilers used Book 54 of the *Commentary on the Praetor's Edict* by the late classical jurist, Paul.

Paul begins his discussion of acquiring possession with detailed statements regarding *who* has the capacity to acquire possession. (D 41.2.1.2-22; D 41.2.2) Compare, for example, D.41.2.1.2-3: "We acquire possession through ourselves. A lunatic or ward acting without the authority of his guardian cannot commence to possess"[7] with D.41.2.1.5: "Likewise we acquire possession through a slave or a son who is in paternal power."[8] Then he gives a brief indication of *what* can be possessed. D.41.2.3 pr.: "Things that are corporeal can be possessed."[9] Finally he turns to the means; i.e., *how* one acquires possession. D.41.2.3.1: "We acquire possession '*corpore et animo*' [with body and intent]."[10]

We shall begin our discussion of possession with the *means* (types of acquisition) and at the conclusion take up the topic of capacity to acquire possession.

---

[5] Translator's note: *res nec mancipi* is property (*res*) that does not (*nec*) require the formal procedures of "mancipation" (*mancipatio*) or "surrender in law" (*in iure cessio*) to effect legal transfer of ownership. On the character of property that *did* require such formalities (*res mancipi*) see fn. 1 in the Introduction to chapter III.

[6] D 41.2: *De adquirenda vel amittenda possessione.*

[7] Paul D 41.2: *Apiscimur autem possessionem per nosmet ipsos. Furiosus et pupillus sine tutoris auctoritate non potest incipere possidere.*

[8] Paul D.41.2.1.5: *Item adquirimus possessionem per servum aut filium, qui in potestate est.*

[9] Paul D.41.2.3 pr.: *possideri autem possunt, quae sunt corporalia.*

[10] Paul D.41.2.3.1: *Et apiscimur possessionem corpore et animo.*

A. Means of Acquisition: *corpore et animo*

Apart from the exceptions to be discussed in subsection B, possession in principle can be acquired only *corpore et animo* (these terms of art are best used in place of translations) *Animus* [the nominative form of *animo*] is the intention to possess; *corpore* [lit. 'with body'] (the nominative form, *corpus*, is practically never used in this connection) means "by bringing about a physical relationship" to the thing that is to be possessed. The *animus* does not have to be expressly declared; often it is implicit in the act that brings about the physical relationship to the thing.

The measure of physical proximity that satisfies the prerequisite of acquiring possession *corpore* is examined by Roman jurists in numerous cases. In this connection one must take account of whether the acquisition concerns a movable piece of property or an immovable (land), and whether the acquisition is with the previous possessor's consent (derivative possession) or without it or against his will (original possession). The ability to exert control over the property is also at issue when there is the possibility of damage to the property by a third party (compare Cases 5 and 6 regarding the transfer of keys to a warehouse, and Cases 8 and 9 on acquiring possession of wild animals). We find both narrower and broader interpretations of this corporeal principle and, in the following discussion, we aim to analyze the most important of the pertinent case-distinctions. The *animus possidendi* ["intention of possessing"] is a topic that Cases 7 and 11 are particularly concerned with.

Literature:

Schulz, F. *Einführung in das studium der Digesten.* Tübingen: Mohr, 1916, 16 ff.
Gordon, W. M. *Studies in the Transfer of Property by* traditio. Aberdeen: University of Aberdeen, 1970, 44 ff.

CASE 1

D 41.2.3.1 (Paulus libro quinquagesimo quarto ad edictum)

Et apiscimur possessionem corpore et animo, neque per se animo aut per se corpore. quod autem diximus et corpore et animo adquirere nos debere possessionem, non utique ita accipendum est, ut qui fundum possidere velit, omnes glebas circumambulet: sed sufficiet quamlibet partem eius fundi introire, dum mente et cogitatione hac sit, uti totum fundum usque ad terminum velit possidere.

Translation: (Paul in book 54 of his *Commentary on the Praetor's Edict*)[11]

And we acquire possession *corpore et animo*, not *animo* alone nor *corpore* alone. But that we have said we must take possession *corpore et animo* should not be understood in an absolute sense to mean that he who wishes to possess a farm must walk around the entire farm (literally "every clod of earth"): it suffices to enter any part of the farm, provided the entry is with the intention and thought that one wishes to possess the whole farm up to its boundary.

Notes on the Text:

The text begins with a broad explanation of the principle "*apiscimur possessionem corpore et animo…*" ["we acquire possession *corpore et animo*, not *animo* alone nor *corpore* alone"]. The abstract principle is then interpreted (*ita accipiendum est*) by means of an example. On the use of *accipiendum est* ["should be understood"], see under Case 72.

The word *fundus* can mean either a country estate or a piece of land. In what follows we usually translate the term as "piece of land."

---

[11] The late classical jurist, Julius Paulus, was a pupil of Cervidius Scaevola and began his career in the same way as Ulpian, as an *adsessor* ["legal advisor"] to the Praetorian Prefect, Papinian. In common with Ulpian, therefore, he belonged to the *consilium* ["advisory council"] of Septimius Severus (193–211). Under Alexander Severus (222–235) he reached the rank of Praetorian Prefect, the highest imperial office. Paul is regarded as more original than the somewhat younger Ulpian, to whom is attributed a stronger tendency to dogmatic hardening of the originally more flexible legal concepts of the classical period.

Apart from his undoubtedly difficult and time-consuming official duties, Paul was an astonishingly productive juristic writer (*Notae* ["Notes"] on Julian, on Marcellus, on Scaevola, on Neratius, 16 books *ad Sabinum* ["Commentary on Sabinus"], 26 books of *Quaestiones* ["Legal Questions"], 23 books of *Responsa* ["Legal Opinions"]). Paul's *Commentary on the Praetor's Edict* is a monumental work of 80 books (papyrus rolls), in which the classical casuistic literature is critically collected, sorted out, and set forth from consistent systematic viewpoints. The compilers took many excerpts from the work into the Digest, thereby mostly removing, however, detailed citations of literature and reports of juristic disagreement. About one third of Paul's book 54, which dealt with possession and prescription, is preserved in the Digest.

Discussion Questions [with model answers]:[12]

1) How does one get possession of a piece of land, according to Paul?
2) What practical considerations argue for walking around the land's boundaries? What ones argue against it?
3) Would you answer the previous question differently depending upon the location and nature of the land?
4) Is Paul thinking of original (i.e., first) possession (without derivation of possession from a predecessor), or derivative (subsequent) possession?
5) Would you require different degrees of physical relationship as between original versus derivative possession of a piece of land?
6) What measures would an acquirer have to take, if the jurists did not let even a "walk around the entire farm" (*omnes glebas circumambulare*) constitute sufficient physical relationship?
7) What measures might satisfy a less strict conception of physical relationship, one that would not require any entry at all onto the property?
8) How could the acquirer express most clearly his intent to take possession of the whole property "up to the boundaries" (*usque ad terminum*)?

   — in the case of original possession?
   — in the case of derived possession?

Answers:

1) By stepping onto any part of the piece of land in question with the purpose of taking possession of the whole piece.
2) Pro: Publicity (acquisition will sometimes be more clearly recognizable by third parties); clear establishment of the boundaries avoids future disagreements with the neighbors. (*Fines demonstrare* ["to point out the boundaries"] is a seller's obligation, the acquisition of possession is of course a separate and independent issue.)
   Con: Impracticality (property boundaries can be clarified in other ways); from the viewpoint of "control" of the property it makes no qualititative difference from mere entry.

3) A "walk around the fields" would scarcely be reasonable in the case of an especially large or impassable property. An argument can be made for or against different treatments using the considerations listed under "2" above.
4) Probably of derivative possession (the normal case). Original possession would be thinkable in the case of a long-abandoned property, also when

---

[12] Translator's note: In the first two cases of this Casebook and occasionally thereafter the authors provide model answers for the Discussion Questions.

possession is acquired through *usucapio pro herede*,[13] as much as in the case of occupation by force (in that connection, however, see under Case 54).

5) Stricter requirements are sometimes needed in the case of original possession, in view of possible acts of third parties who also wish to gain possession. (Smith enters in the morning upon an ownerless piece of property with a view to taking possession, then he leaves it again; in the afternoon Jones begins to plow or fence in the property with a view to taking possession of it.)

6) Fence it in; cultivate it.

7) Point it out (from a neighboring plot or possibly an even greater distance).

8) — In the case of original possession: walk around the boundaries, fence it in, cultivate it, work the land in a manner that expresses a claim to the entire surface (not, say, just walking around or building on a part of the land without ever entering upon the remainder).

— In the case of derivative possession: manifesting directly to the preceding possessor (mostly by express declaration) the intention of taking possession of the whole property.

Compare with this Case:

§ 309 Austrian Civil Code:

Whoever has a piece of property in his control or custody is the holder of that property. If the holder of a piece of property has the intention of keeping it as his own, he is the possessor of it.[14]

§ 312 Austrian Civil Code:

Tangible, movable property is taken into possession by physically grasping it, removing it, or taking it into custody; immovable property is taken into possession by entering upon, marking the boundaries of, fencing, signposting, or working it …[15]

Literature:

Moehler, R. "Der Besitz am Grundstück, wenn der Besitzer es verlässt." *ZRG* 77 (1960) 52–124, 54 ff.

---

[13] Translator's note: *usucapio* (Anglicised as "usucapion" or "usucaption") literally means "taking by use." It refers to the acquisition of ownership through uninterrupted possession for a period fixed by law, a process called "prescription." *Pro herede* means "[acting in good faith as if] in the capacity of an heir."

[14] § 309 ABGB: Wer eine Sache in seiner Macht oder Gewahrsame hat, heißt ihr Inhaber. Hat der Inhaber einer Sache den Willen, sie als die seinige zu behalten, so ist er ihr Besitzer.

[15] § 312 ABGB: Körperliche, bewegliche Sachen werden durch physische Ergreifung, Wegführung oder Verwahrung; unbewegliche aber durch Betretung, Verrainung, Einzäunung, Bezeichnung oder Bearbeitung in Besitz genommen …

CASE 2

D 41.2.18.2 (Celsus libro vicensimo tertio digestorum)

Si venditorem quod emerim deponere in mea domo iusserim, possidere me certum est, quamquam id nemo dum attigerit: aut si vicinum mihi fundum mercato venditor in mea turre demonstret vacuamque se possessionem tradere dicat, non minus possidere coepi, quam si pedem finibus intulissem.

Translation: (Celsus in book 23 of his *Digesta*)[16]

If I have ordered the seller to place in my house that which I have bought, it is certain that I possess it, even if no one has yet touched it. Or if, after I have bought a neighboring piece of land, the seller in my tower points it out and says he is delivering *vacua possessio* ["unimpeded possession"], I begin to possess it no less than if I had set foot on the land.

Notes on the Text and Discussion Questions [with model answers]:

On *certum est* ("it is certain"), see below on Case 27. The text presents two fact-situations that are connected with *aut* ["or"]. It cannot be known if the jurist is responding to an actual question or just dealing with theoretical considerations. A systematic division of the passage recommends itself:

The first fact-situation:

1) The facts: buyer tells the seller to place the goods in the buyer's house. The seller complies with the instruction.
2) Legal question: has the buyer thereby acquired possession?
3) The jurist's decision: self-evidently (*certum est*) he has, even if no one in the house of the buyer has yet touched the goods.
4) Considerations: The buyer's intention to take possession is here unproblematic and will therefore not be discussed. The jurist instead considers how the physical relationship that affects the taking of possession should be established. In the normal case, delivery (*traditio*) of the goods is made

---

[16] Publius Iuventius Celsus (praetor 106, consul for second time 128, Governor in Thrace and Asia, member of Hadrian's *consilium*) is one of the most prolific jurists of the high classical period. His acumen and originality are sometimes accompanied by polemical assertiveness. Although he, like Neratius, was head of the school of juristic thought associated with Proculus, Celsus seems to have made his own contribution to overturning the traditional school controversies. Noteworthy are his abstract declarations regarding instruction in the sources of law and the methods of interpretation.

Celsus' principal work, *Digesta* in 39 books, follows the organization of the Praetor's Edict in books 1–27 and a standard sequence of *leges* ["statutes"] and *senatusconsulta* ["senatorial decrees"] in books 28–39. The work is relatively well preserved in Justinian's Digest (141 fragments).

into the hand of the buyer, who grasps the goods and takes them with him. Here, instead, an arrangement is made for subsequent delivery to the buyer's house.

a) Celsus states it as decided that with delivery of the property into the buyer's house it is not necessary for the buyer to have contact with it. Why is the jurist satisfied with the mere deposit of the goods absent any act of receiving them? Is he thinking only of the case where the seller comes with the goods into the house of the buyer, and the buyer is present and instructs him to put the thing down, or does the opinion also apply to the case of an agreement in the seller's shop with subsequent transfer to the buyer's house (in the buyer's absence)?

b) Does the buyer take possession if the seller leaves the thing *in front of* the house?

c) Does the buyer take possession of a thing left in front of his house if he has expressly agreed to that with the seller?

Answers:

a) The thing transferred into the house of even an absent buyer has clearly entered into his sphere of control.

b) If the buyer has instructed the seller to place the property *in* the house, possession does not count as passing before that point in time, in accordance with the instruction. Although one might sometimes assume a sufficient physical relationship before then, there is no taking of possession, because the buyer did not wish to take possession until that point in time. The seller has the obligation of careful safekeeping (*custodia*) up to that point. He is therefore liable for loss or damage to the property, since he did not deposit the property *in* the house, according to the agreement, but *in front of* the house.

c) The agreement of the parties cannot take the place of the required physical relationship. From the viewpoint of control, since there can be a considerable difference between whether the property is placed *in* or *in front of* the house, the Roman jurists reached different decisions according to the circumstances (the nature of the place, of the property, etc.).

The second fact-situation:

1) The facts: someone has purchased another piece of property that abuts onto his own. The seller points out the property to the buyer from a tower that is on the buyer's land and declares to the buyer that he, the seller, is delivering *vacua possessio* (i.e., turning over the vacated property).

2) Legal question: can one in this case speak of taking possession *corpore*?
3) The jurist's decision: yes, just as if the possessor had entered upon the property.
4) Considerations:

   a) Is it an important detail that a *neighboring* piece of land is at issue?
   b) Is it relevant to the decision that the piece of land is pointed out from *the buyer's* tower?
   c) How does this decision of Celsus relate to that of Paul D 41.2.3.1 (Case 1)?
   d) To what degree is pointing out a piece of property from a tower comparable to placing a thing in the house of the buyer?
   e) In spite of the collocation of the two fact-situations, could one make a distinction between their respective degrees of physical relationship?

Literature:

Gordon, W. M. *Studies in the Transfer of Property by* traditio. Aberdeen: University of Aberdeen, 1970, 50 ff.

CASE 3

D 46.3.79 (Iavolenus libro decimo epistularum)

Pecuniam, quam mihi debes, aut aliam rem si in conspectu meo ponere te iubeam, efficitur, ut et tu statim libereris et mea esse incipiat: nam tum, quod a nullo corporaliter eius rei possessio detinetur, adquisita mihi et quodammodo manu longa tradita existimanda est.

Translation: (Javolenus in book 10 of his *Letters*)[17]

If I should ask you to put down where I can see it the money that you owe me or something else, the effect is that you are immediately free of the debt and the coin or other thing becomes my property; for at the point when physical possession of the thing is retained by no one, it counts as having been acquired by me and having been delivered, in a manner of speaking, "by a long hand."

Notes on the Text:

The compilers have placed this text in Title 46.3 of the Digest, which is entitled "On Payments and Discharges of Debt."[18] The words *aut aliam rem* ["or something else"] could be a later intrusion or perhaps only an imprecise manner of speaking. The following word, *libereris* ["you are free of"] shows that this statement must concern a thing that is *owed*.

Facts of the case. Someone has asked his debtor to lay down the money, or something else that is owed, in front of his eyes. The debtor complies with this command.

Legal question. Is the debtor released from the debt as a result of that action? Does the creditor acquire possession of the thing?

Discussion Questions:

1) Does the command itself serve to release the debtor and give possession to the creditor, or is it necessary to complete the action that is commanded?
2) What significance would you attach to the spatial distance of the creditor from the thing and the possibility of action by a third party?
3) Based on this text, try to develop a definition of *traditio longa manu* ["delivery by means of a long hand"] and then see if pointing out a piece of land from

---

[17] The high classical jurist, L. Javolenus Priscus, worked in the second half of the first century after Christ (consul in 86, later governor of Germania superior, Syria, Africa, member of the *consilium* of Trajan and Hadrian). Chiefly he worked on critical study of the work of earlier jurists (Labeo, Cassius, Plautius). From his *Epistulae* ("Letters," in 14 books; the arrangement of the subject matter is not recoverable), 72 fragments are preserved in the Digest. The original letter form is not preserved in the fragments. Longer excerpts follow the *responsa* format (i.e., presentation of the subject – legal question – jurist's response).

[18] D 46.3: *de solutionibus et liberationibus.*

a tower (D 41.2.18.2 = Case 2) and leaving goods in the house of the buyer (same case) can be subsumed under your definition.

4) What is the meaning and importance of the provision: *quod a nullo corporaliter eius rei possessio detinetur* ["when physical possession of the thing is retained by no one"]?

Literature:

Eckardt, Bernd. *Iavoleni epistulae*. Berlin: Duncker & Humblot, 1978, 231 ff.

CASE 4

D 41.2.1.21 (Paulus libro vicensimo tertio ad edictum)

Si iusserim venditorem procuratori rem tradere, cum ea in praesentia sit, videri mihi traditam Priscus ait, idemque esse, si nummos debitorem iusserim alii dare. non est enim corpore et tactu necesse adprehendere possessionem, sed etiam oculis et affectu argumento esse eas res, quae propter magnitudinem ponderis moveri non possunt, ut columnas, nam pro traditis eas haberi, si in re praesenti consenserint: et vina tradita videri, cum claves cellae vinariae emptori traditae fuerint.

Translation: (Paul in book 54 of his *Commentary on the Praetor's Edict*)[19]

If I should order the seller in the presence of the thing to deliver it to my *procurator*[20] Priscus says that the thing is considered to have been delivered to me. [He says] the same is true if I order the debtor to give the money to another. For it is not necessary to take possession physically and with touching, but it can also be taken by means of the eyes and attitude. That is proved by those things which cannot be moved because of the greatness of their weight, like columns; for these are considered to have been delivered if the parties so agree in the presence of the property. Wine too counts as delivered, if the keys to the wine cellar have been delivered to the buyer.

Note on the Text:

On *videri* ("is considered"), see below under Case 72.

Discussion Questions:

Four cases are joined together here:

1) Acquiring possession by command to the seller in the presence of the property to deliver it to the acquirer's *procurator* ["agent"].

   a) Does the buyer's acquisition of possession occur at the instant of the command to the seller, or at the instant of the delivery to the *procurator*?
   b) Is the presence of the *procurator* at the giving of the command necessary?

---

[19] On the author and work, see Case 1 (D 41.2.3.1). The "Priscus" cited in the text could be Neratius (see Case 71: D 41.3.41) or Javolenus (Case 3: D 46.3.79), both of whom bore this cognomen.

[20] Translator's note: A *procurator* is a kind of agent who acts with the authorization of and on behalf of his principal.

2) Acquiring possession of owed money by the creditor's command to the debtor to deliver it to a third party.

   a) In this case is an agreement in the presence of a visible and counted sum of money necessary?

3) Acquiring possession of especially heavy objects (e.g., columns) by agreement between the seller and the acquirer in the presence of the property.

   a) What is the logical connection of this fact-situation with the first two fact-situations?

4) Acquiring possession of wine by delivering to the buyer the keys to the wine cellar.

   a) Is the jurist thinking of delivery of the keys in the cellar, in front of the cellar, or at any place?
   b) Would all four cases count as *traditio longa manu* (D 446.3.79: Case 3)?
   c) Under what conditions is the statement that one can take possession "by means of the eyes and attitude" valid?

Literature:

Gordon (Case 2 above) 47 ff.

Watson, A. "Acquisition of Ownership by *traditio* to an extraneus," *SDHI* 33 (1967) 194 ff. (reprinted in *Studies in Roman Private Law*. Rio Grande, OH: Hambledon Press, 1991, 114 ff.

CASE 5

D 18.1.74 (Papinianus libro primo definitionum)

Clavibus traditis ita mercium in horreis conditarum possessio tradita videtur, si claves apud horrea traditae sint: quo facto confestim emptor dominium et possessionem adipiscitur, etsi non aperuerit horrea: quod si venditoris merces non fuerunt, usucapio confestim incohabitur.

Translation: (Papinian in the first book of his *Definitions*)[21]

Possession of goods stored in a warehouse counts as delivered with delivery of the keys to the warehouse, provided the keys have been delivered at the warehouse. With this act the buyer immediately takes both ownership and possession, even if he has still not opened the warehouse. But if the wares were not the property of the seller, usucapion will begin from that point.

Note on the Text:

On *videtur* ("counts as"), see below under Case 72.

Discussion Questions:

1) Is delivery of the keys understood as a "symbolic" transfer of the goods (cf. "through symbols" in § 427 of the Austrian Civil Code, quoted below), or as an "actual" one?
2) How does Papinian conceptualize the acquisition of possession, since he requires that the keys be delivered in front of the warehouse and not in some other place?
3) Is it relevant whether other copies of the delivered keys exist, and who has them in hand?
4) Does it make a difference if the goods of more than one owner are in the warehouse? How about if all the goods in the warehouse are being transferred? What if only a part of them?

---

[21] Aemilius Papinianus rose to the summit of the imperial service. He was praetorian prefect from 203 to 212 CE. Paul and Ulpian at different times were his *adsessores*. Papinian was executed in 212 because he allegedly disapproved of the killing of Caracalla's brother and co-Emperor, Geta.

The works of Papinian, especially his 37 books of *Quaestiones* and 19 books of *Responsa*, present casuistic reasoning in its highest perfection. In spite of a difficult style and oftentimes extreme brevity of expression, Papinian is impressive for his brilliance and acumen. He was highly esteemed by the Compilers (numerous excerpts in the Digest) and still today counts in the law as one of the greatest Roman jurists.

Papinian's two books of *Definitiones* are the only juristic writing that survives under this title. As far as can be gleaned from the available excerpts, the work concerned itself with "refinements" of accepted legal principles.

5) Can someone deliver the goods in an unlocked warehouse merely by pointing out the warehouse without delivery of the keys?

Compare with this Case:

§ 426 Austrian Civil Code:

Movable property in general can only be transferred to another by physical delivery from hand to hand.[22]

§ 427 Austrian Civil Code:

However, in the case of goods that cannot be physically handed over because of their nature, like debts, cargoes, warehouse contents, or other collections, the law permits the transfer through symbols—by which the owner gives the transferee documents through which ownership is established, or transfers the means by which the transferee is placed in the position of taking exclusive possession of the goods, or by one's attaching a distinctive mark to the goods from which anyone can clearly recognize that the goods have been passed to another.[23]

Literature:

Gordon (Case 2 above) 57.

---

[22] **§ 426 ABGB:** Bewegliche Sachen können in der Regel nur durch körperliche Übergabe von Hand zu Hand an einen anderen übertragen werden.

[23] **§ 427 ABGB:** Bei solchen beweglichen Sachen aber, welche ihrer Beschaffenheit nach keine körperliche Übergabe zulassen, wie bei Schuldforderungen, Frachtgütern, bei einem Warenlager oder einer andern Gesamtsache, gestattet das Gesetz die Übergabe durch Zeichen; indem der Eigentümer dem Übernehmer die Urkunden, wodurch das Eigentum dargetan wird, oder die Werkzeuge übergibt, durch die der Übernehmer in den Stand gesetzt wird, ausschließend den Besitz der Sache zu ergreifen; oder, indem man mit der Sache ein Merkmal verbindet, woraus jedermann deutlich erkennen kann, daß die Sache einem andern überlassen worden ist.

CASE 6

D 41.1.9.6 (Gaius libro secundo rerum cottidianarum sive aureorum)

Item si quis merces in horreo repositas vendiderit, simul atque claves horrei tradiderit emptori, transfert proprietatem mercium ad emptorem.

Translation: (Gaius in the second book of his *Jurisprudence of Daily Life*, also known as the *Golden Rules*)[24]

Likewise if someone sells goods that are stored in a warehouse, he transfers ownership of the goods to the buyer as soon as he delivers the keys to the warehouse to the buyer.

Discussion Questions:

Gaius speaks of acquiring ownership. Since acquiring possession is a condition of acquiring ownership, the opinion of Gaius implies an affirmation of this means of acquiring possession.

In contrast with Papinian (Case 5), the Gaius passage lacks an indication that the delivery of keys must take place in front of the warehouse. This could be the result of an unintended omission from the text, a conscious juristic controversy regarding the necessity of delivering the keys in the presence of the property, or a difference in the fact-situations of the storage, in which delivery of the keys in front of the warehouse is necessary or not, depending on the circumstances.

Try to reconcile the differences between Gaius and Papinian (Case 5) by proposing appropriately different fact-situations. Could arguments from Case 2 (D 41.2.18.2) and Case 9 (D 41.1.55) be found in support of Gaius' opinion?

Literature:

Gordon (Case 2 above) 57.

---

[24] Gaius (both his full name and origins are unknown) was an outsider of classical jurisprudence. He worked as a teacher of law without the *ius respondendi*. His works (around 20 writings between 150 and 180 CE) are primarily didactic in purpose (easily graspable expressions of subject matter). They also reveal interests in legal history (e.g., a commentary on the Twelve Tables) but avoid discussion of legal controversies and cases. Consequently, among his colleagues and followers Gaius did not count as someone appropriate for citation. The importance of his contribution lies in the formulation of abstract doctrine and systematic description. The *Institutes* of Gaius (an introductory text in four books) have, through the medium of Justinian, decisively influenced law-teaching and codification up to modern times. The *Res Cottidianae* [*Jurisprudence of Daily Life*] (in seven books) is probably a version of the *Institutes* reworked by Gaius himself.

CASE 7

D 18.6.15[14].16 (Paulus libro tertio rerum epitomatorum Alfeni)

Materia empta si furto perisset, postquam tradita esset, emptoris esse periculo respondit, si minus venditoris: videri autem trabes traditas, quas emptor signasset.

Translation: (Paul in the third book of his *Excerpts from Alfenus*)[25]

If material that has been purchased is lost by theft after it has been delivered, he replied that the buyer bears the risk. If it has not yet been delivered, the seller bears it. Beams that the buyer has marked with his seal are understood to have been delivered.

Note on the Text:

On *videri* ("are understood as"), see under Case 72.

Discussion Questions [with model answers]:

1) What is meant by the statement: *periculum est emptoris* ("the buyer bears the risk")?
2) What rule applies with regard to the seller's risk and liability?
3) What objection can be made against acquiring effective possession (*corpore, animo*) of beams by merely "marking them with one's seal" (*signare*)?
4) Is it important how the buyer marks the beams? Whether he provides an explanation or not? Would it be necessary to know the practice of Roman lumber-trading in order to answer this question?
5) Would acquisition of possession also be possible by merely pointing?

Answers:

1) *Periculum est emptoris* means that the buyer bears the "price-risk": the risk of loss of the property through the operation of *force majeure* (fire, flood, robbery, etc.) passes to the buyer as soon as the sale is concluded, not waiting until delivery of the goods to the buyer. The buyer must pay the purchase price even if he does not obtain the goods.
2) Up to the delivery, however, the seller is liable not only for intentional or negligent damage to or destruction of the property, but he has in addition

---

[25] On Paul, see Case 1 (D 41.2.3.1). The republican-period jurist P. Alfenus Varus (cos. 39 BCE) wrote 40 books of *Digesta*, which were excerpted by Paul and supplemented with his own annotations. Alfenus is the only pre-classical jurist whose work is preserved for us in larger fragments (54 passages in the Digest).

a special duty of care, *custodia*, which places upon him the risk of theft in particular. In the case of theft after delivery, the buyer must pay the purchase price to the seller. In the case of theft before delivery, the seller must refund to the buyer any purchase price that has been received.

3) Just attaching one's seal (*signare*) to the beams may not indicate with sufficient clarity that the buyer wishes to take possession at that moment. He might only be intending to distinguish the marked beams from the whole stock and to take possession later (through collection or delivery).

4) By giving an explanation, it would certainly be clear whether the *animus possidendi* ["intention of possessing"] was present. A standard conforming practice in Roman lumber-trading would permit the marking (*signare*), or the manner in which the buyer does it, to serve as an implied expression of his intention one way or another.

5) Yes; the physical relationship would be entirely sufficient: cf. D 41.2.1.21 (columns etc.)—Case 4.

CASE 8

D 41.1.5.1 (Gaius libro secundo rerum cottidianarum sive aureorum)

Illud quaesitum est, an fera bestia, quae ita vulnerata sit, ut capi possit, statim nostra esse intellegatur. Trebatio placuit statim nostram esse et eo usque nostram videri, donec eam persequamur, quod si desierimus eam persequi, desinere nostram esse et rursus fieri occupantis: itaque si per hoc tempus, quo eam persequimur, alius eam ceperit eo animo, ut ipse lucrifaceret, furtum videri nobis eum commisisse. plerique non aliter putaverunt eam nostram esse, quam si eam ceperimus, quia multa accidere possunt, ut eam non capiamus: quod verius est.

Translation: (Gaius in the second book of his *Jurisprudence of Daily Life*, also known as the *Golden Rules*)[26]

The question was asked whether a wild beast that has been wounded sufficiently that it can be caught should be understood as immediately becoming our property (i.e., the property of the person who wounded it). Trebatius was of the opinion that it did and that it remained our property, as long as we continued to pursue the beast. But if we desisted from pursuing it, the beast ceased to be ours and became once again the property of whoever takes it first (*occupatio*). Therefore if, while we are pursuing the beast, another takes it with the intention of securing the profit of it, he is deemed to have committed a theft against us. Most jurists, however, hold that the beast does not become ours until we capture it, since many things can happen to prevent us from capturing it. This is the more correct opinion.

Notes on the Text:

The text stands in Title 41.1 of the Digest, which is entitled "On acquiring ownership of things" (*de adquirendo rerum dominio*). The compilers have used a large fragment from the *res cottidianae* of Gaius to introduce the subject. Gaius first discusses acquisition of *original* ownership according to the *ius gentium* ["law of (all) peoples"], beginning with the statement that one acquires ownership of wild beasts as *res nullius* (ownerless property) by means of *occupatio* (taking possession with the intent of owning): D 41.1.1 and 3 (Case 94). He then considers in the passage above the necessary physical relationship for acquiring possession.

Gaius refers to an old juristic controversy (*quaesitum est* ["it was asked"]) and then expresses his agreement (*verius est* ["is more correct"]) with the dominant opinion of most jurists (*plerique*) against Trebatius. On *intellegatur* ("should be understood"), see on Case 72.

The phrase *verius est* ("[this] is more correct")—i.e., the better juristic opinion or solution to the problem—signals no more than a controversy. The jurist makes

---

[26] On the author and work, see Case 6 (D 41.1.9.6). The jurist who is cited, Gaius Trebatius Testa, was a younger friend of Cicero and legal adviser to Caesar and Augustus.

a choice between two positions that have been expounded by colleagues or predecessors (see Cases 118 and 125), or he contrasts a previous opinion with his own. Occasionally *verius* may just express a judgment after weighing two viewpoints that one and the same jurist has set forth.

Discussion Questions:

1) Express in your own words the fact-situation, legal question, and the two opposed juristic opinions.
2) Is the wounding essential to the view of Trebatius or could mere pursuit of a slow animal (one that is easily caught) be sufficient to acquire possession?
3) Does Gaius take a position contrary to the principle of acquiring possession *longa manu* ["with a long hand"] (Case 3)?
4) How would Gaius have viewed the killing of the animal before any immediate grasping of it?
5) Would Gaius have likely decided differently if the animal had been fatally wounded or his capture had been inevitable as a practical matter?
6) Should one under certain conditions recognize the claim of a pursuer who ought not to be interfered with by another (e.g., as a reward for his time and effort, or in order to avoid conflicts)?

n.b.: Regarding this case see the model case-analysis in the **Appendix** at p. 321.

Compare with this Case:

Pierson v. Post, 3 Cai. R. 175, 2 Am. Dec. 264 (Supreme Court of New York 1805)

Post, a hunter on horseback with a pack of hounds, was pursuing a fox and already near to killing him, when suddenly Pierson, a farmer, jumped in between, killed the fox, and carried him off. Post sued Pierson and won at trial. Pierson appealed the judgment.

The appellate court overturned the decision, saying: "The case now under consideration is one of mere pursuit, and presents no circumstances or acts which can bring it within the definition of occupancy..."

In dissent Judge Livingston wrote: "... [O]ur decision should have in view the greatest possible encouragement to the destruction of an animal so cunning and ruthless in his career. But who would keep a pack of hounds...and for hours... pursue the windings of this wily quadruped, if...a saucy intruder, who had not shared in the honors or labors of the chase, were permitted to come in at the death, and bear away in triumph the object of pursuit?... [A] pursuit like the present... which must inevitably and speedily have terminated in corporal possession, confers such a right to the object of it as to make anyone a wrongdoer who shall interfere and shoulder the spoil."

On this American case and the Roman law foundations of its decision, see most recently Charles Donahue, Jr. "Animalia ferae naturae: Rome, Bologna, Leyden, Oxford, and Queen's County, NY, in *Studies in Memory of A. Arthur Schiller*, Roger S. Bagnall, A. Arthur Schiller, and William Vernon Harris eds., Leiden: Brill, 1986, 39–63.

Literature:

Knütel, Rolf. "Von schwimmende Inseln, wandernden Bäumen, flüchtenden Tieren und verborgenen Schätzen," in *Rechtsgeschichte Und Privatrechtsdogmatik*, R. Zimmermann, R. Knütel, and J. Peter Meincke, eds. Heidelberg: C. F. Müller, 1999, 565 ff.

CASE 9

D 41.1.55 (Proculus libro secundo epistularum)

In laqueum, quem venandi causa posueras, aper incidit: cum eo haereret, exemptum eum asbstuli: num tibi videor tuum aprum abstulisse? et si tuum putas fuisse, si solutum eum in silvam dimisissem, eo casu tuus esse desisset an maneret? et quam actionem mecum haberes, si desisset tuus esse, num in factum dari oporteret, quaero. respondit: laqueum videamus ne intersit in publico an in privato posuerim et, si in privato posui, utrum in meo an in alieno, et, si in alieno, utrum permissu eius cuius fundus erat an non permissu eius posuerim: praeterea utrum in eo ita haeserit aper, ut expedire se non possit ipse, an diutius luctando expediturus se fuerit. summam tamen hance puto esse, ut, si in meam potestatem pervenit, meus factus sit. sin autem aprum meum ferum in suam naturalem laxitatem dimisisses et eo facto meus esse desisset, actionem mihi in factum dari oportere, veluti responsum est, cum quidam poculum alterius ex nave eiecisset.

Translation: (Proculus in the second book of his *Epistles*)[27]

A boar fell into a snare that you had placed there for the purpose of hunting. While he was held there I took him out and brought him away. Are you to understand that I have made off with your boar? If you think that he was your property, would he have ceased to be your property, or remained so, if I had released him into the forest? Further, I ask which action you could bring against me if he ceased to be your property, or whether you could bring an action *in factum*.[28] He answered: Let us see if it makes a difference whether the snare was placed on public or private ground; and if on private ground, whether on mine or someone else's; and if on someone else's, whether with or without the permission of the landowner. Additionally, was the boar so caught in the snare that he could not free himself, or would he have freed himself after more struggle? In my judgment, however, the essence of the case is that the boar has become my property if it has come into my

---

[27] Proculus, an early classical jurist, lived in the first half of the first century CE. He assumed, probably in 33 CE, the leadership of the legal school subsequently named after him. The *Epistles*, his principal work, is represented in the Digest in 33 fragments. Legal problems, issues, and answers were discussed in them. Therefore the practical case at issue is less often in the foreground than theoretical expansions. The drawing of numerous distinctions imparts a didactic and systematizing character to the work.

[28] Translator's note: the reference of *in factum* here is to an action for wrongful damage to, or destruction of, property, as is made clear by the concluding words of this case. The procedural distinction between an action *in factum* (utilizing a formula based "on what was done") as opposed to *in ius* (utilizing a formula based "on the law" as expressed in statutory language) was instituted by the Urban Praetor to provide a remedy in cases that did not fit precisely into one of the statutorily authorized actions. For that reason actions *in factum* are sometimes in English called "actions on the case," which draws attention to the similarity in origin and function between the Roman action *in factum* and the common law tort of "trespass on the case," out of which the common law tort of "negligence" ultimately evolved.

control. If you release my wild boar into his natural state of freedom, and he therefore is my property no longer, an *actio in factum* must be given to me, just as it has been decided when someone threw another's cup off a boat into the sea.

Notes on the Text:

On *videor* ("are you to understand that I ..."), see on Case 72. Consider this passage only from the viewpoint of acquiring possession, in regard to which Proculus provides the following considerations:

1) The boar is caught in the snare, or he could have freed himself.
2) The snare lies on land that is:

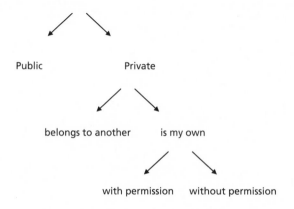

Public   Private

belongs to another   is my own

with permission   without permission

Discussion Questions:

1) Is hunting on another's land permissible in Rome? Cf. Case 94.
2) What effect does the landowner's prohibition have on the hunter's acquisition of possession and ownership?
3) Using the abstract viewpoints of Proculus, try to construct specific fact-situations in which the person who places the snare would and would not acquire possession. Regarding these, compare Case 55.
4) Jones places a snare on Smith's land despite Smith's prohibition. A boar is caught in the snare. Jones sees the boar from a distance and goes to the boar with the intent of seizing him. Suddenly Smith comes up, cuts through the snare, and lets the boar free. Has Jones already acquired possession? Does the decision depend on whether the boar could have freed itself after a short while?
5) How do you decide the case in which someone takes fish out of a net that someone else has put in the sea?

Compare with this Case:

Young v. Hichens, 6 Q. B. 606 (1844)

Fisherman Young discovered a school of mackerel from his boat, laid his net around them in a half-circle, and drew it together leaving a small gap. His men beat the water with their rowing and thereby prevented the fish from escaping. Before they could close the net the boat of defendant Hichens sailed through the gap into the circle and completely fished it out. The court decided: "It does appear almost certain that the plaintiff would have had possession of the fish but for the act of the defendant; but it is quite certain that he had not possession."

Literature:

Krampe, C. *Proculi Epistulae. Eine frühklassische Juristenschrift*. Karlsruhe: C. F. Müller, 1970 (Freiburger rechts- und staatswissenschaftliche Abhandlungen, 34), 65 ff.

CASE 10

D 41.2.51 (Iavolenus libro quinto ex posterioribus Labeonis)

Quarundam rerum animo possessionem apisci nos ait Labeo: veluti si acervum lignorum emero et eum venditor tollere me iusserit, simul atque custodiam posuissem, traditus mihi videtur. idem iuris esse vino vendito, cum universae amphorae vini simul essent. sed videamus, inquit, ne haec ipsa corporis traditio sit, quia nihil interest, utrum mihi an et cuilibet iusserim custodia tradatur. in eo puto hance quaestionem consistere, an, etiamsi corpore acervus aut amphorae adprehensae non sunt, nihilo minus traditae videantur: nihil video interesse, utrum ipse acervum an mandato meo aliquis cutodiat: utrubique animi quodam genere erit aestimanda.

Translation: (Javolenus in the fifth book of his *Excerpts from the Posthumously Published Writings of Labeo*)[29]

Labeo says that one can acquire possession of certain things *animo*: for example, when I buy a pile of logs and the seller authorizes me to take them away, the pile is seen to have been transferred as soon as I have taken custody of them. The same rule [i.e., that one can take possession *animo*] applies to the sale of wine when all the wine-vessels are present at once. But let us consider, he says, whether this is a physical delivery, since it makes no difference whether the safe-keeping is transferred to me or to whomever I appoint. I believe the issue turns on this: whether the pile of logs or the wine is understood to have been delivered, even if they have not been physically touched. I see no difference whether I guard the woodpile myself or someone else does so at my command. In both cases it is to be accepted that possession has been acquired by a kind of mental act (*animo*).

Discussion Questions [with model answers]:

1) Is Labeo thinking of an agreement in the presence of the woodpile or in some other place?
2) Does Labeo require a guard to be placed in order to effect possession of wine vessels?
3) Consider to what degree the decisions in Cases 2, 3, 4, 5, 7, and 9 can be understood as applicable to woodpiles on the one hand and wine vessels on the other.

---

[29] On Javolenus, see Case 3 (D 46.3.79). The jurist M. Antistius Labeo, mentioned in the title and the text, was a pupil of Trebatius. On account of his creative brilliance he became the most prominent representative of early classical jurisprudence. He is supposed to have been barred from the consulship because of his opposition to Augustus. Since he did not have the *ius respondendi*, he worked chiefly as a teacher of law and as a juristic writer. The school that was later called the "Proculians" goes back to him. Labeo's prolific corpus (over 400 books) is known to us through only two abridgments: Paul wrote an epitome and commentary on the *Pithana* in 8 books (see Case 37), and Javolenus did the same with the *posteriores* (i.e., posthumously published works).

4) What do Labeo and Javolenus understand by the term *animo*? Are they thinking of a waiver of the requirement of physical relationship?

5) Does it matter what the personal *status* of the guard is?

Answers:

1) Earlier and in another place, because, as follows from the ensuing example of wine vessels, Labeo also recognizes that possession can be acquired by agreement in the presence of the thing. The buyer of the woodpile could therefore have taken immediate possession by agreement in the presence of the woodpile, without having to appoint a guard, unless he intended to take possession by means of appointing a guard.

2) No. Agreement in the presence of the thing is enough for taking possession.

3) Woodpile (the applicable principle is the coming into the possessor's sphere of control): cf. placement of goods in the house, the boar in the snare. Wine vessels (the applicable principle is agreement in the presence of the thing): cf. pointing out land from a tower, setting something down *in conspectu*, delivery of keys in front of a warehouse.

4) Javolenus and Labeo do not waive the need for a physical relationship. The purchaser's *custodia* ["custody," i.e., taking responsibility for safekeeping] is still required. The waiver applies only to the requirement of physical contact (*adprehensae non sunt* ["they have not been grasped"]), which was called for by an older doctrine and was identified with the words *corpore possidere* ["to possess bodily"].

5) Yes. The later formulated rule that states that possession can be acquired *animo nostro corpore alieno* ["with our intent and another's body"] restricts the physical element to the mediation of a person "in power."

Literature:

Hausmaninger, H. "Besitzerwerb solo animo," in *Festgabe für Arnold Herdlitczka zu seinem 75. Geburtstag. Dargebracht von seinen Schülern und Freunden*, R. Arnold, Franz Horak, and Wolfgang Waldstein, eds. München: W. Fink, 1972, 117 ff.

CASE 11

D 18.6.1.2 (Ulpianus libro vicesimo octavo ad Sabinum)

Si dolium signatum sit ab emptore, Trebatius ait traditum id videri: Labeo contra, quod et verum est: magis enim ne summutetur, signari solere quam ut traditum videatur.

Translation: (Ulpian in the 28th book of his *Commentary on the* Ius Civile *of Sabinum*)[30]

Trebatius says that if the buyer has marked a wine vessel with his seal, it counts as delivered. Labeo says not, which is correct. For the seal is more often affixed in order to prevent substitution rather than to signify delivery.

Note on the Text:

On *videatur* ("signify") see on Case 72. *Signare* means "to seal" or "affix one's seal to"; *summutare* ("to substitute, exchange") could refer to the vessel but also to the wine.

The facts: A wine vessel is marked with the buyer's seal. It remains in the seller's wine cellar.

The legal question: Has the buyer taken possession with his seal?

Discussion Questions:

Trebatius affirms that *traditio* ["delivery"] has taken place and therefore presupposes that the buyer has taken possession by agreement with the seller, who wishes to surrender possession. Labeo says *traditio* has not taken place.

---

[30] The late classical jurist, Domitius Ulpianus, was a pupil and, like Paul, an *adsessor* to the Praetorian Prefect, Papinian. He was a member of the imperial *consilium* and himself finally became Praetorian Prefect under Alexander Severus. In 223 he was killed in a revolt of the praetorians. His *Commentary on the Praetor's Edict* had approximately the same compass as that of Paul and presents a comprehensive discussion of classical legal literature. Ulpian's *Commentary on the* Ius Civile (51 *libri ad Sabinum* ["51 books on 'The Civil Law' by Sabinus"]) breaks off with consideration of *rei vindicatio* [an owner's lawsuit for recovery of property in the possession of the defendant]. We do not know if the work remained unfinished or a part was lost. The Compilers excerpted Ulpian's work more extensively than all other classical writers: almost one third of the entire Digest stems from his work.

Massurius Sabinus, who is cited in the title reference, was an early classical jurist. He obtained the *ius respondendi* ["right of giving authoritative legal opinions"] from Tiberius, being the first person of equestrian rank to do so. The "Sabinian" school of legal teaching goes back to him. His most important work, *tres libri iuris civilis* ["Three books on the *ius civile*"], was studied and discussed throughout the whole classical period and served as the topic of extensive commentaries by Pomponius, Paul, and Ulpian (all of which were entitled *ad Sabinum*).

On Trebatius see Case 8 (D 41.1.5.1); on Labeo see Case 10 (D 41.2.51).

1) Analysis of Trebatius' legal reasoning:

   a) Does a seal suffice to establish the physical relationship?
   b) Is the buyer's *animus possidendi* ["intention of possessing"] present?
   c) Is this *animus* already expressed through the purchase itself?
   d) Do you think that for Trebatius the issue of transfer of possession would also arise even without the sealing or other touching of the vessel (*dolium*) in question?
   e) Can the decision of Trebatius be supported by Alfenus D 18.6.15 [14].1 (Case 7)?

2) Analysis of the contrary view of Labeo:

   a) Does the degree of physical relationship not satisfy him?
   b) How does he assess the factor of intent (both seller's and buyer's) and how does he explain his decision?
   c) Following Labeo, how might someone take possession of a *dolium*?
   d) What legal consequences are tied to the moment of *traditio*?
   e) What considerations support Ulpian's apodictic approval of Labeo's opinion?

B. Special Cases: Acquisition *"animo"*

It seems that the doctrine formulated by the late classical jurist Paul, "we acquire possession *corpore et animo*, not *animo* alone nor *corpore* alone" (D 41.2.3.1: Case 1), is not without exceptions. In some jurists, one finds the notion that possession can be acquired *animo* alone: see the considerations of the early classical Labeo in D 41.2.51 (Case 10), which permit a manifestation of intent to count as acquiring possession without any physical contact. If in such cases (e.g., appointing someone to watch a woodpile) one speaks of acquisition *animo*, of course the requirement of a certain physical relationship has not been waived. Labeo himself raises the question of whether one should speak of acquiring possession *corpore* in these cases too.

If a *detentor* ([a mere"holder of property," such as] a lessee, a tenant, a safekeeper, or a borrower) purchases it from the possessor (or is given it or obtains it on loan, etc.), he obtains possession through simple agreement with the seller, insofar as there is no requirement for the thing to be returned and subsequently delivered by an act of physically handing it over. (See under Case 13 [D 12.1.9.9]: *animo enim coepit possidere* ["he commences to possess it *animo*"].) Even in this case of so-called *traditio brevi manu*[31] ["delivery with a short hand"], however, the physical relationship is not missing; instead it is already present to a sufficient degree, so that there need be no issue of physical delivery and act of acquisition. The formulation, "one can take possession *animo*," is therefore imprecise, since in reality there is no waiver of the physical element.

Although the so-called *constitutum possessorium*[32] ["possessory agreement"] is not identified in the sources as a way of acquiring possession *animo*, it belongs in this section because of its meaning: someone can take possession by mere agreement with the erstwhile possessor, if the latter agrees to hold the property henceforth in the name of the acquirer, who in this way satisfies the physical relationship.[33]

---

[31] The term is not authentic. It is clearly based on D 23.3.43.1 (*brevi manu acceptum a muliere et marito datum*) and is misleading in that no *traditio* (delivery) occurs, although the legal effect of delivery does take place (cf. Case 14 [D 6.2.9.1]: *pro tradita erit accipienda*).

[32] The term dates from the 16th century. It comes from the statement *possessio autem recedit, ut quisque constituit nolle possidere* in D 41.2.17.1.

[33] Translator's note: *traditio brevi manu* and *constitutum possessorium* are reciprocal principles. Both involve intent to transfer possession. Under the former, an existing holder becomes a possessor; under the latter, an existing possessor becomes a holder.

Literature:

Hausmaninger (Case 10 above) 113 ff.
Schulz, F. *Einführung in das studium der Digesten*. Tübingen: Mohr, 1916, 63 ff.
Gordon (Case 2 above) 13 ff.
Wacke, Andreas. *Das Besitzkonstitut als Übergabesurrogat in Rechtsgeschichte und Rechtsdogmatik : Ursprung, Entwicklung u. Grenzen d. Traditionsprinzips im Mobiliarsachenrecht.* Köln: Hanstein, 1974, 8 ff.

a. *Traditio brevi manu*

CASE 12

D 41.1.9.5 (Gaius libro secundo rerum cottidianarum sive aureorum)

Interdum etiam sine traditione nuda voluntas domini sufficit ad rem transferendam, veluti si rem, quam commodavi aut locavi tibi aut apud te deposui, vendidero tibi: licet enim ex ea causa tibi eam non tradiderim, eo tamen, quod patior eam ex causa emptionis apud te esse, tuam efficio.

Translation: (Gaius in the second book of his *Jurisprudence of Daily Life*, also known as the *Golden Rules*)[34]

Sometimes even without *traditio* the simple intention of the owner suffices to accomplish the delivery of the property, as when I sell you something that I have lent or rented to you or deposited with you. Although I did not deliver it to you for this reason, I make it yours by consenting to its remaining with you due to the purchase.

Discussion Questions:

1) On the basis of what shared attribute does Gaius group together loans, tenancies, and deposits? Can you think of further examples?
2) Could Gaius have named other grounds for acquisition besides a purchase?
3) Gaius speaks of acquiring ownership. To what extent does his decision also apply to acquiring possession?
4) Why does Gaius not mention the *animus possidendi* ["possessory intent"] of the acquirer?

Compare with this Case:

§ 428 Austrian Civil Code:

A thing is delivered by declaration, if the transferor makes his will known in a manner capable of proof that henceforth he holds the thing in the name of the acquirer; or the acquirer of the thing henceforth is to possess by legal property-right the thing that he previously held without legal property-right.[35]

Literature:

Gordon (Case 2 above) 37 ff.

---

[34] On the author and work, see Case 6 (D 41.1.9.6).

[35] **§ 428 ABGB:** Durch Erklärung wird die Sache übergeben, wenn der Veräußerer auf eine erweisliche Art seinen Willen an den Tag legt, daß er die Sache künftig im Namen des übernehmers innehabe; oder, daß der übernehmer die Sache, welche er bisher ohne ein dingliches Recht innehatte, künftig aus einem dinglichen Rechte besitzen solle.

CASE 13

D 12.1.9.9 (Ulpianus libro vicensimo sexto ad edictum)

Deposui apud te decem, postea permisi tibi uti: Nerva Proculus etiam antequam move-antur, condicere quasi mutua tibi haec posse aiunt, et est verum, ut et Marcello videtur: animo enim coepit possidere. ergo transit periculum ad eum, qui mutuam rogavit et pot-erit ei condici.

Translation: (Ulpian in the 26th book of his *Commentary on the Praetor's Edict*)[36]

I deposited 10 gold coins with you. Later I permitted you to use the money. Nerva and Proculus say that even before the coins have been removed from where you were keeping them, they can be the subject of a *condictio*,[37] like loans of money (*mutua*). And that is correct, as Marcellus too agrees: for he [the depositary] has begun to possess them *animo*. Therefore the risk has passed to whoever requested the loan, and one can bring a *condictio* against him.

Notes on the Text:

Ulpian's discussion occurs in D 12.1: *de rebus creditis si certum petetur et de condictione* ["Concerning loaned property and the action called *condictio* when a sum certain will be sought"], in the context of discussing lawsuits based on loans.

The facts: Smith and Jones make a contract regarding the safekeeping of 10 pieces of gold. Later the depositor permits the money to be used by the depositary at the latter's request.

Making a contract	Altering the contract by	Actual use
for safekeeping	allowing use of the money	of the money

Legal question: What are the legal consequences of agreeing to permit use of the money? To what degree do these consequences take place already before actual use of the money?

---

[36] On Ulpian see Case 11 (D 18.6.1.2). The jurist mentioned in the text, M. Cocceius Nerva (the father) died in 33 CE. He preceded Proculus as the leader of the law school that was later called the "Proculian" school. He was a close adviser of the Emperor Tiberius and is cited by later authors. The title of his work is not known. On Proculus see Case 9 (D 41.1.55). On Marcellus see Case 18 (D 41,2,19. pr).

[37] Translator's note: A *condictio* is a lawsuit for recovery of the value of property. The key point here is that ownership of the lent money, and therefore possession too, has been transferred without further physical movement simply by the transferor's grant of permission to use the money.

Discussion Questions:

A *depositum* (contract for safekeeping) is a "real contract"[38] that comes into existence with the transfer of a movable to the care of a safekeeper, who is obligated to safekeep the item without compensation and to return it at any time. The receiver of the property becomes a *detentor* ["holder"], and he holds the property in the name of the depositor. He may not use the property.

A *mutuum* (contract for loan) is a "real" contract by which a sum of money (or other fungible property) is transferred to the ownership of a receiver, and it is agreed that the receiver is to return the same sum (or quantity of fungible property) in the future. The receiver of the loan becomes the owner. He may use the property.[39]

Nerva and Proculus accept that a contract originally for safekeeping [*depositum*] is transformed into a contract for loan [*mutuum*] by the granting of permission to use the [deposited] property.[40] They therefore proceed from the assumption that the safekeeper has requested the depositor to permit use of the money (*qui mutuam rogavit* ["whoever requested the loan"]). A contract comes into being through mutual agreement. A depositor's permission to use the property, if it had not been requested, would be an offer that required acceptance [by the depositary]. The safekeeper's acceptance could follow expressly or by implication (spending the money), but prior to this acceptance there would be no contract.

A *mutuum* requires transfer of ownership, and this presupposes acquiring possession. Since the safekeeper of the 10 coins is a *detentor*, it is not necessary that he give the money back to the depositor and obtain the loan amount by re-delivery: in fact he need not remove the money even once from his cashbox. Already the early classical Nerva and Proculus allowed him to obtain possession by the fiction of a *traditio brevi manu* ("delivery with a short hand"). Marcellus and ultimately Ulpian agreed with this solution. (Possibly a different opinion was held by the rival Sabinian school: see under Case 16).

Animo coepit possidere ["he has begun to possess *animo*"] expresses the idea that acquiring possession requires no physical activity if there already exists a sufficient physical relationship to the property. The *detentor* obtains possession for himself solely by mutual agreement with the existing possessor.

---

[38] Translator's note: "Real contracts" (*obligationes re contractae*) in Roman law are a type of contract that arises from the entrusting of property to the custody of another person. They are called "real" because the contractual obligation is linked to the disposition of the property (*res* in Latin) itself.

[39] Translator's note: A contract for the loan of money (*mutuum*) must be distinguished from a contract for the loan of non-fungible property. The latter is called *commodatum* and does not transfer ownership. See D.13.6.8 (Pomponius): *rei commodatae et possessionem et proprietatem retinemus* ("we retain both the possession and the ownership of property that is loaned as *commodatum*")

[40] In this context we need not consider further whether *quasi mutua* ["as if loaned"] means that the jurists have treated the legal relationship not as *mutuum* but as like *mutuum*.

Periculum means the risk of accidental loss of the property. Basically "the owner bears the risk" (*casum sentit dominus*). Since the recipient of a loan becomes the owner of the loan's value, he must return the sum obtained, should it be lost even without his fault (e.g., by fire, theft, etc.). But as safekeeper of the money, he would have been liable only for intentional or grossly negligent action that prevented its return. This narrower liability can be explained by the difference in interests: a *depositum* serves the needs of the depositor alone, whereas a loan without interest [*mutuum*] benefits only the loan recipient.[41]

A reason for the preceding legal distinction would be the case in which the sum deposited is unexpectedly lost (e.g., it is stolen) after the permission to use it was granted but before its actual use.

Literature:

MacCormack, Geoffrey. "The Role of Animus in the Classical Law of Possession." *ZRG* 86 (1969) 105–145.

von Lübtow, Ulrich. *Die Entwicklung des Darlehensbegriffs im römischen und im geltenden Recht mit Beiträgen zur Delegation und Novation,* Vol. Bd. 10. Berlin: Duncker & Humblot, 1965, 55 ff.

---

[41] Translator's note: If interest is to be charged, it is normally the subject of a separate promissory contract.

CASE 14

D 6.2.9.1 (Ulpianus libro sexto decimo ad edictum)

Si quis rem apud se depositam vel sibi commodatam emerit vel pignori sibi datam, pro tradita erit accipenda, si post emptionem apud eum remansit.

Translation: (Ulpian in the 16th book of his *Commentary on the Praetor's Edict*)[42]

If someone buys a thing that has been deposited with himself or loaned [*commodatam*][43] or given as a pledge to himself, the property is to be understood as having been delivered, if it remains with him after the purchase.

Note on the Text:

The appended clause, *vel pignori sibi datam* ("or given as a pledge to himself"), could be due to the correction of a copyist's oversight or the addition of a later reworking.

Discussion Questions:

State the fact-situation and legal question and justify the jurist's reasoning. In your discussion refer to D 41.1.9.5 (Case 12) and D 12.1.9.9 (Case 13).

Literature:

> V. Lübtow (Case 13) 57 ff.

---

[42] On the author and work, see Case 11 (D 18.6.1.2).

[43] Translator's note: *commodatam* is another form of the word *commodatum*. See fn. 39 of Case 13.

This rule had already been expressed by jurists of the republican period (called *veteres* "the old [jurists]"). The rule means that no one can unilaterally alter for his own benefit the legal basis of his possession. *Causa possessionis* ["the legal basis of possession"] is therefore not to be understood technically as the basis of possessory title but quite generally as the reason for being in possession. The rule applies particularly to a *detentor* (*naturalis possessor*—i.e., someone who holds the property but does not have *possessio* of it). So, for example, a lessee or renter [neither of whom is technically a "possessor" of the property] would not be in a position to acquire the property by prescription *pro herede* ("[as if] in the capacity of an heir") following the death of the owner.

The classical jurists felt that the rule was too broadly fashioned and needed to be limited. Julian (D 41.3.33.1) did allow a tenant to acquire the property by prescription as a possessor *pro herede*, if the tenant believed in good faith that he was the heir. The jurist had to employ a flimsy argument to justify this solution: *viz.* since the tenant did not have *possessio*, he could not run afoul of the prohibition against a *mutatio causae possessionis* ("change of the reason for his possession")! The rule was therefore not simply abandoned. Celsus had to reconcile it with the theoretical premise of the *constitutum possessorium* (D 41.2.18 pr.: Case 17). Still later, Paul was troubled by the rule's continuing influence and was obliged to distinguish the doctrine of *traditio brevi manu* from it. Compare Julian's ill-considered reasoning with the following case (D 41.2.3.20) (*qui ne possidebam quidem* = "since I did not even possess [the property]"), which could lead to the irrational result that a *detentor* may indeed unilaterally change the legal basis for his claim to possession (in order thereafter to acquire ownership through prescription), while a possessor cannot!

The rule is still present in § 319 of the Austrian Civil Code (quoted under Case 17).

Literature:

Hausmaninger, H. "Nemo sibi ipse causam possessionis mutare potest—eine Regel der veteres in der Diskussion der Klassiker," in *Aktuelle Fragen Aus Modernem Recht Und Rechtsgeschichte: Gedächtnisschrift Für Rudolf Schmidt*, E. Seidl and Rudolf Schmidt, eds. Berlin: Duncker & Humblot, 1966, 399 ff.

Schmidlin, Bruno. *Die Römischen Rechtsregeln; Versuch Einer Typologie*, Vol. Abh. 29. Köln: Böhlau Verlag, 1970, 90 ff., 114 ff.

Nörr, Dieter. "Spruchregel Und Generalisierung." *ZRG* 89 (1972) 18–93.

MacCormack, G. "Nemo Sibi Ipse Causam Possessionis Mutare Potest." *BIDR* 75 (1972) 71–96, 71 ff.

---

[44] "No one can change to his own benefit the legal basis of his possession" (translator's note).

CASE 15

D 41.2.3.19 and **20** (Paulus libro quinquagensimo quarto ad edictum)

(19) *Illud quoque a veteribus praeceptum est neminem sibi ipsum causam posses-*
sionis mutare posse.

(20) *Sed si is, qui apud me deposuit vel commodavit, eam rem vendiderit mihi vel dona-*
verit, non videbor causam possessionis mihi mutare, qui ne possidebam quidem.

Translation: (Paul in the 54th book of his *Commentary on the Praetor's Edict*)[45]

(19) The older jurists have also taught that no one can change for his own benefit the legal basis of his claim to possession.

(20) But if someone who has deposited property with me or lent it to me [*com-*
modavit] later sells or gives me the property, I do not count as someone
who has changed the basis of possession for himself, since I did not even
possess [the property before].

Note on the Text:

On *videbor* ("I ... count as ..."), see on Case 72.

Discussion Questions:

1) Explain the distinction between the doctrine of *traditio brevi manu* and the rule
"*nemo sibi ipse ...*"

2) Replace the inapposite argument of "*qui ne possidebam quidem*" ("since I did
not possess the property before") with a more suitable one.

Literature:

Hausmaninger, H. "Nemo sibi ipse causam possessionis mutare potest—eine Regel
der veteres in der Diskussion der Klassiker," in *Aktuelle Fragen aus modernem Recht und
Rechtsgeschichte: Gedächtnisschrift für Rudolf Schmidt*, E. Seidl and Rudolf Schmidt eds. Berlin:
Duncker & Humblot, 1966, 404.

---

[45] On the author and work, see Case 1 (D 41.2.3.1).

CASE 16

D 41.2.3.18 (Paulus libro quinquagensimo quarto ad edictum)

Si rem apud te depositam furti faciendi causa contrectaveris, desino possidere. Sed si eam loco non moveris et infitiandi animum habeas, plerique veterum et Sabinus et Cassius recte responderunt possessorem me manere, quia furtum sine contrectatione fieri non potest nec animo furtum admittatur.

Translation: (Paul in the 54th book of his *Commentary on the Praetor's Edict*)[46]

If you, intending to steal property that I deposited with you, have removed it, I cease to possess it. But if you have not removed it from its place and intend to make a denial, most of the older jurists, along with Sabinus and Cassius, have correctly replied that I remain the possessor, since there is no theft without handling the property, nor can a theft take place *animo* alone.

Note on the Text:

On *plerique* ("most"), see on Case 72.

Discussion Questions:

Consider this text in connection with the holding of D 12.1.9.9 (*animo enim coepit possidere*, Case 13) and with the rule *nemo sibi ipse causam possessionis mutare potest*. Do you detect in the two texts a school-conflict between the Sabinians and the Proculians regarding the permissibility of acquiring possession *solo animo*?[47]

Literature

Thomas J. A. C. "Infitiando Depositum Nemo Facit Furtum" in *Studi in onore di Edoardo Volterra*, Pubblicazioni della Facoltà di Giurisprudenza dell'Università di Roma, Vol. 41, Milano: Giuffrè, 1971, 759–768, at 762 ff.

---

[46] On the author and work, see Case 1 (D 41.2.3.1); on Sabinus, see Case 11 (D 18.6.1.2); on his pupil Cassius, see Case 19 (D 41.2.21.3).

[47] Translator's note: In citing Sabinus and Cassius, Paul is implicitly stating the position of the "Sabinians," one of two rival "schools" of juristic thought that are often explicitly identified with opposing opinions in the Digest. The "Proculians," named for the jurist Proculus, who is the author of Case 13, formed the other "school." See also fn. 29 to Case 10, the second parag. of fn. 30 to Case 11, and fn. 51 to Case 19. For examples of specific differences of opinion, see Case 120, Case 122 (w. "Note on the Text"), and Case 127 (following the Discussion Questions).

b. *Constitutum possessorium*

CASE 17

D 41.2.18 pr. (Celsus libro vicensimo tertio digestorum)

Quod meo nomine possideo, possum alieno nomine possidere: nec enim muto mihi causam possessionis, sed desino possidere et alium possessorem ministerio meo facio. Nec idem est possidere et alieno nomine possidere: nam possidet, cuius nomine possidetur, procurator alienae possessioni praestat ministerium.

Translation: (Celsus in the 23d book of his *Digesta*)[48]

What I possess in my own name I can also commence to possess in the name of another. I do not change thereby the *causa* ["legal basis"] of my possession, but I cease to be the possessor and I make another the possessor by my aid. To possess and to possess in the name of another are not the same thing. For only he in whose name the possession is held is the "possessor" (in a strict sense); a *procurator* only provides the means for another's possession.

Note on the Text:

The theoretical foundation of the *constitutum possessorium* ["possessory agreement"] that is offered here by Celsus might originally have been linked to an actual case that has been deleted by the compilers. The abrupt appearance of the *procurator* in the last clause is an indication of such abbreviation.

Discussion Questions [with model answers]:

1) How does Celsus distinguish the *constitutum possessorium* from the rule of "*nemo sibi ipse ...*"?
2) Construct a concrete case to which the abstract argument of Celsus would apply.
3) Could the decision of Trebatius in D 18.6.1.2 (Case 11) be understood as an acceptance of the *constitutum possessorium*?
4) Do you think that Celsus would consider an abstract agreement, by which the current possessor henceforth holds the property in the name of the new possessor, sufficient to effect a transfer of possession in the absence of a concrete *causa detentionis* ["reason to continue holding"] (e.g., a contract to keep the property, lease agreement, etc.)?
5) What policy argument speaks in favor of requiring a legal transaction and against the sufficiency of an abstract possessory agreement?

---

[48] On the author and work, see Case 2 (D 41.2.18.2).

6) Does the *constitutum possessorium* violate the Roman principle that excludes acquisition of possession through the agency of another person who is not "in power?"

7) What logical connection is there between *constitutum possessorium* and *traditio brevi manu*?

Answers:

1) The transferor is not changing the basis of his possession; he is transferring his possession.

2) A *procurator* first acquires a piece of property in his own name and then informs the *dominus* ["owner"]; thereafter he holds the property at the latter's disposal.

3) No. There would have to have been an express agreement that the seller would henceforth hold the *dolium* ["wine jar"] in the name of the buyer. The presence of the property, or even affixing a seal to it, would be superfluous if possession were acquired in this manner.

4) No. A concrete *causa* is the basis of the text that follows: i.e., the *procurator* of the Celsus text indicates that a *mandatum* [i.e., a principal's instruction to his agent] is the *causa detentionis*.

5) Inadequate publicity.

6) Yes.

7) Waiver of physical transfer.

Compare with this Case:

§ 319 Austrian Civil Code:

The holder of a piece of property is not authorized to change unilaterally the basis of his custody and thereby to lay claim to title; however, the person who lawfully possessed a piece of property in his own name up to that point in time can transfer the right of possession to another and thereafter hold it in the other's name.[49]

---

[49] **§ 319 ABGB:** Der Inhaber einer Sache ist nicht berechtigt, den Grund seiner Gewahrsame eigenmächtig zu verwechseln, und sich dadurch eines Titels anzumaßen; wohl aber kann derjenige, welcher bisher eine Sache im eigenen Namen rechtmäsig besaß, das Besitzrecht einem andern überlassen und sie künftig in dessen Namen innehaben.

§ 428 (first half) **Austrian Civil Code** (quoted at Case 12)

§ 930 German Civil Code:

If the owner is in possession of the property, delivery of possession can be replaced by agreement of a legal relationship between him and the acquirer, in virtue of which the acquirer gets indirect possession.[50]

Literature:

Hausmaninger (Case 15) 405 ff.

Gordon (Case 2) 27 ff.

Weyand, S. *Der Durchgangserwerb in der juristischen Sekunde: Systemdenken Oder Problemdenken Im Klassischen römischen Recht,* Vol. Bd. 143. Göttingen: O. Schwartz, 1989, 108 ff.

---

[50] **§ 930 BGB:** Ist der Eigentümer im Besitze der Sache, so kann die Übergabe dadurch ersetzt werden, daß zwischen ihm und dem Erwerber ein Rechtsverhältnis vereinbart wird, vermöge dessen der Erwerber den mittelbaren Besitz erlangt.

CASE 18

D 41.2.19 pr. (Marcellus libro septimo decimo digestorum)

Qui bona fide alienum fundum emit, eundem a domino conduxit: quaero, utrum desinat possidere an non. Respondi: in promptu est, ut possidere desierit.

Translation: (Marcellus in the 17th book of his *Digesta*)[51]

Someone has bought another's piece of land in good faith and later leases the property back from the owner. I ask whether he ceases to be in possession or not. I answered: it is clear that he has ceased to be in possession.

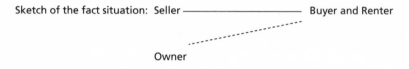

Sketch of the fact situation: Seller ———————————— Buyer and Renter

Owner

Discussion Questions:

1) What legal position has the buyer of the land first obtained [cf. fn. 3 on p. 1]
2) What later causes him to execute a lease agreement?
3) Why does he cease to be in possession?
4) What happens with the possession after conclusion of the lease agreement?

Literature:

Gordon (Case 2) 22 ff.

---

[51] The high classical Ulpius Marcellus belonged to the *consilium* of Antoninus Pius (138–161) and Marcus Aurelius (161–180). His principal work was 31 books of *Digesta*, a collection of legal problems that was patterned on the *Digesta* of Julian.

CASE 19

D 41.2.21.2 (Iavolenus libro septimo ex Cassio)

Qui alienam rem precario rogavit, si eandem a domino conduxit, possessio ad dominum revertitur.

Translation: (Javolenus in the seventh book of his *Abridgement of Cassius*)[52]

If someone's request to use property has been granted, and he later leases the same property from the owner, the possession reverts to the owner.

Discussion Questions:

Formulate the factual situation and legal question. Justify the jurist's decision (cf. Case 18).

Literature:

Manthe, U. *Die Libri Ex Cassio Des Iavolenus Priscus*, Vol. n.F., Bd. 4. Berlin: Duncker & Humblot, 1982, 200 ff.
Gordon (Case 2) 22 ff.

---

[52] On Javolenus, see Case 3 (D 46.3.79). The early classical C. Cassius Longinus came from one of the foremost families of Rome. He was consul in 30 CE, later proconsul and legate in the provinces of Asia and Syria, and ultimately exiled to Sardinia by Nero in 65 CE. He was a pupil of Sabinus and led the Sabinian school in common with the latter or as his successor. As a result the members of the school came to be called *Cassiani*. His books on the *ius civile*, which are known to us in fragments from a reworking by Javolenus, were his chief work.

CASE 20

D 6.1.77 (Ulpianus libro septimo decimo ad edictum)

Quaedam mulier fundum non marito donavit per epistulam et eundem fundum ab eo conduxit: <...>[53] *posse defendi in rem ei competere, quasi per ipsam adquisierit possessionem veluti per colonam. Proponebatur, quod etiam in eo agro qui donabatur fuisset, cum epistula emitteretur: quae res sufficiebat ad traditam possessionem, licet conductio non intervenisset.*

Translation: (Ulpian in the 17th book of his *Commentary on the Praetor's Edict*)[54]

A woman has by means of a letter both given a piece of land to a man who is not her husband[55] and leased the property back from him: <[someone replied that]> it could be argued that he has standing to bring an *actio in rem*,[56] since he acquired possession through her as through a tenant. It was proposed that he was even on the land that had been given when the letter was sent. This circumstance sufficed to transfer possession, even if there had not been a lease agreement.

Discussion Questions:

1) Formulate the two different fact-situations that are considered by Ulpian.
2) What *actio in rem* is meant, and why does the man have standing to bring it?[57]
3) What significance does the letter have for acquisition of possession?
4) At what time and in what manner has the donee acquired possession?
5) Compare the conditions of acquisition (*corpore et animo*) as between the two fact-situations.

Literature:

Gordon (Case 2) 15 ff.

---

[53] A main clause has fallen out before *posse* (perhaps *respondi* ["I replied"] or X *respondit* ["X replied"]).

[54] On the author and work, see Case 11 (D 18.6.1.2).

[55] Translator's note: The significance of this detail is that gifts between spouses were legal nullities in Roman law.

[56] Translator's note: See the Translator's Glossary for an explanation of the difference between *in rem* versus *in personam* actions.

[57] Translator's note: The indicated *actio in rem* is the *rei vindicatio*, an owner's suit to recover possession of his property that is currently in the possession of another. For more information see the Introduction and Section A of Chapter IV.

CASE 21

D 41.2.48 (Papinianus libro decimo responsorum)

Praedia cum servis donavit eorumque se tradidisse possessionem litteris declaravit. Si vel unus ex servis, qui simul cum praediis donatus est, ad eum, qui donum accepit, pervenit, mox in praedia remissus est, per servum praediorum possessionem quaesitam ceterorumque servorum constabit.

Translation: (Papinian in the 10th book of his *Opinions*)[58]

Someone has given away a farm with its slaves and declared by letter that he has transferred possession of them. Now if even one of the slaves who was given along with the farm came to the donee and was immediately sent back to the farm, it will be certain that possession of the farm and its other slaves has been acquired.

Note on the Text:

On *constabit* ("it will be certain that"), see under Case 41.

Discussion Questions:

1) At what time and in what manner has the donee acquired possession?
2) Why is *constitutum possessorium* not considered?

Literature:

Gordon (Case 2) 26 ff.

---

[58] On the author and work, see Case 5 (D 18.1.74).

C. Capacity to Acquire Possession

Legal competence is the capacity to acquire rights and obligations through one's own legally effective transactions. It is entirely or partially lacking in those persons to whom the legal order denies the capacity to make rational, legally enforceable commitments. Generally speaking, such persons in Roman law are children, the insane, women, and spendthrifts. Although the concepts of "legal competence" and "legal capacity" did not yet explicitly exist in Roman law, the texts clearly show the beginnings of their expression. Certainly the Roman jurists distinguish between acquiring possession as a factual event (acquisition of actual control over a thing) and acquiring possession as a legal matter. In the case of the latter, they placed more restrictive requirements on the acquirer's maturity of volition (see Case 22 on this issue).

Persons-in-power (the *uxor in manu*,[59] family children, slaves) could not manage their own property rights. Due to its legal character they also could not exercise *possessio* for themselves—see Case 23 (D 41.2.49.1 Papinian). They could, however, serve as "tools" or "instruments" through which to acquire rights or possession on behalf of the person in whose power they were. The classical jurists reached various decisions and provided divergent rationales in developing the doctrine of acquiring possession through persons-in-power. Apart from the question of the degree to which the acquisition of possession by a person holding power depended to greater or lesser extent on the person's actual knowledge and wishes, the jurists chiefly considered the problem of what legal or factual connection between the power-holder and the person-in-power ([the issues of] *potestas* ["legitimate power"], *possessio,* actual possibility of control, participation in the management of affairs) justified considering the taking of physical possession by a person-in-power as sufficient *corpore* for the power-holder. As far as concerned the personal intentions of the person-in-power, the general rules on legal competence and capacity to acquire possession were applicable.

Acquiring possession through a person who is not in power is possible only exceptionally in classical Roman law. If Titius authorizes his friend, Seius, to buy something for him, he does not take possession at the time when the property is delivered to Seius, but only when Seius hands the property over to Titius (see Case 35); however, if a guardian takes possession for his ward, the late classical jurists

---

[59] Translator's note: *uxor in manu* means "wife in a *manus* marriage." The *manus* marriage was an archaic and, over time, relatively uncommon form of marriage in which the wife became subject to the "hand" (*manus*) of the husband and came to occupy essentially the same legal position as a daughter vis-à-vis her husband. Far more common was marriage *sine manu* ("without *manus*"), in which the wife's property remained legally separate from the husband's.

will count this as possession by the ward. The same applies to the *curator*[60] and even the *procurator*.

Literature:

Benöhr, Hans-Peter. *Der Besitzerwerb durch Gewaltabhängige im Klassischen römischen Recht.* Berlin: Duncker & Humblot, 1972.

Wieacker, Fr. *IURA* 12 (1961) 371 ff. (rev. of Nicosia, G. *L'Acquisto Del Possesso Mediante i Potestati Subiecti.* Milano: Giuffrè, 1959).

Watson, A. "Acquisition of Possession Per Extraneam Personam." *RHD* 29 (1961) 22–42 (reprinted in *Studies in Roman Private Law.* Rio Grande, OH: Hambledon Press, 1991, 63 ff.).

_____. "Acquisition of Ownership by Traditio to an Extraneus," *SDHI* 33 (1967) 189–209 (reprinted in *Studies in Roman Private Law.* Rio Grande, OH: Hambledon Press, 1991, 109 ff.).

Berneisen, E. "Per Liberam Personam," *RIDA* 6 (1959) 249–291.

Claus, Axel. *Gewillkürte Stellvertretung Im Römischen Privatrecht*, Vol. Bd. 25. Berlin: Duncker & Humblot, 1973.

Krüger, Wolfgang. *Erwerbszurechnung kraft Status.* Berlin: Duncker & Humblot, 1979.

Krenz, Uwe. "Der Besitzerwerb 'Per Procuratorem'," *Labeo* 43.3 (1997) 345–364.

---

[60] Translator's note: In this connection a *curator* is a person charged with looking after the affairs of someone who might be legally competent but for some infirmity—e.g., an insane person or spendthrift.

CASE 22

D 41.2.1.3 (Paulus libro quinquagensimo quarto ad edictum)

Furiosus et pupillus sine tutoris auctoritate non potest incipere possidere, quia affectionem tenendi non habent, licet maxime corpore suo rem contingant, sicuti si quis dormienti aliquid in manu ponat. Sed pupillus tutore auctore incipiet possidere. Ofilius quidem et Nerva filius etiam sine tutoris auctoritate possidere incipere posse pupillum aiunt: eam enim rem facti, non iuris esse: quae sententia recipi potest, si eius aetatis sint, ut intellectum capiant.

Translation: (Paul in the 54th book of his *Commentary on the Praetor's Edict*)[61]

A madman, just like a child without the approval of his guardian, cannot begin to have possession, because they lack the possessory intent, even if they are in bodily contact with the property to the greatest possible degree: just as if someone should place something in the hand of a sleeping person. But the child with the *auctoritas tutoris* ("authorization of the guardian") can begin to have possession. Ofilius, indeed, and the younger Nerva say that a child can take possession even without the *auctoritas tutoris* and that this is an issue of fact and not of law. This opinion can be accepted if they are of such an age that they have understanding.

Discussion Questions:

1) To what degree is it illuminating to treat a madman, a child, and a sleeping person alike with respect to acquiring possession?
2) Do only Nerva and Ofilius distinguish between capacity to acquire possession and legal capacity, or does Paul also?
3) Do you think that Ofilius and Nerva would have permitted a four-year-old child to acquire possession without *auctoritas tutoris*? (On age and legal capacity, see Case 86).
4) Is there a firm age of understanding that you would apply in this case?

---

[61] On the author and work, see Case 1 (D 41.2.43.1). Aulus Ofilius was a pupil of Servius and was befriended by Caesar. There are no excerpts of his work in the *Digest*, but he is cited by other jurists over 50 times. M. Cocceius Nerva (*filius*) was son of the jurist of the same name (Case 13) and father of the Emperor Nerva. He did not attain the juristic importance of his father.

Compare with this Case:

§ 310 Austrian Civil Code:

Children under seven years of age and persons over seven who do not have the use of reason can—except in the cases of § 151 subsec. 3—only take possession through their legally recognized representative. In other cases the capacity for independent acquisition of possession is granted.[62]

§ 151 subsec. 3 Austrian Civil Code:

If an underage child concludes a business transaction that is customarily concluded by underage children of his age, and concerns a minor matter of daily life, this business transaction … retroactively becomes legally effective with the fulfillment of the obligations that concern the child.[63]

---

[62] **§ 310 ABGB:** Kinder unter sieben Jahren und Personen über sieben Jahre, die den Gebrauch der Vernunft nicht haben, können—außer in den Fällen des **§ 151 Abs. 3**—Besitz nur durch ihren gesetzlichen Vertreter erwerben. Im übrigen ist die Fähigkeit zum selbständigen Besitzerwerb gegeben.

[63] **§ 151 Abs. 3 ABGB:** Schließt ein minderjähriges Kind ein Rechtsgeschäft, das von Minderjährigen seines Alters üblicherweise geschlossen wird, und eine geringfügige Angelegenheit des täglichen Lebens betrifft, so wird dieses Rechtsgeschäft … mit der Erfüllung der das Kind treffenden Pflichten rückwirkend rechtswirksam.

b. Acquiring Possession through Persons-in-Power

i. Acquiring Possession and Capacity to Own Property

CASE 23

D 41.2.49.1 (Papinianus libro secundo definitionum)

Qui in aliena potestate sunt, rem peculiarem tenere possunt, habere possidere non possunt, quia possessio non tantum corporis, set et iuris est.

Translation: (Papinian in the second book of his *Definitions*)[64]

Whoever is in another's power (*potestas*) can keep a *peculium*[65] but not possess it, because possession is not only a physical but also a legal condition.

Discussion Questions:

1) Are sons of the family and slaves equally lacking financial capacity?
2) What economic goal does *peculium* serve and what legal position does it confer on the holder?
3) Explain the basis of Papinian's decision (cf. Case 22: *rem facti, non iuris esse* "an issue of fact and not of law").

Literature:

Benöhr, Hans-Peter. *Der Besitzerwerb durch Gewaltabhängige im klassischen römischen Recht.* Berlin: Duncker & Humblot, 1972, 66, 77 ff.

---

[64] On the author and work, see Case 5 (D 18.1.74).

[65] Translator's note: *peculium* is a sum of money or other property that is granted to a son-in-power or to a slave for the recipient's more-or-less discretionary use and management, though with the notional purpose of benefiting the grantor. Although technically still owned by the father or master, *peculium* constitutes a separate property and is subject to different legal treatment.

ii. Acquisition through One's Slaves and Children

CASE 24

D 41.2.3.12 (Paulus libro quinquagensimo quarto ad edictum)

Ceterum animo nostro, corpore etiam alieno possidemus, sicut diximus per colonum et servum, nec movere nos debet, quod quasdam etiam ignorantes possidemus, id est quas servi peculiariter paraverunt: nam videmur eas eorundem et animo et corpore possidere.

Translation: (Paul in the 54th book of his *Commentary on the Praetor's Edict*)[66]

Moreover we possess with our own *animo* but with *corpore* of another, as we have said through a tenant farmer or a slave; and it should not distract us that we possess certain things even without our knowledge: i.e., the property which our slaves have acquired for their *peculium*. For we possess such property by means of the *corpus* and the *animus* of the slaves.

Discussion Questions [with model answers]:

1) Do you think that Paul is thinking of the *constitutum possessorium* in reference to acquiring possession through a tenant?
2) With the formulation "*animo nostro, corpore alieno*" is Paul considering slaves as merely tools or also as representatives of the wishes of the *dominus*?
3) Can one [reasonably] say that in the case of acquisition on the basis of *peculium* the *animus possidendi* of the slave represents the *animus possidendi* of the *dominus*?
4) Read Paul's reasoning in D 42.1.2.5 (Case 25) and evaluate it against the reasoning of this case (D 41.2.3.12).

Answers:

1) Possibly yes. Certainly the "possessory agreement" (*constitutum possessorium*) is a special way of acquiring possession, one in which the person who formerly possesses in his own name transfers possession to the acquirer while retaining the property for his own use, thereafter holding it (e.g., as a tenant) in the name of the new possessor.

   In the present case Paul seems to be thinking of a *dominus* who sends to a purchased piece of land a tenant or a slave, through whom he acquires physical possession of the property by means of a "long hand" or a "tool." Nevertheless, acquisition of possession through persons who are not in power is only exceptionally recognized as valid, even if they are functioning as mere "tools." Perhaps in the case of a *colonus* ["tenant farmer"], as with a

---

[66] On the author and work, see Case 1 (D 41.2.3.1).

procurator, a representative is allowed to acquire possession because of the great practical dependence on such persons.

2) To act as a representative is to give or receive an expression of intent on behalf of another person and in that person's name, so that the effects of the legal transaction apply to the other person directly. Mere assistants (e.g., messengers who only communicate information) are not representatives of another's wishes. In view of this, if one should speak of representation only in terms of legally binding transactions, and if one can speak of a person-in-power, especially a slave who has no legal competence, as a "representative," it becomes clear from Paul's formulation that he is here thinking of the slave as only a tool. Yet even if the slave is only an instrument, one must expect of him a "natural awareness" of the acquisition, an intention to exercise actual control. It is not necessary (or relevant) whether the intent is to acquire possession for the *dominus*.

3) Yes. *Concessio peculii* ["a grant of *peculium*"] means handing over total control for the management of property for conducting a business, etc. The person-in-power in this situation also represents the power-holder's will. A general and abstract possessory will of the *dominus* inheres in the grant of full control. That intent can then be concretized in a specific case.

4) The acquisition of property for a *peculium* without the specific knowledge of the *dominus* also follows from the principle of *animo nostro, corpore alieno*. The abstract and general *animus* of the *dominus* naturally requires concretization through the person-in-power, so that one can speak of acquisition of possession *animo servorum* ["with the *animus* of one's slaves"] (D 41.2.3.12 *eorundem et animo et corpore* ["with the *animus* and *corpus* of the same persons"]) in the same way as acquisition *animo nostro* ["with our *animus*"] (D 41.2.1.5 *nostra voluntate* ["with our will"] in Case 25).

Literature:

Benöhr (Case 23) 46 ff.
MacCormack (Case 13) 131 ff.

CASE 25

D 41.2.1.5 (Paulus libro quinquagensimo quarto ad edictum)

Item adquirimus possessionem per servum aut filium, qui in potestate est, et quidem earum rerum quas peculiariter tenent, etiam ignorantes, sicut Sabino et Cassio et Iuliano placuit, quia nostra voluntate intellegantur possidere, qui eis peculium habere permiserimus. Igitur ex causa peculiari et infans et furiosus adquirunt possessionem et usucapiunt, et heres, si hereditarius servus emat.

Translation: (Paul in the 54th book of his *Commentary on the Praetor's Edict*)[67]

Likewise through a slave or a son-in-power we acquire possession, even of those things that they hold in their *peculium* without our knowledge—which is the view of Sabinus, Cassius, and Julian—because they are understood to take possession according to the intentions of us, who permitted them to have a *peculium*. Therefore, even an infant or a madman can take possession and usucapt on the basis of *peculium*, as can an heir, if a slave belonging to the estate makes a purchase.

Note on the Text:

On *intellegantur* ("they are understood to ..."), see Case 72.

Discussion Questions:

1) Titius instructs his slave to purchase a ring and then goes on a trip. The slave acquires the ring the next day. Titius first learns of the acquisition upon his return. At what point in time has he obtained possession of the ring?
2) Why does one in principle expect the *dominus* to have knowledge of the slave's taking of possession?
3) Why does one not ascribe to the *dominus* the intention of possessing anything that any of his slaves acquires by any means?
4) Using economic arguments, provide a rationale for Paul's decision that a *dominus* acquires possession "even of those things that [persons in our power] hold in their *peculium* without our knowledge."
5) How can acquisition for a *peculium* in favor of an *infans* ["infant": i.e., a child below the age of seven] or a *furiosus* ["insane person"] come about, given that these cannot give a *peculium* nor express legally binding wishes?
6) Paul speaks here only of a slave and a son-in-power. Do you think possession could be acquired through a daughter-in-power or a female slave? Through a *servus furiosus* ["an insane slave"]? A *servus impubes* ["a minor slave"]? A four-year-old slave-child?

Literature:

Benöhr (Case 23) 91.

---

[67] On Paul, see Case 1 (D 41.2.3.1); on Sabinus, see Case 11 (D 18.6.1.2); on Cassius, see Case 19 (D 41.2.21.3); on Julian, see Case 70 (D 41.1.36).

CASE 26

D 41.2.44.1 (Papinianus libro vicensimo tertio quaestionum)

Quaesitum est, cur ex peculii causa per servum ignorantibus possessio quaereretur. Dixi utilitatis causa iure singulari receptum, ne cogerentur domini per momenta species et causas peculiorum inquirere. Nec tamen eo pertinere speciem istam, ut animo videatur adquiri possessio: nam si non ex causa perculiari quaeratur aliquid, scientiam quidem domini esse necessariam, sed corpore servi quaeri possessionem.

Translation: (Papinian in the 23rd book of his *Legal Questions*)[68]

It has been asked why even unwitting possession should be acquired through the *peculium* of a slave. I answered that this exceptional rule has been adopted for practical reasons: in order that the power-holder not be required to investigate each and every transaction affecting the *peculium*. However, the case in which possession counts as acquired *animo* does not belong here: indeed, if something is acquired other than for the *peculium*, the knowledge of the power-holder is necessary—although physically the possession is acquired through the slave.

Notes on the Text:

Papinian gives a rationale for the decision combined with acknowledgment that the decision stands as an anomaly of juristic law (*utilitatis causa iure singulari receptum* ["this exceptional rule has been adopted for practical reasons"]). He then tries to distinguish between acquiring possession through a person-in-power and acquiring possession *animo*.

Roman jurists often appeal to *utilitas* (usefulness, consideration of practical needs) as an argument for justifying a decision. In doing so they not infrequently give preference to a practical solution over one that is logically consistent.

Discussion Questions:

1) What does *utilitatis causa* ["for practical reasons"] actually mean? Can you expand on the viewpoint of Papinian's considerations?
2) *Ius singulare* is an "exceptional rule" which takes precedence over an established legal principle (Paulus D 1.3.16). Try to give the principle and the exception a precise formulation. On *receptum est* ["has been adopted"], see Case 31.
3) Like Paul (D 41.2.3.12 = Case 24), Papinian sees the acquisition of possession through a person-in-power as effected *animo nostro corpore alieno.*

---

[68] On the author and work, see Case 5 (D 18.1.74).

How can one distinguish this from acquisition *animo*? Where would you place the case in which someone appoints a slave to watch a woodpile (cf. D 41.2.51 = Case 10)?

Literature:

Benöhr (Case 23) 92 ff.

Wubbe, F. B. J. "Ius Singulare Quid Sit," in *Ars Boni Et Aequi : Festschrift für Wolfgang Waldstein zum 65. Geburtstag.* Stuttgart: F. Steiner, 1993, 451–469, at 460 ff.

iii. Acquisition through *bona fide serviens* and through *usufructuarius*[69]

CASE 27

Gai. Inst. 2.94

De illo quaeritur, an per eum servum, in quo usumfructum habemus, possidere aliquam rem et usucapere possimus, quia ipsum non possidemus. Per eum vero, quem bona fide possidemus, sine dubio et possidere et usucapere possumus. Loquimur autem in utrisque personis secundum definitionem, quam proxume exposuimus; id est si quid ex re nostra vel ex operis suis adquirant, id nobis adquiritur.

Translation: (Gaius in the second book of his *Institutes*)[70]

There is a question whether we can possess and acquire by prescription through a slave in whom we have only a usufruct, since we do not possess the slave itself. Certainly we can possess and acquire by prescription through someone whom we possess in good faith. As regards both types of persons, however, we observe the distinction that we have already made: i.e., whatever they acquire with means that we have provided, or by means of their own labor, is acquired for us.

Notes on the Text:

Gaius refers to his statements at Inst. 2.91 that (according to established doctrine) the slave in whom someone has a usufruct acquires ownership for the usufructuary [if the purchase is] *ex re nostra vel ex operis suis* ["with means that we have provided, or by means of their own labor"], but *extra eas causas* ["apart from those reasons"] (e.g., property acquired by inheritance or legacy) the acquisition is for the slave's owner.

In Inst. 2.92 Gaius continues: "The same applies in reference to a person who is acting in the good faith belief that he is our slave (*bona fide serviens*), whether he is a free man or another's slave . . . Therefore what has been acquired by him apart from these two grounds of acquisition belongs either to himself (if he is free) or to his owner (if he is a slave)."[71] The *homo liber bona fide serviens* is a free man who

---

[69] Translator's note: A *usufructuarius* ("usufructuary") is a person who has the legal right to use and take the profits (usufruct) of another's property. A *bona fide serviens* is defined in the "Notes on the Text" of this case.

[70] On author and work, see Case 6 (D 41.1.9.6).

[71] Gaius Inst. 2.92: *Idem placet de eo, qui a nobis bona fide possidetur, sive liber sit sive alienus servus . . . itaque quod extra duas istas causas adquiritur, id vel ad ipsum pertinet, si liber est, vel ad dominum, si servus sit.*

mistakenly believes he is a slave and who is also in good faith thought to be a slave by the person whom he serves.

With negative statements like "doubtless" (*sine dubio*) or "there is no doubt" (*nulla dubitatio est, procul dubio est, non dubitatur,* etc.), as frequently as with positive ones like "it is established" (*constat*), "the established doctrine" (*placet, placuit*), "it is accepted" (*receptum est*), "it is certain" (*certum est*), Roman jurists rely upon established juristic doctrine that removes any need for further argument.

Discussion Questions:

1) Does Gaius consider possession of the slave to be a precondition for acquiring possession through a slave?
2) On the basis of what factors does Gaius let the slave in whom someone owns a usufruct acquire possession sometimes for the usufructuary and sometimes for the owner?
3) With reference to the *possessor* do you think it makes sense to consider the *homo liber bona fide serviens* ["free man who mistakenly believes he is a slave"] to be in the same position as another's slave who is mistakenly possessed (i.e., as one's own) in good faith?

Literature:

Benöhr (Case 23) 35 ff.

CASE 28

D 41.2.1.6 (Paulus libro quinquagensimo quarto ad edictum)

Sed et per eum, quem bona fide possidemus, quamvis alienus sit vel liber, possessionem adquiremus. Si mala fide eum possideamus, non puto adquiri nobis possessionem per eum: sed nec vero domino aut sibi adquiret, qui ab alio possidetur.

Translation: (Paul in the 54th book of his *Commentary on the Praetor's Edict*)[72]

But we acquire possession through the person whom we possess *bona fide*, whether he be another's slave or a free man. If we possess him *mala fide* ["in bad faith"], I do not think that possession will be acquired through him. But someone who is possessed by another acquires property neither for himself nor for his true *dominus*.

Discussion Questions:

1) Does Paul let the *bona fide serviens* acquire only for his possessor?
2) Compare Paul's decision with that of Gai. Inst. 2.94 (Case 27) and try to make sense of the different views.

Literature:

Benöhr (Case 23) 30, 39, 78 ff.

---

[72] On author and work, see Case 7 (D 41.2.3.1).

CASE 29

D 41.1.21 pr. (Pomponius libro undecimo ad Sabinum)

Si servus meus tibi bona fide serviret et rem emisset traditaque ei esset, Proculus nec meam fieri, qui servum non possideam, nec tuam, si non ex re tua sit parata. Sed si liber bona fide tibi serviens emerit, ipsius fieri.

Translation: (Pomponius in the 11th book of his *Commentary on the* Ius Civile *of Sabinus*)[73]

If my slave, who is serving you in good faith, buys property and it is delivered to him, Proculus says that the property neither passes into my ownership, because I do not possess the slave, nor into yours, unless the property is acquired with your money. But if a free person, who is acting as your slave in good faith, has bought property, it passes into his own ownership.

Discussion Questions:

1) According to Proculus and Pomponius, does the *homo liber bona fide serviens* acquire only for himself?
2) Can the *homo liber bona fide serviens* acquire possession for himself even if he believes that he is a slave and that he is acquiring for his *dominus*? (The problem of *animus possidendi* ["possessory intent"].)
3) For whom would Proculus and Pomponius let a *servus usufructuarius* ["slave of whom someone has the usufruct"] acquire possession?

Literature:

Benöhr (Case 23) 68 ff.

---

[73] Sextus Pomponius is a contemporary of Gaius and, like him, a representative of the academic tradition of Roman jurisprudence. He did not possess the *ius respondendi*, but he is important as the author of wide-ranging works of commentary (39 books *ad Quintum Mucium*; a first exhaustive commentary *ad Sabinum*; his *Commentary on the Praetor's Edict* may have reached the imposing dimension of 150 books). Pomponius is cited by Ulpian more frequently than anyone else, and numerous excerpts of Pomponius are preserved in the Digest.

CASE 30

D 41.2.1.8 (Paulus libro quinquagensimo quarto ad edictum)

Per eum, in quo usum fructum habemus, possidere possumus, sicut ex operis suis adquirere nobis solet: nec ad rem pertinet, quod ipsum non possidemus: nam nec filium.

Translation: (Paul in the 54th book of his *Commentary on the Praetor's Edict*)[74]

We can acquire possession through a slave in whom we have the usufruct, just as he regularly acquires for us through his efforts. And it is irrelevant that we do not possess him: we also do not possess a son.

Discussion Questions:

Try to provide a sure foundation for Paul's decision in favor of acquiring possession through a usufructuary slave, and compare your argument with Gaius Inst. 2.94 (Case 27), Proculus/Pomponius D 41.1.21 pr. (Case 29), and Paul D 41.2.1.6 (Case 28).

Literature:

Benöhr (Case 23) 37, 80

---

[74] On author and work, see Case 1 (D 41.2.3.1).

iv. Acquisition through *servus fugitivus* ["fugitive slave"]

CASE 31

D 41.2.1.14 (Paulus libro quinquagensimo quarto ad edictum)

Per servum, qui in fuga sit, nihil posse nos possidere Nerva filius ait, licet respondeatur, quamdiu ab alio non possideatur, a nobis eum possideri ideoque interim etiam usucapi. Sed utilitatis causa receptum est, ut impleatur usucapio, quamdiu nemo nactus sit eius possessionem. Possessionem autem per eum adquiri, sicut per eos, quos in provincia habemus, Cassii et Iuliani sententia est.

Translation: (Paul in the 54th book of his *Commentary on the Praetor's Edict*)[75]

The younger Nerva says that we can possess nothing through a fugitive slave, although it should be decided that as long as another does not possess him, he would be possessed by us and therefore in time acquired by prescription. But for reasons of practicality the view prevails that the prescription could be completed only as long as no one has taken possession of him. It is the opinion of Cassius and Julian that possession is acquired through him just as through those slaves that we have in the province.

Note on the Text:

Receptum est "it is recognized that," "the view prevails that" refers to an established judicial doctrine that can support the decision in future cases without further argumentation. On *utilitatis causa* "for reasons of practicality," see Case 26.

Discussion Questions:

1) Does Nerva let possession by the *dominus* of the *servus fugitivus* be extinguished? (cf. Case 46)
2) The fugitive slave has taken away property of his *dominus*. Has the *dominus* thereby lost possession of the property?
3) On what grounds could Nerva deny acquisition of possession through a *servus fugitivus*?
4) What parallels can be drawn between a *servus fugitivus* and a slave in the province?
5) The *fugitivus* is taken by a third party. Can he acquire possession for that person? (Cf. Case 28)

Literature:
   Benöhr (Case 23) 129 ff.

---

[75] On author and work, see Case 1 (D 41.2.2.1); on Nerva *filius*, see Case 22 (D 41.2.1.3); on Cassius, see Case 19 (D 41.2.21.3); on Julian, see Case 70 (D 41.1.36).

CASE 32

Gai. Inst. 2.95

Ex iis apparet per liberos homines, quos neque iuri nostro subiectos habemus neque bona fide possidemus, item per alienos servos, in quibus neque usumfructum habemus neque iustam possessionem, nulla ex causa nobis adquiri posse. Et hoc est, quod vulgo dicitur per extraneam personam nobis adquiri non posse; tantum de possessione quaeritur, an per procuratorem nobis adquiratur.

Translation: (Gaius in the second book of his *Institutes*)[76]

It follows from these considerations that there are no grounds on which possession can be acquired for us through free men who are neither in our power nor possessed in good faith by us, or through another's slaves of whom we have neither the usufruct nor *iusta possessio* ["valid possession"]. And that means, as is commonly said, one cannot acquire possession through other persons. The only issue regarding possession is whether it can be acquired for us through a *procurator*.

Note on the Text:

Vulgo dicta ("as is commonly said") are legal maxims (rules of thumb) that are occasionally taken by the jurists as overly broad and are therefore narrowed by critical commentary (cf. Case 90).

Discussion Questions:

1) Considering Cases 23 to 31, make a list of persons through whom a Roman *pater familias*[77] can acquire possession.
2) Can one unite all these cases under a unified viewpoint?
3) Why exactly does the *procurator* present a new issue regarding acquisition of possession through a person not in power?

Compare with this Case:

§ 855 German Civil Code:

If someone exercises the actual control over a piece of property for another, in whose household or business or similar relationship on account of which he has

---

[76] On author and work, see Case 6 (D 41.1.9.6).

[77] Translator's note: A *pater familias* ("father of the family") is the head of the household and *sui juris* –i.e., in the "power" of no one.

to follow the other's instructions concerning the property, then only the other is the possessor.[78]

Literature:

Watson, Alan. "Acquisition of Possession per Extraneam Personam." *RHD* 29 (1961) 22–42, at 27 ff. (reprinted in *Studies in Roman Private Law*. Rio Grande, OH: Hambledon Press, 1991, 68 ff.

---

[78] **§ 855 BGB:** Übt jemand die tatsächliche Gewalt über eine Sache für einen anderen in dessen Haushalt oder Erwerbsgeschäft oder in einem ähnlichen Verhältnis aus, vermöge dessen er den sich auf die Sache beziehenden Weisungen des anderen Folge zu leisten hat, so ist nur der andere Besitzer.

CASE 33

Pauli Sententiae 5.2.2

Per liberas personas, quae in potestate nostra non sunt, adquiri nobis nihil potest. Sed per procuratorem adquiri nobis possessionem posse utilitatis causa receptum est. Absente autem domino comparata non aliter ei, quam si rata sit, quaeritur.

Translation: (*Opinions of Paul*)[79]

We *cannot* acquire anything through a free person who is not in our power. It is accepted, however, that for reasons of practicality we can acquire possession through a *procurator*. Still, in the absence of the *dominus*, possession counts as acquired by him only when he ratifies it.

Discussion Questions:

Compare the historical development of the doctrine of *utilitatis causa receptum est* ["it is accepted for reasons of practicality"] with Gai. Inst. 2.95 (Case 32) and Neratius (around a generation prior to Gaius) D 41.3.41 *iam fere conveniat* ["it is now generally recognized"] in Case 73. On *utilitatis causa receptum,* see also Case 26 and Case 31.

1) How is acquisition of possession *per procuratorem* different from acquisition for a *peculium* through persons-in-power?
2) Can the *procurator* also act as a representative of the intentions of the *dominus*?
3) What utilitarian grounds speak in favor of acquisition of possession through a *procurator*?
4) Try to explain the proviso: "*absente autem domino*" ["in the absence of the owner"].

Literature:

Watson (Case 32) 32 (reprinted in *Studies* 73).
Krenz, Uwe. "Der Besitzerwerb 'Per Procuratorem.'" *Labeo* 43.3 (1997): 345–364, at 352 ff.

---

[79] On Paul, see Case 1 (D 41.2.3.1). The *Pauli Sententiae* (*Opinions of Paul*) are today considered to be an early post-classical compilation of excerpts—chiefly, though not exclusively, from the works of Paul—that was reworked more than once between the third and fifth centuries. For a long time the *Sententiae* exerted great influence as a simple, practical handbook.

CASE 34

D 41.2.1.20 (Paulus libro quinquagensimo quarto ad edictum)

Per procuratorem tutorem curatoremve possessio nobis adquiritur. Cum autem suo nomine nacti fuerint possessionem, non cum ea mente, ut operam dumtaxat suam accomodarent, nobis non possunt adquirere. Alioquin si dicamus per eos non adquiri nobis possessionem, qui nostro nomine accipiunt, futurum, ut neque is possideat cui res tradita sit, quia non habeat animum possidentis, neque is qui tradiderit, quoniam cesserit possessione.

Translation: (Paul in the 54th book of his *Commentary on the Praetor's Edict*)[80]

We acquire possession through a *procurator*, a *tutor*, or a *curator*:[81] however, if such persons acquire possession in their own name, not with the intention of merely providing a service, they cannot acquire possession for us. Otherwise, if we decide that we cannot acquire possession through such persons, it would follow that neither he to whom the property has been transferred would have possession, since he lacks the intention to possess, nor would he who has transferred the property, since he has surrendered the possession.

Note on the Text:

Paul employs an *argumentum ad absurdum*: he seeks to support the correctness of his decision by showing the contrary view or alternative to be absurd (irrational, untenable). The *argumentum ad absurdum* is not infrequently introduced with the phrase *alioquin dicendum* ("otherwise one has to say"). Compare with Paul's decision, however, Celsus D 41.2.18.2 (Case 43) and Paul D 41.2.1.6 (Case 28).

Discussion Questions:

1) With persons-in-power, is intent necessary for possession to be acquired for another?
2) Can an *infans* [a child under seven] acquire possession for himself, or only through his *tutor* ["guardian"]? Cf. Case 22 on this question.
3) What arguments speak for treating the *tutor* and the *curator* alike? What arguments to the contrary do you think are possible?

Literature:

Watson (Case 32) 30 ff. (reprinted in *Studies* 71 ff.); Krenz (Case 33) 359 ff.

---

[80] On author and work, see Case 1 (D 41.2.3.1).

[81] Translator's note: a *procurator* is a type of agent who acts for another under the other's authority (D 3.3.1 pr.). A *tutor* is a guardian, most commonly for minors under the age of puberty, although often for adult women in legal transactions. A *curator* is someone appointed to administer the affairs of another, typically a minor over the age of puberty or someone otherwise adjudged to be incompetent, such as a spendthrift (*prodigus*) or insane person (*furiosus*). The term *curator* is also used more generally to refer to persons charged with resonsibilities of oversight in various other contexts.

CASE 35

D 41.1.59 (Callistratus libro secundo quaestionum)

Res ex mandatu meo empta non prius mea fiet, quam si mihi tradiderit qui emit.

Translation: (Callistratus in the second book of his *Legal Questions*)[82]

A thing that has been purchased pursuant to my directions does not become my property until he who purchased it delivers it to me.

Discussion Questions:

Interpret this text of the late classical Callistratus in light of the three texts discussed above: Gai. Inst. 2.95 (Case 32); PS 5.2.2 (Case 33); Paulus D 41.2.1.20 (Case 34).

Literature:

Watson (Case 4) 199 (reprinted in *Studies* 119).
Claus, Axel. *Gewillkürte Stellvertretung im Römischen Privatrecht,* Vol. Bd. 25. Berlin: Duncker & Humblot, 1973, 183 ff.

---

[82] Callistratus came from the Greek-speaking eastern empire and worked under Septimius Severus and Caracalla. In addition to his two books of *Quaestiones* ["Legal Questions"], he wrote three books of *Institutiones* ["Institutes"], six books *De Cognitionibus* ["On Trials"], four books *De Jure Fisci et Populi* ["On the law of the Treasury and the People"], and six books on *Edictum Monitorium* ["Advisory Edict"] (a title of unclear meaning).

CASE 36

D 41.1.20.2 (Ulpianus libro vicensimo nono ad Sabinum)

Si ego et Titius rem emerimus eaque Titio et quasi meo procuratori tradita sit, puto mihi quoque quaesitum dominium, quia placet per liberam personam omnium rerum possessionem quaeri posse et per hanc dominium.

Translation: (Ulpian in the 29th book of his *Commentary on the* Ius Civile *of Sabinus*)[83]

If Titius and I have bought something and it has been delivered to Titius [as buyer] and as if [he were] my *procurator*, I think that I too have acquired the ownership, since according to the established doctrine possession of anything can be acquired through a free person, and therewith also ownership.

Discussion Questions:

1) Formulate the fact-situation and then determine the logical connections between *quasi…procuratori* ["as if my *procurator*"], *puto* ["I think"], and *placet* ["the established doctrine is"].

2) In connection with a jurist's name, *placet* expresses an individual legal opinion (e.g., *Trebatio placuit* "Trebatius was of the opinion that" Case 8). Without a jurist's name *placet* (*placuit*) refers to a generally established legal doctrine: "it is the established doctrine that." Considering this usage and the late classical texts above (Cases 33 to 35), what is your conclusion regarding the authenticity of this text? Has there been a post-classical reworking? In this connection compare Inst. Iust. 2.9.5: *et hoc est, quod dicitur per extraneam personam nihil adquiri posse: excepto eo, quod per liberam personam veluti per procuratorem placet non solum scientibus, sed etiam ignorantibus vobis adquiri possessionem secundum divi Severi constitutionem* ("And this means, as is said, that nothing is acquired through an outside person: but with the exception, based on a constitution of the Emperor Severus, of what is acquired for you through a free person like a *procurator*—and not only with your knowledge, but also without it").

Literature:

Watson (Case 4) 202 ff. (reprinted in *Studies* 122 ff.).

Flume, Werner. *Rechtsakt und Rechtsverhältnis: Römische Jurisprudenz und Modernrechtliches Denken.* n.F., Heft 56. Paderborn: F. Schöningh, 1990, 87.

Claus (Case 35) 189 ff.

---

[83] On author and work, see Case 11 (D 18.6.1.2).

CASE 37

D 41.1.65 pr. (Labeo libro sexto pithanon a Paulo epitomatorum)

Si epistulam tibi misero, non erit ea tua, antequam tibi reddita fuerit. Paulus: immo contra: nam si miseris ad me tabellarium tuum et ego rescribendi causa litteras tibi misero, simul atque tabellario tuo tradidero, tuae fient. Idem accidet in his litteris, quas tuae dumtaxat rei gratia misero, veluti si petieris a me, uti te alicui commendarem, et eas commendaticias tibi misero litteras.

Translation: (Labeo in the sixth book of Paul's Epitome of his *Pithana*)[84]

If I send you a letter, it does not become your property before it is delivered to you. Paul: quite the opposite. For if you have sent me your courier, and I send you a letter in reply, the letter becomes your property as soon as I give it to your courier. The same applies to those letters that I send you in compliance with your wishes, as when you ask me to recommend you to someone and I send you the letter of recommendation.

Discussion Questions:

1) Do you think that Labeo and Paul are making a distinction, as regards acquiring possession, between a person not in power and a *tabellarius* ["courier"] who is in power (i.e., a slave)?
2) Why does Paul specify an answering letter and a letter of recommendation, but does not attribute to the *dominus* possession and ownership of all letters that are given to the *tabellarius* of another?

Literature:

Watson (Case 4) 201 ff. (reprinted in *Studies* 121 ff.)

Benöhr, Hans-Peter. "Der Brief: Korrespondenz, Menschlich und Rechtlich Gesehen: Ciceros Briefe an Atticus und die Rechte an Briefen in Rom," *ZRG* 115 (1998): 115–149, at 132 ff.

Claus (Case 35) 11f ff., 203 ff.

---

[84] On Paul, see Case 1 (D 41.2.3.1); on Labeo, see Case 10 (D 41.2.51). *Pithana* are plausible aphorisms that, although not precisely provable, are nevertheless illuminating. They belong to the literary genre of *libri regularum* ("Books of Rules/Maxims"). Paul published an epitome of Labeo's work with commentary in eight books. He gives excerpts of Labeo *verbatim* and frequently attaches his own critical comments to them.

CASE 38

D 47.2.14.17 (Ulpianus libro vicensimo nono ad Sabinum)

Si epistula quam ego tibi misi, intercepta sit, quis furti actionem habeat? Et primum quaerendum est, cuius sit epistula, utrum eius qui misit, an eius ad quem missa est? Et si quidem dedi servo eius, statim ipsi quaesita est, cui misi: si vero procuratori, aeque (quia per liberam personam possessio quaeri potest) ipsius facta est, maxime si eius interfuit eam habere. Quod si ita misi epistulam, ut mihi remittatur, dominium meum manet, quia eius nolui amittere vel transferre dominium ...

Translation: (Ulpian in the 29th book of his *Commentary on the* Ius Civile *of Sabinus*)[85]

If a letter that I sent to you is intercepted, who has the action for theft? And first it must be determined to whom the letter belongs, whether to him who sent it or him to whom it was sent. If I have given it to the slave of the addressee, the addressee has immediately acquired the ownership. Likewise, if I gave it to his *procurator* (because possession can be acquired through a free person), it has become his property, especially if it was a matter affecting his interests. But if I sent the letter with the intention of having it returned to me, the ownership remains mine, since I did not wish either to surrender or to transfer it.

Discussion Questions:

Write a short explanation of this case with reference to D 41.1.65 pr. (Case 37).

Literature:

>   Watson (Case 4) 204 ff. (reprinted in *Studies* 124 ff.)
>   Claus (Case 35) 194 ff.
>   Benöhr (Case 37) 137 ff.

---

[85] On author and work, see Case 11 (D 18.6.1.2).

Keeping Possession and Losing Possession

Introduction

Loss of possession is dealt with in the same title of the *Digest* as acquisition of possession: D 41.2 *de adquirenda vel amittenda possessione* ["Concerning the Acquisition or Loss of Possession"]. Attempts at systematic theoretical treatment recur in the late classical jurists.

Paul D 41.2.8 believes that possession would be lost in the same way as acquired: *corpore et animo*,[1] although the limited application of this principle soon reveals itself. Frequently the loss of just one element (e.g., the physical relationship in situations of involuntary loss of possession; the possessory intent in certain cases of voluntary surrender of possession through delivery of property) can already by itself bring about the end of possession.

As with acquiring possession, the issue of the physical relationship necessary for keeping possession will be examined through cases. From these there emerges a more flexible conception of physical relationship than that which applies to acquiring possession. Indeed, despite great attenuation of the physical relationship, any spatial connection can serve to preserve possession (e.g., of summer and winter pasturage, and especially of fugitive slaves).

Naturally the possessory intention plays a particularly important role in this connection. Paul's longer discussion of the element of intent in bk. 54 *ad edictum* ["On the Praetor's Edict"] was reproduced by the compilers in obviously abbreviated form at D 41.2.3.6–11.[2] The structure of the late classical overlay comes out most clearly from an (also abbreviated) excerpt of the Papinian tractate at D 41.2.44.2ff (Case 51). According to the latter, one must distinguish in regard

---

[1] *Quemadmodum nulla possessio adquiri nisi animo et corpore potest, ita nulla amittitur, nisi in qua utrumque in contrarium actum est.* ("Just as no possession is acquired without *animo* and *corpore*, so none is lost, unless where the opposite of both elements obtains.") Same point at Paul D 50.17.153.

[2] See D 41.2.3.6 (under Case 40), D 41.2.3.8 (Case 65), D 41.2.3.9 (Case 39), D 41.2.3.11 (Case 48).

to loss of possession whether (1) someone possesses the property itself *corpore et animo*; or (2) whether the physical relationship is established through an intermediary (*possessio animo nostro, corpore alieno*); or (3) whether someone retains the possession *solo animo*.

Because of the grave consequences of losing possession (interruption of prescription, loss of the advantageous position in litigation over ownership, dependency of acquiring possession through a slave on having possession of the slave, etc.), the Roman jurists made great efforts to enable the preservation of possession for as long as possible. This protection of the possessor following the loss of physical control must have come into conflict with the principle of possession as actual control over the property. Juristic controversies and divergent interpretations resonate in the sources, but the lines of development are recoverable only with difficulty, if at all.

Literature:

Rabel, Ernst. "Zum Besitzverlust nach klassicher Lehre," in *Studi in Onore Di Salvatore Riccobono Nel XL Anno Del Suo Insegnamento*, vol. 4, Salvatore Riccobono and Giovanni Baviera eds. Palermo: Arti grafiche G. Castiglia (1936) 203 ff. (reprinted in *Gesammelte Aufsätze* IV [1971] 580 ff.).

Wieacker, Fr. "Der Besitzverlust am Den Heimlichen Eindringling," *Festschrift Für H. Lewald*. Basel: Helbing & Lichtenhahn, 1953, 185–200, at 185 ff.

Moehler, R. "Der Besitz am Grundstück, Wenn der Besitz es verlässt." *ZRG* 77 (1960) 52–124.

MacCormack, G. "The Role of Animus in the Classical Law of Possession." *ZRG* 86 (1969) 105–145.

Ankum, Hans. "Das Verlassen von Liegenschaften." *ZRG* 114 (1997) 402–422.

A. Voluntary Surrender of Possession (unilaterally or through delivery; movable or immovable property)

CASE 39

D 41.2.3.6 (Paulus libro quinquagensimo quarto ad edictum)

Et si alii tradiderim, amitto possessionem. Nam constat possidere nos, donec aut nostra voluntate discesserimus aut vi deiecti fuerimus.

Translation: (Paul in the 54th book of his *Commentary on the Praetor's Edict*)[3]

And if I transfer (a piece of land) to another, I lose the possession. For it is certain that we possess only until we either voluntarily give up the possession or are forcibly driven from it.

Note on the Text:

On *constat* ("it is certain"), see under Case 41.

Discussion Questions:

1) According to Paul, is possession of land extinguished if it is temporarily relinquished with a view to its return?
2) At what point in time does Smith's possession end if he sells and delivers the land to Jones?

   — With Smith's decision to give up the possession?
   — With the announcement of this decision?
   — With the vacating of the land by Smith?
   — With Jones' taking possession of the land?

3) When does Smith's possession end, if he decides—(a) on his own land, (b) in another place—that he does not wish to possess the land any longer?
4) At what point does Smith's possession end, if he is forcibly driven from his land by Jones?

   — With Jones' occupation of the land?
   — With Smith's vacating of the land?
   — With the failure of Smith's attempts to regain the land?
   — With the cessation of Smith's attempts to regain the land?
   — With the abandonment of Smith's intention to re-exert control over the land?

---

[3] On author and work, see Case 1 (D 41.2.3.1).

Compare with this Case:

§ 349 Austrian Civil Code:

The possession of a physical thing is normally lost, if the thing is lost without hope of being found; if it is voluntarily given up; or if it comes into another's possession.[4]

§ 856 German Civil Code:

The possession is terminated if the possessor gives up or otherwise loses actual control over the thing.[5]

---

[4] **§ 349 ABGB:** Der Besitz einer körperlichen Sache geht insgemein verloren, wenn dieselbe ohne Hoffnung, wieder gefunden zu werden, in Verlust gerät; wenn sie freiwillig verlassen wird; oder, in fremden Besitz kommt.

[5] **§ 856 BGB:** Der Besitz wird dadurch beendigt, daß der Besitzer die tatsächliche Gewalt über die Sache aufgibt oder in anderer Weise verliert.

CASE 40

D 41.2.3.6 (Paulus libro quinquagensimo quarto ad edictum)

In amittenda quoque possessione affectio eius qui possidet intuenda est: itaque si in fundo sis et tamen nolis eum possidere, protinus amittes possessionem. Igitur amitti et animo solo potest, quamvis adquiri non potest.

Translation: (Paul in the 54th book of his *Commentary on the Praetor's Edict*)[6]

Also in connection with the loss of possession one must look to the intention of the possessor. So, if you are on your piece of land and yet do not wish to possess it, you immediately lose the possession. Therefore one can lose the possession *solo animo*, although one cannot acquire possession in this way.

Discussion Questions:

1) Do you think Paul considers that an expression of one's intent is required?
2) What are some possible ways of voluntarily surrendering possession:

   — to a piece of land?
   — to movable property?

3) Is Paul thinking of an abandonment or a delivery, or does his decision apply to both situations?
4) Is Paul possibly thinking of a possessory agreement (*constitutum possessorium*)?

Literature:

MacCormack (Case 13) 134 ff.

---

[6] On the author and work, see Case 1 (D 41.2.3.1).

CASE 41

D 41.2.29 (Ulpianus libro trigensimo ad Sabinum)

Possessionem pupillum sine tutoris auctoritate amittere posse constat, non ut animo, sed ut corpore desinat possidere: quod est enim facti, potest amittere. Alia causa est, si forte animo possessionem velit amittere: hoc enim non potest.

Translation: (Ulpian in the 30th book of his *Commentary on the* Ius Civile *of Sabinus*)[7]

It is established that a *pupillus* can lose possession without the *auctoritas tutoris* ["guardian's authorization"]. He cannot do so *animo*, but he can give up possession *corpore*. For what is of a purely factual character, he can lose. The situation is different if he should wish to give up the possession *animo*: that he cannot do.

Note on the Text:

Constat ("it is established that") refers to an uncontested judicial doctrine that is invoked as valid law. Comparable formulations are *receptum est* ("it is recognized," see Case 31) or *eo iure utimur* ("we follow this rule," see Case 156).

Discussion Questions:

1) In which of the following cases does the *pupillus* lose possession (and why)?

— He unintentionally lets a ring fall into the sea.
— He deliberately throws the ring into the sea.
— He gives and delivers the ring to a friend.
— He gives his ring to a friend, who up to that point had been guarding the ring for him (with the *auctoritas tutoris*).
— He leaves his own land with a view to giving up possession of it.
— He gives and delivers the land to a friend.
— He gives the land to his tenant.

Literature:

MacCormack (Case 13) 138 ff.

---

[7] On author and work, see Case 11 (D 18.6.1.2).

CASE 42

D 41.1.11 (Marcianus libro tertio institutionum)

Pupillus quantum ad adquirendum non indiget tutoris auctoritate: alienare vero nullam rem potest nisi praesente tutore auctore, et ne quidem possessionem, quae est naturalis, ut Sabinianis visum est: quae sententia vera est.

Translation: (Marcian in the third book of his *Institutes*)[8]

As far as concerns acquisition of possession, the *pupillus* does not require any *auctoritas tutoris*; he cannot, however, alienate anything without the presence of his guardian as *auctor* ["authorizer"]: not even the possession, which is a factual matter, as the Sabinians thought. This judgment is correct.

Discussion Questions:

1) To what degree is the reference to the factual nature of the possession relevant here?
2) To what degree is acquisition of possession by a *pupillus* without *auctoritas tutoris* recognized? (See Case 22.)
3) How is it worthwhile to have different rules governing the acquisition as opposed to the surrender of possession by a *pupillus*?
4) Is Marcian holding that the *possessio* of a *pupillus* remains in force despite the loss of control through delivery of the property to an acquirer?

---

[8] Nothing is known of the person and career of Aelius Marcianus. Like Modestinus, he belonged to the last generation of the classical jurisprudence. In addition to his conspicuously voluminous *Institutes* (16 books) he wrote some brief essays.

CASE 43

D 41.2.18.2 (Celsus libro vicensimo tertio digestorum)

Si furioso, quem suae mentis esse existimas, eo quod forte in conspectu inumbratae quietis fuit constitutus, rem tradideris, licet ille non erit adeptus possessionem, tu possidere desinis; sufficiet quippe dimittere possessionem, etiamsi non transferas. Illud enim ridiculum est dicere, quod non aliter vult quis dimittere, quam si transferat: immo vult dimittere, quia existimat se transferre.

Translation: (Celsus in the 23rd book of his *Digesta*)[9]

If you have delivered a thing to a madman that you understood to be sane, say while he was in a state of complete tranquility, you have surrendered possession, although that one has not obtained the possession. For it is enough that you gave up the possession, even if you did not transfer anything to him. Surely it is laughable to say that someone does not wish to surrender possession other than when he transfers it: on the contrary, he surrenders possession all the more because he believes he is transferring it.

Note on the Text:

Emotionally tinged criticism of the judicial opinions of other jurists with expressions like *ridiculum* ("laughable"), *stultum* ("stupid") is very infrequently found in classical jurisprudence. Celsus seems to occupy an exceptional position with his polemical streak.

Discussion Questions:

1) Following the opinion of Celsus, who is the possessor? Who is the possessor according to the contrary opinion that Celsus considers "laughable"?
2) How might one argue in favor of the contrary opinion? Cf. D 41.2.34 pr. (Case 44) and D 43.16.18 pr. (Case 58).
3) What persuasive effect does the *argumentum ad absurdum* of Celsus have? (On this question see Case 34.)

Literature:

Wieacker, Fr. "Amoenitates Iuventianae." *IURA* 13 (1962) 1–21, at 15 ff.
Hausmaninger, H. "Publius Iuventius Celsus: Persönlichkeit und juristische Argumentation," *ANRW* II/15 (1976) 394 ff.

---

[9] On author and work, see Case 2.

CASE 44

D 41.2.34 pr. (Ulpianus libro septimo disputationum)

Si me in vacuam possessionem fundi Corneliani miseris, ego putarem me in fundum Sempronianum missum et in Cornelianum iero, non adquiram possessionem, nisi forte in nomine tantum erraverimus, in corpore consenserimus. Quoniam autem in corpore consenserimus, an a te tamen recedet possessio, quia animo deponere et mutare nos possessionem posse et Celsus et Marcellus scribunt, dubitari potest: et si animo adquiri possessio potest, numquid etiam adquisita est: sed non puto errantem adquirere: ergo nec amittet possessionem, qui quodammodo sub condicione recessit de possessione.

Translation: (Ulpian in the seventh book of his *Disputations*)[10]

If you have directed me to the *vacua possessio* ["unimpeded possession"] of the *fundus Cornelianus* ["Cornelian farmstead"], and I go to it in the belief that I have been sent to the *fundus Sempronianus* ["Sempronian farmstead"], then I do not acquire possession, unless we have erred only about the name but agree about the physical property.[11] However, since we agree about the physical property, the question arises whether you lose the possession, because one can surrender and alter possession *animo*, as both Celsus and Marcellus write. And if possession can be acquired *animo*, has it been acquired at all [in this case]? But I do not think that the mistaken person does acquire: therefore he who has surrendered the possession under a kind of condition will not lose it.

Discussion Questions [with model answers]:

1) Which of the following three fact situations is Ulpian discussing?

   a) Smith wants to acquire the *fundus Sempronianus*.
   Jones wants to alienate the *fundus Cornelianus* and sends Smith to the *fundus Cornelianus*.
   Smith enters the *fundus Cornelianus* in the belief that he is entering the *Sempronianus*.

   b) Smith wants to acquire the *fundus Cornelianus*.
   Jones wants to alienate the *fundus Cornelianus* and also sends Smith to the *Cornelianus*.

---

[10] On Ulpian, see Case 11 (D 18.6.1.2). *Disputationes* are discussions of legal problems in education or in a judge's *consilium*. Ulpian contributed 10 books to this genre. On Celsus, see Case 2 (D 41.2.18.2). On Marcellus, see Case 18 (D 41.2.19 pr.).

[11] Translator's note: the final clause of this sentence ("unless ... property") has been conjectured to be an interpolation. Omitting the words removes an apparent contradiction between this clause and the remainder of the paragraph. Without the clause, however, the correct answer to Discussion Question "1" becomes "a", and the answers to some of the other questions too would be different.

Smith enters the *Cornelianus*, but believes the farm is called *Sempronianus* (or both parties spoke erroneously of the *Sempronianus* but meant the *Cornelianus*).

c) Smith wants to acquire the *fundus Sempronianus*.

Jones wants to alienate the *fundus Sempronianus* but erroneously sends Smith to the *Cornelianus*.
Smith enters the *Cornelianus* in the belief that it is the *Sempronianus*.

2) Point out the kinds of errors represented by each of the three fact-situations.
3) According to Ulpian, has Jones lost possession of the *fundus Cornelianus*?
4) Has Jones surrendered possession of the *fundus Sempronianus* "*animo?*"
5) Has Smith acquired possession of the *fundus Cornelianus*?
6) Did Smith get possession of the *fundus Sempronianus*?
7) What is the relationship of Ulpian's decision with Celsus D 41.2.18.1 (Case 43)?

Answers:

1) Fact situation "c."
2) Variant "a": disagreement over the object of the transaction.
   Variant "b": *falsa demonstratio* ["erroneous identification"].
   Variant "c": shared error over the object of the transaction.
3) No. Jones retains possession of the *Cornelianus*, since he did not wish to surrender possession of the *Cornelianus* but of the *Sempronianus*. Smith has not entered the *Cornelianus* as possessor; therefore Jones' possession has not been disturbed.
4) No. Jones has, so to say, given up the *Sempronianus* under a condition that Smith takes possession of it. Jones is therefore still the possessor.
5) No. Smith has not acquired possession despite his entry upon the *Cornelianus*, since he lacked the corresponding *animus*. He did not in fact wish to take possession of this plot but another, the *Sempronianus*.
6) No. Smith has not acquired possession of the *Sempronianus*, since acquisition *solo animo* is only exceptionally recognized. (A question of *constitutum possessorium* would arise, and in this case the requisite mutual intent is otherwise lacking.)
7) Ulpian opposes the opinion of Celsus, according to whom Jones loses possession in the *Sempronianus*, even if Smith does not acquire the possession of it. For Celsus it is legally irrelevant that Jones wanted to surrender the possession only so that Smith could acquire it. Ulpian thinks that the issue is not a trivial error of intent, but something like a condition of losing possession. Since the condition is not satisfied, Jones remains the possessor.

Literature:

MacCormack (Case 13) 136 ff.

Benöhr, Hans-Peter. "Irrtum und guter Glaube der Hilfsperson beim Besitzerwerb" in *Studien im römischen Recht: Max Kaser Zum 65. Geburtstag gewidmet von seinen hamburger Schülern*, Kaser, Max, Dieter Medicus, and Hans Hermann Seiler, edd., Heft 65. Berlin: Duncker & Humblot, 1973, 11 ff.

Watson, A. "Two Studies in Textual History." *RHD* 30 (1962) 209–242 (reprinted in *Studies in Roman Private Law*. Rio Grande, OH: Hambledon Press, 1991, 363 ff).

Raap, Christian. "Der Irrtum beim Erwerb und beim Verlust des Besitzes: ein Deutungsversuch Zu D. 41, 2, 34 Pr." *ZRG* 109 (1992) 501–504.

B. Involuntary Surrender of Possession

a. Movable Property

CASE 45

D 41.2.25 pr. (Pomponius libro vicensimo tertio ad Quintum Mucium)

Si id quod possidemus ita perdiderimus, ut ignoremus, ubi sit, desinimus possidere.

Translation: (Pomponius in the 23rd book of his *Commentary on the* Ius Civile *of Q. Mucius*)[12]

If we lose that which we possess in such a way that we do not know where it is, we cease to possess it.

Discussion Questions:

1) Distinguish among the terms "forget," "misplace," and "lose."
2) Consider whether possession is lost in the following fact situations:

   a) It occurs to a Roman on his way home from the baths that he left his book in the baths.
   b) A Roman woman realizes after returning from the city that she lost a piece of jewelry on the journey.
   c) Someone looks for a certain letter among his papers and in his haste fails to find it.

3) Does the statement of Pomponius fit one of the cases described in "2"?

Compare with this Case:

§ 388 Austrian Civil Code:

1) Movable property that is in no one's custody and has left the holder's control without his intent is lost property.
2) Movable property that has been left behind without the holder's intent in a place under another's care, and that thereby has come into another's control, is forgotten property.[13]

---

[12] On author and work, see Case 29 (D 41.2.21 pr.); on Q. Mucius Scaevola, see Case 136 (D 43.24.1.5).

[13] § 388 ABGB:

(1) Verloren sind bewegliche, in niemandes Gewahrsame stehende Sachen, die ohne den Willen des Inhabers aus seiner Gewalt gekommen sind.

(2) Vergessen sind bewegliche Sachen, die ohne den Willen des Inhabers an einem fremden, unter der Aufsicht eines anderen stehenden Ort zurückgelassen worden und dadurch in fremde Gewahrsame gekommen sind.

CASE 46

D 41.2.3.13 (Paulus libro quinquagensimo quarto ad edictum)

Nerva filius res mobiles excepto homine, quatenus sub custodia nostra sint, hactenus possideri, id est quatenus, si velimus naturalem possessionem nancisci possimus. Nam pecus simul atque aberraverit aut vas ita exciderit, ut non inveniatur, protinus desinere a nobis possideri, licet a nullo possideatur: dissimiliter atque si sub custodia mea sit nec inveniatur, quia praesentia eius sit et tantum cessat interim diligens inquisitio.

Translation: (Paulus in the 54th book of his *Commentary on the Praetor's Edict*)[14]

The younger Nerva writes that we possess movable property, with the exception of slaves, as long as we find the property in our *custodia*—i.e., if we, as soon as we wish, can take natural possession [*naturalis possessio*: i.e., "actual physical possession"] of it. So a cow that has wandered off, or a vase that is missing in such a way that we cannot find it, immediately ceases to be possessed by us, even if it has been taken into possession by no one else. It is different if the property is in my *custodia* but has not been found, since it is present and in the meantime only a careful search for it is lacking.

Discussion Questions:

1) Do you think that, following Nerva's formulation, a peasant possesses the plow that he lets stand in a field overnight, or a woodpile that he leaves in the forest?
2) How is possession of a slave lost?
3) How can Nerva's distinction between a cow that has wandered off and a slave that has run off be supported?

---

[14] On author and work, see Case 1 (D 41.2.3.1); on Nerva *filius*, see Case 22 (D 41.2.1.3).

CASE 47

D 41.2.13 pr. (Ulpianus libro septuagensimo secundo ad edictum)

Pomponius refert, cum lapides in Tiberim demersi essent naufragio et post tempus extracti, an dominium in integro fuit per id tempus, quo erant mersi. Ego dominium me retinere puto, possessionem non puto, nec est simile fugitivo: namque fugitivus idcirco a nobis possideri videtur, ne ipse nos privet possessione: at in lapidibus diversum est.

Translation: (Ulpian in the 72nd book of his *Commentary on the Praetor's Edict*)[15]

Pomponius treats the problem of whether ownership of stones that have sunk in the Tiber as a result of shipwreck and after some time have been raised again remains in force during the time they were submerged. I think that the ownership is maintained, but the possession is not. The case is not comparable with a *servus fugitivus* ["fugitive slave"], because possession of the *fugitivus* counts as continuing in order that he himself cannot rob us of the possession.

Discussion Questions:

1) The solution that Pomponius proposed is missing: it was clearly omitted by the compilers. How might it have run?
2) Do you keep possession or ownership in a ring that falls:

   — into a swimming pool?
   — into the sea?

3) How is the case to be decided if the stones were thrown into the Tiber in order to avoid the shipwreck?
4) Where is the similarity, denied by Ulpian but clearly believed by other jurists, between the sunken stones and a *servus fugitivus*?
5) Examine the logical and legal-policy aspects of Ulpian's distinction (between ownership and possession) in reference to D 41.2.3.13 (Case 46) and D 41.2.1.14 (Case 31).

   n.b.: Regarding this case see the model case-analysis in the **Appendix** at p. 324.

---

[15] On author and work, see Case 11 (D 18.6.1.2); on Pomponius, see Case 29 (D 41.1.21 pr.).

CASE 47a

D 41.2.44 pr. (Papinianus libro vicensimo tertio quaestionum)

Peregre profecturus pecuniam in terra custodiae causa condiderat: cum reversus locum thensauri immemoria non repeteret, an desisset pecuniam possidere, vel, si postea recognovisset locum, an confestim possidere inciperet, quaesitum est. dixi, quoniam custodiae causa pecunia condita proponeretur, ius possessionis ei, qui condidisset, non videri preremptum, nec infirmitatem memoriae damnum adfere possessionis, quam alius non invasit: alioquin responsuros per momenta servorum, quos non viderimus, interire possessionem. Et nihil interest, pecuniam in meo an in alieno condidissem, cum, si alius in meo condidisset, non alias possiderem, quam si ipsius rei possessionem supra terram adeptus fuissem. Itaque nec alienus locus meam propriam aufert possessionem, cum, supra terram an infra terram possideam, nihil intersit.

Translation: (Papinian in the 23rd book of his *Legal Questions*)[16]

Before traveling abroad someone had buried money in the ground for safekeeping. After returning, when he did not locate the place due to his forgetfulness, it was asked whether he had ceased to possess the money, and whether he would immediately begin to possess it again if he should later remember the location.

I said that, since it is proposed that the money was buried for safekeeping, the right of possession was not lost by him who buried it, and also that a failure of memory would cause no impairment to the possession of property that no one else had entered upon.

Otherwise the jurists would have to decide that possession of slaves is lost the moment we no longer see them.

And it makes no difference whether I buried the money on my own or another's land, since I, if another had buried money on my land, would possess it only if I had taken hold of it above ground. Therefore [the fact of burial on] another's land does not remove my possession, since it makes no difference whether I possess property that is above or below ground.

Note on the Text:

On the *argumentum ad absurdum* "*alioquin responsuros*" ("otherwise the jurists would have to decide"), see on Case 34.

Discussion Questions:

1) Do I lose possession of my buried money if another takes possession of my land during my absence?

---

[16] On author and work, see Case 5 (D 18.1.74).

2) Do I lose possession if I bury my money on another's land and the owner blocks my reentry?
3) Do I lose possession if the owner of the land digs up my money?

Literature:

Mayer-Maly, T. "Thesaurus Meus," in *Studia in Honorem Velimirii Pólay Septuagenarii*, Elemér Pólay, Ödön Both, and József Attila Tudományegyetem, eds., Állam- és Jogtudományi Kar. t.33, fasc.1-31. Szeged: Szegedi József Attila Tudományegyetem Állam- és Jogtudományi Kara, 1985, 283–289, at 287 ff.

b. Land

i. Keeping and Losing Possession of Summer and Winter Pasturage

CASE 48

D 41.2.3.11 (Paulus libro quinquagensimo quarto ad edictum)

Saltus hibernos aestivosque animo possidemus, quamvis certis temporibus eos relinquamus.

Translation: (Paul in the 54th book of his *Commentary on the Praetor's Edict*)[17]

We retain possession of summer and winter pastures, even if we leave them for certain periods of time.

Discussion Questions:

1) Is Paul proceeding from the proposition that the physical relationship is lost as a result of leaving the *saltus* ["pastures"]?
2) How long can one retain one's possession of the *saltus* "*animo?*"
3) Could one also make the argument that possession of the *saltus* would be retained *corpore et animo*?
4) Possession of a house or field remains in force during short periods when they are left. To what extent do summer and winter pastures represent a borderline case?

Literature:

Rabel, Ernst. "Zum Besitzverlust nach klassicher Lehre," in *Studi in Onore Di Salvatore Riccobono Nel XL Anno Del Suo Insegnamento*, vol. 4, Salvatore Riccobono and Giovanni Baviera, eds. Palermo: Arti grafiche G. Castiglia, 1936, 203 ff. (reprinted in *Gesammelte Aufsätze*, 4 [1971] 580 ff., at 585 ff.).

---

[17] On author and work, see Case 1 (D 41.2.3.1).

CASE 49

D 41.2.27 (Proculus libro quinto epistularum)

Si is, qui animo possessionem saltus retineret, furere coepisset, non potest, dum fureret, eius saltus possessionem amittere, quia furiosus non potest desinere animo possidere.

Translation: (Proculus in the fifth book of his *Epistles*)[18]

If he who retains the possession of a pasture *animo* becomes mad, he cannot give up the possession of the pasture during the period of his madness, since a *furiosus* cannot cease to possess *animo*.

Discussion Questions:

1) Why does the "loss" of the *animus* through madness not bring about the loss of possession? Compare this with the issue of acquisition of possession by a *furiosus* at D 41.2.3 (Case 22).
2) How could he nevertheless lose possession?
3) Would the loss of possession by a *pupillus* be handled in the same way? (Cf. Cases 41 and 42.)

Literature:

MacCormack (Case 13) 110 ff.
Krampe (Case 9) 79.

---

[18] On author and work, see Case 9 (D 41.1.55).

CASE 50

D 43.16.1.25 (Ulpianus libro sexagensimo nono ad edictum)

Quod volgo dicitur aestivorum hibernorumque saltuum nos possessiones animo reti-nere, id exempli causa[19] didici Proculum dicere: nam ex omnibus praediis, ex quibus non hac mente recedemus, ut omisisse possessionem vellemus, idem est.

Translation: (Ulpian in the 69th book of his *Commentary on the Praetor's Edict*)[20]

I learned that Proculus said of the rule of thumb, "we retain *animo* the possession of summer and winter pastures," that it was presented as an example; for it is the same in respect of all farm property that we do not leave with the intention of abandoning it.

Note on the Text:

On *volgo dicitur* ["rule of thumb;" literally, "it is commonly said"], see Case 32 .

Discussion Questions:

1) Explain the exemplary character (the broadening of its application) of the *saltus*-decision.
2) Is the duration of the possessor's absence from the land relevant to his reten-tion of possession?

Literature:

Rable (Case 48) 210 ff. (reprinted in *Gesammelte Aufsätze* 585 ff.).

---

[19] <*dici*> ["it was presented"] has certainly fallen out here through a copyist's error.
[20] On author and work, see Case 11 (D 18.6.1.2); on Proculus, see Case 9 (D 41.1.55).

D 41.2.44.2 (Papinianus libro vicensimo tertio quaestionum)

Quibus explicitis, cum de amittenda possessione quaeratur, multum interesse dicam, per nosmet ipsos an per alios possideremus: nam eius quidem, quod corpore nostro teneremus, possessionem amitti vel animo vel etiam corpore, si modo eo animo inde digressi fuissemus, ne possideremus: eius vero, quod servi vel etiam coloni corpore possidetur, non aliter amitti possessionem, quam eam alius ingressus fuisset, eamque amitti nobis quoque ignorantibus. Illa quoque possessionis amittendae separatio est. nam saltus hibernos et aestivos, quorum possessio retinetur animo,

D 41.2.45 (Idem libro secundo definitionum)

licet neque servum neque colonum ibi habeamus,

D 41.2.46 (Idem libro vicensimo tertio quaestionum)

quamvis saltus proposito possidendi fuerit alius ingressus, tamdiu priorem possidere dictum est, quamdiu possessionem ab alio occupatam ignoraret. Ut enim eodem modo vinculum obligationum solvitur, quo quaeri adsolet, ita non debet ignoranti tolli possessio quae solo animo tenetur.

Translation: (Papinian in the 23rd book of his *Legal Questions*)[21]

Consistent with this discussion, regarding the issue of loss of possession I would say that much depends on whether we possess through ourselves or another. For we can lose that which we possess *corpore nostro* ("our *corpore*") either *animo* or also *corpore*—provided we have left it with the intention of not possessing it. But possession of property that is held physically through a slave or a tenant can be lost only if some other has entered upon it, and this possession is lost even if we are ignorant of it. And the following distinction must be made regarding the loss of possession: summer and winter pastures, of which the possession is retained *animo,*

(the same in the second book of his *Definitions*)
     even if we have neither slave nor tenant there,
(the same in the 23rd book of his *Legal Questions*)
     remain in the possession of the former possessor, despite the entry of another with possessory intent, so long as the former possessor does not know that the possession has been taken by another. In order that the bond of obligations be broken in the same way that it is accustomed to be made, possession that is held *solo animo* ought not to be removed from someone who is ignorant of it.

---

[21] On author and works, see Case 5 (D 18.1.74).

Note on the Text:

D 41.2.45 is the compilers' self-evident (i.e., superfluous) addition of an excerpt from another work of Papinian. The whole thread of text is clearly a severely abbreviated excerpt by the compilers of what was a fuller discussion by Papinian.

Discussion Questions:

1) Papinian discusses loss of possession in property that is possessed a) *corpore nostro* ["with our *corpus*"], b) *animo nostro, corpore alieno* ["with our *animus* but another's *corpus*"], c) *solo animo* ["with our *animus* alone"]. Does he distinguish thereby between voluntary and involuntary loss of possession?

2) Does he also take into consideration the case of someone who travels to a market and, upon his return, finds his land possessed by another? Cf. D 41.2.6.1 (Case 52) and D 41.2.25.2 (Case 53).

3) Is the decision regarding the *saltus* ["pasture(s)"] comparable with the decisional doctrine regarding the *servus fugitivus* ["fugitive slave"]? Cf. Cases 31, 46, and 47.

4) Does the "symmetry principle" (*contrarius actus*)[22] strengthen Papinian's argument?

5) How else can one justify that the possessor of a *saltus* loses possession only when he first learns of the dispossession, while possession is immediately lost with the ouster of a tenant (even without the possessor's knowledge of the ouster)?

Literature:

MacCormack (Case 13) 128 ff.

---

[22] Translator's note: the *contrarius actus* ["contrary act"] refers to the principle of reciprocity by which a change of legal condition that is brought about by a formal act can be reversed by a reciprocating contrary act.

ii. Keeping and Losing Possession of Other Land by the Possessor in Person

CASE 52

D 41.2.6.1 (Ulpianus libro septuagensimo ad edictum)

Qui ad nundinas profectus neminem reliquerit et, dum ille a nundinis redit, aliquis occupaverit possessionem, videri eum clam possidere Labeo scribit: retinet ergo possessionem is, qui ad nundinas abit: verum si revertentem dominum non admiserit, vi magis intellegi possidere, non clam.

Translation: (Ulpian in the 70th book of his *Commentary on the Praetor's Edict*)[23]

If someone goes to the market and leaves no one at home, and, before he returns from the market, someone else seizes the possession, Labeo writes that the latter is understood to be in possession *clam* ["by stealth"]. Therefore the one who travels to the market retains the possession. If the intruder does not admit the returning owner to the property, he should instead be understood to be in possession *vi* ["by force"], not *clam*.

Note on the Text:

On *videri, intellegi* ("is understood"), see under Case 72.

Discussion Questions:

1) At D 41.2.3.5 Labeo denies (contrary to Trebatius and Sabinus) that the same property can have two possessors (i.e., a *iustus* ["lawful"] and an *iniustus* ["unlawful"] *possessor*). What conclusions do you draw from this regarding the interpretation of the present case?
2) Exactly when, following Labeo, does the traveler to the market lose possession?
3) What is the significance of *neminem reliquerit* ["leaves no one"] in the fact situation?
4) May the returning owner forcibly drive out the intruder? On this issue, see the Excursus on "Protecting Possession" following Case 55.
5) Does Labeo's decision that the intruder first possesses *clam*, but later *vi*, have any practical consequences?
6) The characterization of the possession as *vi, clam, precario, bonae fidei* ["by force, by stealth, by request, in good faith"], etc. is applied after the time when possession is acquired. Does the decision contradict the rule: *"nemo sibi ipse causam possessionis mutare potest?"* (See Cases 15 and 16); [For more on *vi* and *clam*, see Section "D" of Chapter IV.]

Literature:

Rabel (Case 48) 217 (reprinted in *Gesammelte Aufsätze* 593 ff.).

---

[23] On author and work, see Case 11 (D 18.6.1.2); on Labeo, see Case 10 (D 41.2.51).

CASE 53

D 41.2.25.2 (Pomponius libro vicensimo tertio ad Quintum Mucium)

Quod autem solo animo possidemus, quaeritur, utrumne usque eo possideamus, donec alius corpore ingressus sit, ut potior sit illius corporalis possessio, an vero (quod a Q. Mucio probatur) usque eo possideamus, donec revertentes nos aliquis repellat aut nos ita animo desinamus possidere, quod suspicemur repelli nos posse ab eo, qui ingressus sit in possessionem: et videtur utilius esse.

Translation: (Pomponius in the 23rd book of his *Commentary on the* Ius Civile *of Q. Mucius*)[24]

Regarding property that we possess *solo animo*, a question arises whether we possess it only so long as another does not enter it *corpore*, with the result that his physical possession is stronger, or instead (as was approved by Q. Mucius) we possess it until someone blocks our return or we surrender the possession *animo* because we suspect that we will be blocked by the person who has entered into possession. This is understood to be the more practical solution.

Note on the Text:

On *utilius* ("more practical"), see on Case 26.

Discussion Questions:

1) Do you think Pomponius was here speaking of keeping possession in a *saltus*?
2) How can someone resist an intruder's acquisition of possession where the intruder has nevertheless taken physical control of the property with possessory intent?
3) Distinguish the legal from the policy arguments in favor of an absent possessor's retention of possession.
4) Is it correct to characterize the cessation of attempts to recover control of the property as *animo desinere possidere* ["surrender the possession *animo*"]?
5) This decision of Pomponius is discussed elsewhere, including by Neratius/Paul at D 41.2.7. How does it stand in relation to Labeo/Ulpian at D 41.2.6.1 (Case 52), Papinian at D 41.2.44.2 (Case 51), and Celsus at D 41.2.18 (Case 54)?

Literature:

MacCormack (Case 13) 121 ff.

---

[24] On author and work, see Case 29 (D 41.2.21. pr.); on Q. Mucius Scaevola, see Case 136 (D 43.24.1.5).

CASE 54

D 41.2.18.3 and 4 (Celsus libro vicensimo tertio digestorum)

(3) *Si, dum in alia parte fundi sum, alius quis clam animo possessoris intraverit, non desisse ilico possidere existimandus sum, facile expulsurus finibus, simul sciero.*

(4) *Rursus si cum magna vi ingressus est exercitus, eam tantummodo partem quam intraverit optinet.*

Translation: (Celsus in the 23rd book of his *Digesta*)[25]

(3) If someone secretly enters upon my land while I am away on another part of the same, it is not to be thought that I have immediately lost possession, if I can easily drive him off as soon as I learn of it.

(4) If, moreover, an army marches in with great force, it gets only that part of the land that it has entered.

Discussion Questions:

1) Can the decision of Celsus at D 41.2.18.3 [i.e., the first part of this case] be seen as an intermediate position between Labeo at D 41.2.6.1 (Case 52) and Pomponius at D 41.2.25.2 (Case 53)?

2) Do you think Celsus would let the possession terminate, if the possessor did not immediately drive out the secret intruder upon learning of him?

3) Does the decision at D 41.2.18.4 [second part of this case] also apply to the case where the army has the intent of possessing the entire property?

4) Discuss the relationship of Celsus D 41.2.18.4 to Paul at D 41.2.3.1 (Case 1)—*sufficit quamlibet partem eius fundi introire* ["it suffices to enter any part of the farm"].

Literature:

Rabel (Case 48) 217 ff. (reprinted in *Gesammelte Aufsätze* 594 ff.).

---

[25] On author and work, see Case 2 (D 41.2.18.2).

CASE 55

D 41.2.22 (Iavolenus libro tertio decimo ex Cassio)

Non videtur possessionem adeptus is qui ita nactus est, ut eam retinere non possit.

Translation: (Javolenus in the 13th book of his *Epitome of Cassius*)[26]

That man is not deemed a possessor, who has obtained the possession in such a way that he is unable to retain it.

Note on the Text:

On *videtur* ("is deemed"), see under Case 72.

Discussion Questions:

1) See whether the statement of Javolenus yields a decision in the following cases:

   a) A wild boar is ensnared in such a way that he can free himself within a foreseeable time (Case 9).
   b) While the possessor of a piece of land is visiting the market, an intruder establishes himself on the land (Case 52).

2) Does the statement of Javolenus have any application to Cases 53 and 54?

---

[26] On Javolenus, see Case 3 (D 46.3.79); on Cassius, see Case 19 (D 41.2.21.3).

Excursus: Protecting Possession through Legal Process

Starting from the necessity of protecting the *possessor* of leased public land against the unauthorized incursion of a third party, there developed early a special legal process for protecting possession. Although this process did not do away with the need for self-help by the *possessor*, it did confine self-help within a legal framework that was supported and expanded by government enforcement.

In classical law, as before and later, the *possessor* may not only forcefully repel an intrusion on his possession (defense of possession), but also forcefully recover his lost property by means of offensive self-help (recovery of possession). If the forceful recovery by the dispossessed possessor takes place within a moderately short time, by classical doctrine the intruder will not have acquired possession, since his control of the property fails to satisfy the element of duration (see Javolenus D 41.2.22, Case 55).

The person whose possession of land is interfered with or from whom the possession is taken secretly or by force can also request from the Praetor the *interdictum uti possidetis* [i.e., the interdict of the form: "Since you now possess . . ."]. This interdict forbids the use of force against the last fault-free possessor:

"*Uti nunc eas aedes* (or *eum fundum* etc.), *quibus de agitur, nec vi nec clam nec precario alter ab altero possidetis, quo minus ita possideatis, vim fieri veto.*"

("Since you now possess the house [or the farm, etc.], concerning which this dispute exists, having obtained it from the other party neither by force nor by stealth nor by request, I forbid the use of force against your possession.")

With this decree the Praetor permits the person who has lost his possession *vi, clam,* or *precario* ["by force, stealth, [or] request"], to take it back by force if necessary. If the opponent hinders this, he is first assessed a fine and later, in a subsequent procedure, condemned to return the property or its monetary equivalent.

The *exceptio vitiosae possessionis*[27] (*nec vi nec clam nec precario alter ab altero*)[28] protects the possessor, who has recovered the control of his property through self-help, against the interdict of his opponent: he who has himself wrongfully taken possession from the interdict-opponent enjoys no possessory protection against the same. Such an intruder can, however, successfully defend and recover his possession against third parties through self-help or praetorian interdict. (This demonstrates the relativity of possessory protection, the protection of the one with better entitlement in an actual conflict of claimants.)

The *interdictum uti possidetis* served as the model for a later *interdictum utrubi* [i.e., interdict of the form: "With whichever of the two parties . . ."] that protected

---

[27] Translator's note: *exceptio vitiosae possessionis* means "affirmative defense of wrongful possession" by the interdict opponent.

[28] Translator's note: *nec vi nec clam nec precario alter ab altero* means "the one having obtained it from the other neither by force, nor by stealth, nor by request."

possession of movable property. The latter, however, did not order a return to the last possessory situation, but to the longer of the rightful possessions during the previous year.

He who was forcibly driven from his property could choose, as an alternative to the *uti possidetis*, an *interdictum unde vi* [i.e., interdict of the form: "From where by force . . ."].[29] The historical relationship of the two interdicts has not been entirely clarified. It is believed that the *unde vi* was introduced because the *uti possidetis* did not provide restitution but only permission for forceful recovery by self-help and a monetary fine for hindrance thereof.

The most important aspects of self-help and possessory protection should be clear in the following cases involving the *interdictum unde vi*.

Compare this topic to the special procedure for loss of possession in the Austrian *Code of Civil Procedure* (§§ 454–460):

§ 454 (1) Austrian Code of Civil Procedure:

In legal proceedings arising from interference with possession of property and of rights, in which the claim is directed only to the protection and the recovery of the last state of possession, and which are initiated within 30 days after the plaintiff becomes aware of the interference . . . [30]

§ 457 (1) Austrian Code of Civil Procedure:

The proceedings are limited to explanation and proof of the facts regarding the last state of possession and the ensuing interference, and all discussion of the right to possession, of title, of the reasonableness or unreasonableness of the possession, or of claims of possible compensation, are excluded.[31]

Literature:

Wesener, G. "Offensive Selbsthilfe im klassischen römischen Recht," *Festschrift Artur Steinwenter, Zum 70. Geburtstag.* Bd.3. Graz: H. Böhlaus Nachf., 1958, 100–120, at 114 ff.

Wesener, G. Review of G. Nicosia, *Studi Sulla Deiectio* (Milano: Giuffrè, 1965), in *SDHI* 32 (1966) 357–362.

---

[29] Translator's note: on the full form of this interdict see the textual note to Case 56.

[30] **§ 454 (1) ZPO:** Im Verfahren über Klagen wegen Störung des Besitzstandes bei Sachen und bei Rechten, in welchen das Klagebegehren nur auf den Schutz und die Wiederherstellung des letzten Besitzstandes gerichtet ist und welche innerhalb 30 Tagen anhängig zu machen sind, nachdem der Kläger von der Störung Kenntnis erlangte . . .

[31] **§ 457 (1) ZPO:** Die Verhandlung ist auf die Erörterung und den Beweis der Tatsache des letzten Besitzstandes und der erfolgten Störung zu beschränken, und es sind alle Erörterungen über das Recht zum Besitze, über Titel, Redlichkeit und Unredlichkeit des Besitzes oder über etwaige Entschädigungsansprüche auszuschließen.

CASE 56

D 43.16.1.30 (Ulpianus libro sexagensimo nono ad edictum)

Qui a me vi possidebat, si ab alio deiciatur, habet interdictum.

Translation: (Ulpian in the 69th book of his *Commentary on the Praetor's Edict*)[32]

If the man who possesses from me by force is himself driven from possession by another, he has the [benefit of the possessory] interdict.

Note on the Text:

Section 43.16 of the *Digest* is entitled *de vi et de vi armata* ["Concerning force and concerning armed force"].

The form of the *interdictum unde vi* in the Hadrianic edict reads: *Unde in hoc anno tu illum vi deiecisti aut familia tua aut procurator tuus deiecit, cum ille possideret, quod nec vi nec clam nec precario a te possideret, eo illum quaeque tunc ibi habuit restituas.* ("From where you have forcefully driven that man in the past year, or members of your *familia* or your procurator have driven him, since he was in possession of property that he obtained from you neither by force, nor by stealth, nor by request, to that place you must return him and restore everything else that he had there at that time.")

Discussion Questions:

Smith possesses a piece of land. Jones drives him from the possession. Then Brown comes and ousts Jones.

1) Who succeeds against whom with the *interdictum unde vi*:
   Jones against Brown? Smith against Brown? Smith against Jones?
2) Who may forcibly drive out whom by means of self-help:
   Jones drive out Brown? Smith drive out Brown?

Compare with this Case:

§ 339 Austrian Civil Code:

Whatever the quality of the possession, no one is authorized to interfere with the same on his own authority. The person who is interfered with has the right to a legal claim for prohibition of the interference and compensation for provable damages.[33]

---

[32] On author and work, see Case 11 (D 18.6.1.2).

[33] **§ 339 ABGB:** Der Besitz mag von was immer für einer Beschaffenheit sein, so ist niemand befugt, denselben eigenmächtig zu stören. Der Gestörte hat das Recht, die Untersagung des Eingriffes, und den Ersatz des erweislichen Schadens gerichtlich zu fordern.

§ 345 Austrian Civil Code:

If someone invades the possession, or through cunning or entreaty stealthily insinuates himself, and seeks to change into a lasting right what a person allowed him to have as a favor without any continuing obligation, then his illegitimate and unreasonable possession becomes invalid as well . . . [34]

§ 346 Austrian Civil Code:

Against every invalid possessor both restoration and indemnification for damages can be sued for. Pursuant to legal process, the court must order both, without regard to a stronger right to the property that the defendant possibly has.[35]

§ 861 I German Civil Code:

If the possession is taken from the possessor through unlawful force, then he can demand restoration of the possession from the person who wrongfully possesses in relation to him.[36]

§ 862 I German Civil Code:

If the possessor is disturbed in his possession through unlawful force, then he can demand cessation of the disturbance by the interferer. If further disturbances are feared, then the possessor can sue for prohibition.[37]

---

[34] § 345 ABGB: Wenn sich jemand in den Besitz eindringt, oder durch List oder Bitte heimlich einschleicht, und das, was man ihm aus Gefälligkeit, ohne sich einer fortdauernden Verbindlichkeit zu unterziehen gestattet, in ein fortwährendes Recht zu verwandeln sucht; so wird der an sich unrechtmäßige und unredliche Besitz noch überdies unecht; . . .

[35] § 346 ABGB: Gegen jeden unechten Besitzer kann sowohl die Zurücksetzung in die vorige Lage, als auch die Schadloshaltung eingeklagt werden. Beides muß das Gericht nach rechtlicher Verhandlung, selbst ohne Rücksicht auf ein stärkeres Recht, welches der Geklagte auf die Sache haben könnte, verordnen.

[36] § 861 I BGB: Wird der Besitz durch verbotene Eigenmacht dem Besitzer entzogen, so kann dieser die Wiedereinräumung des Besitzes von demjenigen verlangen, welcher ihm gegenüber fehlerhaft besitzt.

[37] § 862 I BGB: Wird der Besitzer durch verbotene Eigenmacht im Besitze gestört, so kann er von dem Störer die Beseitigung der Störung verlangen. Sind weitere Störungen zu besorgen, so kann der Besitzer auf Unterlassung klagen.

CASE 57

D 43.16.17 (Iulianus libro quadragensimo octavo digestorum)

Qui possessionem vi ereptam vi [in ipso congressu] reciperat, in pristinam causam reverti potius quam vi possidere intellegendus est: ideoque si te deiecero, [ilico] <tunc> tu me, deinde ego te, unde vi interdictum tibi utile erit.

Translation: (Julian in the 48th book of his *Digesta*)[38]

If someone has recovered by force a possession that had been forcibly taken from him [in the same conflict], he counts as returned to his earlier condition rather than possessing by force. Therefore if I drive you out, and [on the spot] you <then> drive me out, and then I drive you out, you will be able to use the *interdictum unde vi*.

Note on the Text:

Justinian removed the *exceptio vitiosae possessionis* ["affirmative defense of defective possession"] from the form of the *interdictum unde vi*. Therefore the compilers narrowed Julian's statement by interpolating[39] the phrases *in ipso congressu* ["in the same conflict"] and *ilico* ["on the spot"]. On *intellegendus* ("counts as"), see under Case 72.

Discussion Questions:

1) Explain Julian's decision.
2) Consider the following fact-situation: Jones drives Smith from possession of a piece of land. Smith returns after a day and drives out Jones. Jones then moves for the *interdictum unde vi* against Smith. How does the praetor decide? How does Justinian decide?
3) Do the compilers forbid every "recovery of possession," or does their formulation extend beyond simple "defense of possession"?

---

[38] On author and work, see Case 70 (D 41.1.36).

[39] Translator's note. Square brackets in the Latin text and translations of Latin text enclose words that are considered by the editor to be an "interpolation"—i.e., an error that has been introduced into the text during the transmission, or a deliberate change introduced by either a pre-Justinianic copyist of the source-text or by the Justinianic compilers. However, since the putative interpolation is in the manuscripts, the editor continues to reproduce it, so as not to misrepresent what has actually been transmitted by the manuscript tradition. Angled brackets, in turn, enclose text that is considered to have fallen out of the manuscript tradition—i.e., a textual error of omission. Text in angled brackets is not actually transmitted by the manuscript tradition, but the editor thinks it, or something of similar meaning, must have been there originally.

Compare with this Case:

§ 344 Austrian Civil Code:

To the rights of possession belong also the right to protect oneself in one's possession, and in the case that the judicial help would come too late, to resist force with
commensurate force (§ 19). . . .[40]

§ 859 German Civil Code:

I   The possessor may defend himself against unlawful force with force.

II If a movable piece of property is separated from the possessor by means
    of unlawful force, he may take it back by force from the wrongdoer who
    is caught in the very act or pursued.

III If the possession of land is wrested from the possessor through unlawful
    force, he may immediately upon the dispossession recover the possession
    by displacing the wrongdoer.[41]

---

[40] **§ 344 ABGB:** Zu den Rechten des Besitzes gehört auch das Recht, sich in seinem Besitze
zu schützen, und in dem Falle, daß die richterliche Hilfe zu spät kommen würde, Gewalt mit
angemessener Gewalt abzutreiben (§ 19) . . .

[41] **§ 859 BGB:**

I Der Besitzer darf sich verbotener Eigenmacht mit Gewalt erwehren.

II Wird eine bewegliche Sache dem Besitzer mittels verbotener Eigenmacht weggenommen,
so darf er sie dem auf frischer Tat betroffenen oder verfolgten Täter mit Gewalt wieder
abnehmen.

III Wird dem Besitzer eines Grundstücks der Besitz durch verbotene Eigenmacht entzogen,
so darf er sofort nach der Entziehung sich des Besitzes durch Entsetzung des Täters
wieder bemächtigen.

CASE 58

D 43.16.18 pr. (Papinianus libro vicensimo sexto quaestionum)

Cum fundum qui locaverat vendidisset, iussit emptorem in vacuam possessionem ire, quam colonus intrare prohibuit: postea emptor vi colonum expulit: de interdictis unde vi quaesitum est. placebat colonum interdicto venditori teneri, quia nihil interesset, ipsum an alium ex voluntate eius missum intrare prohibuerit: neque enim ante omissam possessionem videri, quam si tradita fuisset emptori, quia nemo eo animo est, ut possessionem omittere propter emptorem, quam emptor adeptus non fuisset. Emptorem quoque, qui postea vim adhibuit, et ipsum interdicto colono teneri: non enim ab ipso, sed a venditore per vim fundum esse possessum, cui possessio esset ablata. Quaesitum est, an emptori succurri debeat, si voluntate venditoris colonum postea vi expulisset. Dixi non esse iuvandum, qui mandatum illicitum susceperit.

Translation: (Papinian in the 26th book of his *Legal Questions*)[42]

When someone sold a farm that he had let out on lease, he ordered the buyer to take *vacua possessio* ["unimpeded possession"], which the tenant prohibited him from entering. Thereafter the buyer drove off the tenant with force. The issue concerns the interdict *unde vi*. It was held that the tenant is liable to the seller under the interdict, since it makes no difference whether he prevented the seller himself to enter or another who was sent at the seller's wish. For the possession does not count as surrendered before it is delivered to the buyer, since no one intends to surrender possession in favor of a buyer who would not have received it. The buyer who afterward used force is also liable under the interdict, but to the tenant. For the farm was possessed by force not from him but from the seller, who has been deprived of the possession. It was asked whether the buyer ought to be assisted [by the interdict], if he afterward expelled the tenant at the seller's wish. I replied that he who has taken up an illegal commission should not be assisted.

Note on the Text:

On *placebat* ("it was held that"), see on Case 36; on *videri* ("count as"), see on Case 72.

Discussion Questions:

Analyze Papinian's decision.

---

[42] On author and work, see Case 5 (D 18.1.74).

CASE 59

D 43.16.1.27 (Ulpianus libro sexagensimo nono ad edictum)

Vim vi repellere licere Cassius scribit idque ius natura comparatur: apparet autem, inquit, ex eo arma armis repellere licere.

Translation: (Ulpian in the 69th book of his *Commentary on the Praetor's Edict*)[43]

One may repel force with force, Cassius writes, and this right exists from nature. From this it follows, he says, that it is permitted to repel arms with arms.

Note on the Text:

The operation of the rule *vim vi repellere licet* ("one may resist force with force") is not limited to defense of possession: it expresses generally the right of self-defense (defense by appropriate means against a present or immediately imminent unlawful threat to life, health, or property)—cf. Gaius D 9.2.4 pr. *adversus periculum naturalis ratio permittit se defendere* ("natural reason permits the defense of oneself against danger"); Paul D 9.2.45.4 *vim enim vi defendere omnes leges omniaque iura permittunt* ("all laws and legal regimes permit defense by force against force").

Discussion Questions:

1) In the case of the *interdictum de vi armata* ["interdict concerning armed force"] the praetor granted no *exceptio vitiosae possessionis* ["affirmative defense of defective possession"]. What considerations might have moved him to make this distinction as compared with the *interdictum unde vi*?
2) Smith is driven off by Jones with *vis armata* ["armed force"] and thereafter recovers his possession with armed force. Will the praetor grant Jones the *interdictum de vi armata* against Smith?
3) Rarely the praetor granted an *exceptio "quod tu prior vi hominibus armatis non veneris"* ("insofar as you did not first invade with armed men"). Is Cassius making reference to this *exceptio*?
4) What considerations might have led the praetor to grant an *exceptio "quod tu prior . . . ,"* but not an *exceptio vitiosae possessionis*?

Literature:

Manthe (Case 19) 96 ff.

---

[43] On Ulpian, see Case 11 (D 18.6.1.2); on Cassius, see Case 19 (D 41.2.21.3).

iii. **Keeping and Losing Possession through Intermediaries (Slaves, Tenants)**

CASE 60

D 19.2.60.1 (Labeo posteriorum libro quinto a Iavoleno epitomatarum)

Heredem coloni, quamvis colonus non est, nihilo minus domino possidere existimo.

Translation: (Labeo in the 15th book of the *Epitome of [Labeo's] Posthumously Published Writings* prepared by Javolenus)[44]

I believe that the heir of a tenant, although not himself the tenant, nevertheless possesses for the *dominus* ["owner"].

Discussion Questions:

Explain Labeo's decision.

---

[44] On author and work, see Case 10 (D 41.2.51).

CASE 61

D 41.2.25.1 (Pomponius libro vicensimo tertio ad Quintum Mucium)

Et per colonos et inquilinos aut servos nostros possidemus: et si moriantur aut furere incipiant aut alii locent, inellegimur nos retinere possessionem. Nec inter colonum et servum nostrum, per quem possessionem retinemus, quicquam interest.

Translation: (Pomponius in the 23rd book of his *Commentary on the* Ius Civile *of Q. Mucius*)[45]

We possess also through tenants and renters or our slaves. And if they die or go mad or lease to another, it is understood that we retain the possession. And there is no difference between a tenant and our slave, through whom we retain possession.

Note on the Text:

On *intellegimur* ("it is understood that we"), see under Case 72.

Discussion Questions:

1) How can one make a legal argument for retention of possession despite the death of the slave who works the land?
2) How did the Roman jurists explain the retention of possession by a madman?
3) How long does possession after the death or madness of the slave remain in force?
4) How can the tenant be compared with the slave as regards retention of possession?
5) Why is the owner's possession not impaired by a sublease?

Literature:

Benöhr (Case 23) 51.

---

[45] On author and work, see Case 29 (D 41.1.21 pr.).

CASE 62

D 41.2.30.6 (Paulus libro quinto decimo ad Sabinum)

Si ego tibi commodavero, tu Titio, qui putet tuum esse, nihilo minus ego id possidebo. Et idem erit, si colonus meus fundum locaverit aut is, apud quem deposueram, apud alium rursus deposuerit. Et id quamlibet per plurium personam factum observandum ita erit.

Translation: (Paul in the 15th book of his *Commentary on the* Ius Civile *of Q. Mucius*)[46]

If I lend you something and you lend it thereafter to Titius, who thinks it is yours, I remain the possessor nonetheless. It is the same if my tenant sublets the land, or the person with whom I have deposited a thing, gives it to another for safekeeping. And this holds true in the case of any greater number of persons.

Discussion Questions:

1) Is it without significance that Titius means to exercise the possession not for *ego* [me] but for *tu* [you]?
2) How is it that *tu* [you] do not commit a theft that terminates possession by *ego* [me]?
3) What speaks in favor of an indefinite length of the possessory chain? What speaks against it?

---

[46] On author and work, see Case 1 (D 41.2.3.1).

CASE 63

D 41.2.32.1 (Paulus libro quinto decimo ad Sabinum)

Si conductor rem vendidit et eam ab emptore conduxit et utrique mercedes praestitit, prior locator possessionem per conductorem rectissime retinet.

Translation: (Paul in the 15th book of his *Commentary on the* Ius *Civile of Q. Mucius*)[47]

If a lessee sells the property and leases it back from the buyer and pays rent to both lessors, the first lessor keeps valid possession through the lessee.

Discussion Questions:

　　1) Has the second party here not transferred possession to the third?
　　2) Does it make a difference whether land or a movable is at issue?
　　3) Consider the relationship between this decision and D 41.2.30.6 (Case 62).

---

[47] On author and work, see Case 1 (D 41.2.3.1).

CASE 64

D 41.2.9 (Gaius libro vicensimo quinto ad edictum provinciale)

Generaliter quisquis omnino nostro nomine sit in possessione, veluti procurator hospes amicus, nos posidere videmur.

Translation: (Gaius in the 25th book of his *Commentary on the Provincial Edict*)[48]

Generally speaking, if anyone at all possesses in our name, like a procurator, a guest, or a friend, we count as the possessor.

Note on the Text:

On *videmur* ("we count as"), see under Case 72.

Discussion Questions:

Possession cannot be acquired through guests or friends. How is it that possession can be retained through these persons?

---

[48] On Gaius, see Case 6 (D 41.1.9.6). His 30 books on the provincial edict constituted an exhaustive commentary on the model edict for the provinces. Hadrian caused the provincial edict to be revised and published, as he did with the Praetor's edict too, making the former very similar to the latter.

CASE 65

D 41.2.3.8 (Paulus libro quinquagensimo quarto ad edictum)

Si quis nuntiet domum a latronibus occupatam et dominus timore conterritus noluerit accedere, amisisse eum possessionem placet. Quod si servus vel colonus, per quos corpore possidebam, decesserint discesserintve, animo retinebo possessionem.

Translation: (Paul in the 54th book of his *Commentary on the Praetor's Edict*)[49]

If someone should report that the house is occupied by thieves, and the owner does not wish to return from fear, he has lost the possession according to established doctrine; but if a slave or a tenant, through whom I have the possession *corpore*, dies or departs, I retain the possession *animo*.

Note on the Text:

On *placet* ("according to established doctrine"), see on case 36.

Discussion Questions:

1) Try to find a more substantial reason for the "established doctrine" that Paul cites.
2) Is it relevant for Paul's decision whether robbers actually do occupy the house?
3) From what perspective does Paul contrast the cases discussed here?
4) Can one retain possession *animo*, if his tenant is ousted by an intruder?
5) At D 41.2.40.1 (quoted below) Julian lets possession be lost if a tenant willingly surrenders it. What speaks in favor of Julian's opinion? What in favor of Paul's?

Compare with this Case:

D 41.2.40.1 (Africanus libro septimo quaestionum)

Si forte colonus, per quem dominus possideret, decessisset, propter utilitatem receptum est, ut per colonum possessio et retineretur et contineretur: quo mortuo non statim dicendum eam interpellari, sed tunc demum, cum dominus possessionem apisci neglexerit. Aliud existimandum ait, si colonus sponte possessione discesserit.

---

[49] On author and work, see Case 1 (D 41.2.3.1).

Translation: (Africanus in the seventh book of his *Legal Questions*)[50]

If by chance a tenant, through whom the owner possesses, dies, it is accepted for reasons of practicality that the possession is kept and continues through the tenant; and it is not to be said that the possession is interrupted as soon as the tenant dies, but only when the owner fails to take possession. [Julian] says it should be decided differently if the tenant willfully leaves the possession.

---

[50] On author and work, see Case 90 (D 41.4.11).

CASE 66

D 4.3.31 (Proculus libro secundo epistularum)

Cum quis persuaserit familiae meae, ut de possessione decedat, possessio quidem non amittitur, sed de dolo malo iudicium in eum competit, si quid damni mihi accesserit.

Translation: (Proculus in the second book of his *Epistles*)[51]

If someone persuades my household servants to depart from the possession, the possession is not lost; however, I have an *actio de dolo* ["lawsuit for fraud"] against him, if I suffer any damage.

Discussion Questions:

1) Jones persuades Smith's slaves to leave the latter's land and he himself occupies it. Has Smith lost possession?
2) Jones persuades Smith's household servants to give him a riding horse. Has Smith lost possession?
3) Smith's slaves capture a wild boar; Jones persuades them to let the boar free. Has Smith lost possession? Can he demand the value of the boar from Jones?
4) Add precision to Proculus' opinion and defend it against the objection that control of the property is lost with the departure of the entire household, and therefore the possession is lost too. Also take note of Cases 65 and 51.

Literature:

Krampe (Case 9) 78.
MacCormack, G. "Dolus in the Law of the Early Classical Period (Labeo-Celsus)." *SDHI* 52 (1986) 236–285, at 243 ff.

---

[51] On author and work, see Case 9 (D 41.1.55).

CHAPTER III

Acquiring Ownership and Losing Ownership

Introduction

Acquisition and loss of ownership, the most extensive and strongly protected right that a person could have over property, were regulated by the Roman legal order with particular thoroughness. For the transfer of *res mancipi*,[1] the formal procedures of *mancipatio* ["mancipation"] and *in iure cessio* ["surrender in law"] continued to be used into the classical period. These procedures were replaced in the Justinianic reworking of the sources by informal *traditio* [i.e., mere delivery, which had become more common already in classical practice.

The procedure of *traditio* was applicable, according to the parties' wishes, to the transfer of "detention" (i.e., simple holding), possession, or ownership. It has therefore already been partially discussed in Chapter I [in connection with possession]. *Traditio* was certainly the most frequent and important method of transferring ownership in general. As a form of derivative acquisition of rights, its effectiveness depended upon the legal capacity of the previous owner, his authority to alienate the property, certain prohibitions to alienation, and a valid meeting

---

[1] Translator's note: *res mancipi* (property subject to the type of ownership known as *mancipium*) is a category of property that was transferable only by means of the ancient and highly formal procedures of "mancipation" or a judicial proceeding. It is defined at Gai. Inst. II.14a: "Things are further divided into *mancipi* and [not] *mancipi*. *Mancipi* are lands and houses on Italic soil; likewise slaves and animals that are commonly broken to draught or burden, such as oxen, horses, mules, and asses." F. de Zulueta, *The Institutes of Gaius*, Part 1, Oxford (1946) p. 69.

of the minds. The classical jurists required in addition a *iusta causa* ["legitimate reason"] for the transfer of ownership.

The process of *usucapio* brought about ownership independently of—in fact, in opposition to—existing ownership rights. The function of this means of original acquisition lay principally in rectifying a defective derivative acquisition, and therewith in guaranteeing legal certainty in the interests of the regulated exchange of goods. Roman law did not recognize any immediate acquisition of ownership in good faith by those without entitlement. However, after a relatively short period of prescription, during which the actual owner could pursue his rights, the good-faith possessor acquired ownership of another's property that he had obtained without proper title but on the basis of a *iusta causa*. The texts collected in subsection B of this chapter should shed light on three issues [concerning *usucapio*]: the content of the requisite *bona fides*, the problem of putative title, and the exposition of [the statute known as] the *lex Atinia*.

Hunting and fishing are typical examples of acquiring original ownership through *occupatio* of *res nullius* ["ownerless property"]. This category was more widely defined in Rome than in many other legal systems, which [often] provide for reservations in favor of the state or of certain groups.

Finding, on the other hand, only exceptionally led to acquisition of ownership in Rome: viz. when the [found] property had been abandoned by the owner, and when a *thensaurus* ["treasure-trove"] was involved.

Just as with *occupatio* through hunting and fishing, treasure-trove, and the taking-up of *res derelictae* ["abandoned property"], the acquisition of fruits by separation from the source-property or by taking possession of them was reckoned to be one of the so-called natural ways of acquiring ownership, by which the Roman jurists traced acquisition of original ownership to *naturalis ratio* ["natural reason"] and *ius gentium* ["law recognized by all peoples"].

The same was true of acquiring and losing ownership through accession and mixing. One group of cases under this head concerns the accession of movables to land (*superficies solo cedit* ["the surface goes with the ground"]). A second group concerns the accession of movables to movables; and a third, the blending and mixing of things. Acquiring ownership of money constitutes a special case of the latter.

The problem of who owns a new kind of thing that someone has made out of material belonging to another will be discussed as the last type of natural acquisition. This is known as "transformation" (or "specification").

Loss of ownership is not treated in one place but is discussed in connection with the various types of acquisition where one's acquisition of ownership is linked to another's loss of the same. In this connection possible claims for compensation are occasionally discussed, although they cannot always substitute fully for the lost position of ownership. As a property right, ownership can also come about upon the default of a debtor and thereby be exercised against third party transferees.

Literature:

A. *Traditio*

Kaser, Max. "Zur Iusta Causa Traditionis." *BIDR* 64 (1961) 61–97.

Wolf, Joseph Georg. *Error Im römischen Vertragsrecht*, Vol. 12. Abh. Köln: Böhlau, 1961, 100 ff.

Jahr, G. "Zur Iusta Causa Traditionis." *ZRG* 80 (1963) 141–174.

Benke, Nikolaus. "Zur 'traditio' als zentralem Modell privatrechtlicher Vermögensübertragung," in *Gedächtnisschrift Herbert Hofmeister*, Herbert Hofmeister, Werner Ogris and Walter H. Rechberger, eds. Wien: Manzsche Verlags-und Universitätsbuchhandlung, 1996, 31 ff.

B. *Usucapio*

Thomas, J. A. C. "The Theftuous Pledger and the Lex Atinia," in *Studi in Onore Di Gaetano Scherillo,* I. Milano: Cisalpino - La Goliardica, 1972, 395–404.

Hausmaninger, Herbert. *Die bona fides des Ersitzungsbesitzers im klassischen römischen Recht,* Wien: Herold, 1964; and the review by Wubbe, *RHD* 32 (1964) 597 ff.

Mayer-Maly, Theo. *Das Putativtitelproblem bei der Usucapio,* Graz; Köln: Böhlaus, 1962.

Winkel, Laurens C. *Error Iuris Nocet.* Zutphen, Holland: Terra, 1985.

Bauer, Karen. Ersitzung und Bereicherung im klassischen römischen Recht : *und die Ersitzung im BGB,* n.F., Bd. 11. Berlin: Duncker & Humblot, 1988.

Jakobs, H. H. "Error Falsae Causae," in *Festschrift für Werner Flume zum 70. Geburtstag, 12. September 1978,* I, H. H. Jakobs, ed., Köln: Schmidt, 1978, 43–99.

C. *Occupatio*

Kaser, Max. "Die natürlichen Eigentumserwerbsarten im altrömischen Recht." *ZRG* 65 (1947) 219–260.

Knütel, Rolf. "Von schwimmende Inseln, wandernden Bäumen, flüchtenden Tieren und verborgenen Schätzen," in *Rechtsgeschichte und Privatrechtsdogmatik*, R. Zimmermann, R. Knütel, and J. Peter Meincke, eds. Heidelberg: C.F. Müller, 1999, 549 ff.

D. Abandonment and Finding

Düll, R. "Auslobung und Fund im antiken Recht." *ZRG* 61 (1941) 19–43.

E. Treasure-trove

Hausmaninger, H. "Besitzerwerb solo animo," in *Festgabe für Arnold Herdlitczka zu seinem 75. Geburtstag. Dargebracht von seinen Schülern und Freunden,* Arnold Rudolf Herdlitczka, Franz Horak, and Wolfgang Waldstein, eds. München: W. Fink, 1972, 113–119.

Hill, George. *Treasure Trove in Law and Practice from the Earliest Time to the Present Day.* Oxford: Clarendon Press, 1936.

F. Acquisition of Fruits

Kaser, Max. "Zum Fruchterwerb des Usufruktuars," *Studi in Onore Di Gaetano Scherillo* 1. Milano: Cisalpino - La Goliardica,1972, 405–426.

———. "Partus Ancillae." *ZRG* 75 (1958) 156–200.

Thielmann, G. "Produktion als Grundlage des Fruchterwerbs," *ZRG* 94 (1977) 76–100.

G. Joining, Blending, and Mixing

Meincke, J. P. "Superficies Solo Cedit," *ZRG* 88 (1971) 136–183.

Kaser, Max. Review of Melillo, G. *Tignum Iunctum*, Napoli: Jovene (1964), in *Labeo* 12 (1964) 104 ff.

Hinker, H. "Tignum Iunctum" *ZRG* 108 (1991) 94–122.

Kaser, Max. "Tabula Picta." *RHD* 36 (1968) 31–56.

Watkin, T. G. "Tabula Picta: Images and Icons," *SDHI* 50 (1984) 383–399.

Kaser, Max. "Das Geld im römischen Sachenrecht," *RHD* 29(1961) 169–229.

Fuchs, J. G. "Consumptio Nummorum," in *Mélanges Ph. Meylan*, I, Lausanne: Imprimerie centrale, 1963, 125–137.

Wacke, A. "Die Zahlung mit fremden Geld. Zum Begriff des Pecuniam Consumere." *BIDR* 79 (1976) 49–144.

Bürge, Alfons. Retentio im römischen Sachen- und Obligationenrecht. Zürich: Schulthess, 1979, 14 ff.

Schermaier, Martin Josef. Materia: Beiträge zur Frage der Naturphilosophie im klassischen römischen Recht. Wien: Böhlau, 1992.

H. Transformation

Wieacker, Fr. "Zum Thema der Spezifikation." *Festschrift Für E. Rabel, II: Geschichte Der Antiken Rechte Und Allgemeine Rechtslehre*, Tübingen: Mohr, 1954, II. 263–293.

Mayer-Maly, Th. "Spezifikation. Leitfälle, Begriffsbildung, Rechtsinstitut." *ZRG* 73 (1956) 120–154.

Thielmann, G. "Zum Eigentumserwerb durch Verarbeitung im römischen Recht," in *Sein und Werden im Recht: Festgabe für Ulrich von Lübtow zum 70. Geburtstag am 21. August 1970*, Walter Gustav Becker and Ludwig Schnorr von Carosfeld, eds., Berlin: Duncker & Humblot, 1970, 187–232.

Schermaier, Martin Josef. "D. 41,1,24 und 26 Pr. Ein Versuch zur Verarbeitungslehre des Paulus." *ZRG* 105 (1988) 436–487.

―――. "Teilvindikation oder Teilungsklage? Auf der Suche nach dem klassischen Vermischungs-recht." *ZRG* 110 (1993) 124–183.

Behrends, Okko. "Die Spezifikationslehre, ihre Gegner und die Media Sententia in der Geschichte der römischen Jurisprudenz." *ZRG* 112 (1995) 195–238.

A. *Traditio*

CASE 67

D 41.1.20 pr. (Ulpianus libro vicensimo nono ad Sabinum)

Traditio nihil amplius transferre debet vel potest ad eum qui accipit, quam est apud eum qui tradit. Si igitur quis dominium in fundo habuit, id tradendo transfert, si non habuit, ad eum qui accipit nihil transfert

Translation: (Ulpian in the 29th book of his *Commentary on the* Ius Civile *of Sabinus*)[2]

The act of *traditio* should not transfer more to the transferee than the transferor has, nor does it. Therefore if someone has ownership in a piece of land, he transfers it through *traditio*; if he does not have it, he transfers nothing to the transferee.

Discussion Questions:

1) Do you think the text originally concerned *mancipatio* and has been changed by Justinian? Compare Gaius Inst. 2.22: *mancipi vero res sunt, quae per mancipationem ad alium transferuntur . . .* ("*res mancipi* are things that are transferred to another by means of *mancipatio*").
2) Is at least possession transferred by the non-owner?
3) Can every owner transfer his property with legal effect?
4) Smith tells Jones to sell a book of Smith's for 100. Jones sells the book to Brown for 80 and delivers it to him. Has Brown acquired ownership?

Compare with this Case:

D 50.17.54 (Ulpianus libro quadragensimo sexto ad edictum)

Nemo plus iuris ad alium transferre potest quam ipse haberet.

Translation: (Ulpian in the 46th book of his *Commentary on the Praetor's Edict*)

No one can transfer to another a greater right than he himself has.

§ 442 Austrian Civil Code:

. . . In general no one can cede to another a greater right than he himself has."[3]

---

[2] On author and work, see Case 11 (D 18.6.1.2).

[3] **§ 442 ABGB:** . . . Überhaupt kann niemand einem anderen mehr Recht abtreten, als er selbst hat.

§ 367 Austrian Civil Code:

The ownership suit for movable property does not lie against the reasonable possessor, if he proves that he acquired the property either in a public auction, or from a merchant authorized to engage in this business, or as compensation from someone to whom the plaintiff himself entrusted the property for use, for safekeeping, or for any other purpose. In these cases the ownership will have been acquired by the reasonable possessor, and to the former owner there is available only the right of indemnification against that party who is answerable to him for the loss.[4]

---

[4] § 367 ABGB: Die Eigentumsklage findet gegen den redlichen Besitzer einer beweglichen Sache nicht statt, wenn er beweist, daß er diese Sache entweder in einer öffentlichen Versteigerung, oder von einem zu diesem Verkehre befügten Gewerbsmanne, oder gegen Entgelt von jemandem an sich gebracht hat, dem sie der Kläger selbst zum Gebrauche, zur Verwahrung, oder in was immer für einer andern Absicht anvertraut hätte. In diesen Fällen wird von den redlichen Besitzern das Eigentum erworben, und dem vorigen Eigentümer steht nur gegen jene, die ihm dafür verantwortlich sind, das Recht der Schadloshaltung zu.

CASE 68

D 39.5.25 (Iavolenus libro sexto epistularum)

Si tibi dederim rem, ut Titio meo nomine donares, et tu tuo nomine eam ei dederis, an factam eius putes? Respondit, si rem tibi dederim, ut Titio meo nomine donares, eamque tu tuo nomine ei dederis, quantum ad iuris suptilitatem accipientis facta non est, et tu furti obligaris: sed benignius est, si agam contra eum qui rem accepit, exceptione doli mali me summoveri.

Translation: (Javolenus in the sixth book of his *Letters*)[5]

If I give you something in order for you to make a gift of it to Titius in my name, and you then make a gift of it to him in your own name, do you think that it has become his property? He answered: If I give you something in order for you to make a gift of it to Titius in my name, and you then make a gift of it to him in your own name, by strict application of law the property has not become the transferee's, and you are liable to a suit for theft. But it is fairer, if I do bring a suit against the transferee, for me to be barred by the *exceptio doli* ["affirmative defense of fraud"].

Note on the Text:

Observe the style of a *responsum* ["jurist's opinion in reply to a legal question"] as well as the interesting contrast that is drawn between *suptilitas iuris* ["strict application of law"] and *benignius est* ["more generous"]. The high classical jurists Javolenus, Celsus (see under Case 146), and Julian refer to *benignitas* or *benigna interpretatio* (the kind/charitable/generous construction or interpretation), if they wish to mitigate the severity of an applicable rule (*subtilitas iuris*), especially when a strictly invalid legal transaction should be recognized as legal in the interests of commerce (later called *favor negotii*).

Discussion Questions:

1) Why has Titius not acquired ownership according to the strict application of law?
2) In what way is the decision of Javolenus *benignior* ["more generous"]?
3) Does Javolenus regard Titius as the owner?
4) Against which lawsuit does Javolenus consider the *exceptio doli* to be appropriate?
5) In what does Javolenus see a *dolus* ["fraud/trick/deceit"] of the giver? Cf. Case 71.

Literature:

Eckardt (Case 3) 25 ff.

Hausmaninger, H. "Subtilitas iuris," in *Iuris professio. Festgabe für Max Kaser zum 80. Geburtstag*. Wien: Böhlau, 1986, 59–72, at 64 ff.

---

[5] On author and work, see Case 3 (D 46.3.79).

CASE 69

D 41.1.31 pr. (Paulus libro trigensimo primo ad edictum)

Numquam nuda traditio transfert dominium, sed ita, si venditio aut ali[qu]a iusta causa praecesserit, propter quam traditio sequeretur.

Translation: (Paul in the 31st book of his *Commentary on the Praetor's Edict*)[6]

Never does simple delivery [*traditio*] transfer ownership: it will be transferred only if a sale or other recognized grounds of acquisition precedes the transfer, on the basis of which the transfer follows.

Discussion Questions:

1) Which of the following *causae traditionis* ["reasons for delivery"] do not qualify as bases for acquiring ownership: conferral of a gift—delivery of a dowry—loan of money—loan of a thing—deposit of a pledge—letting of immovable property—payment of a debt?
2) Titius gives and delivers a ring to his wife. After divorce he demands the ring back with a *rei vindicatio*.[7] Will his lawsuit succeed?
3) Smith in error delivers to Jones property that is not owed. Jones knows that Smith does not owe the property, but he says nothing. Does Smith have the *rei vindicatio*?
4) Smith in error delivers un-owed property to Jones, who accepts it in the good faith belief that it is owed. Can Smith vindicate it [i.e., successfully bring the *rei vindicatio*]?

Compare with this Case:

§ 380 Austrian Civil Code:

Without title and without a legal type of acquisition no ownership can be obtained.[8]

§ 929 German Civil Code:

To transfer ownership of a movable it is necessary that the owner deliver the thing to the transferee and that both are in agreement that the ownership is supposed to transfer. . . ."[9]

---

[6] On author and work, see Case 1 (D 41.2.3.1).

[7] Translator's note: The *rei vindicatio* is the action by which an owner sues for recovery of possession of his property. It is discussed in detail in Section "A" of Chapter IV.

[8] **§ 380 ABGB:** Ohne Titel und ohne rechtliche Erwerbungsart kann kein Eigentum erlangt werden.

[9] **§ 929 BGB:** Zur Übertragung des Eigentums an einer beweglichen Sache ist erforderlich, daß der Eigentümer die Sache dem Erwerber übergibt und beide darüber einig sind, daß das Eigentum übergehen soll . . .

Art. 1138 French Civil Code:

The obligation to deliver the thing is perfected by the agreement alone of the contracting parties.

It makes the creditor the owner. . . .[10]

Literature:

Kaser, M. "Zur iusta causa traditionis," *BIDR* 64 (1961) 61–97, at 66 ff.

---

[10] **Art. 1138 C. civ.:** L'obligation de livrer la chose est parfaite par le seul consentement des parties contractantes.

Elle rend le créancier propriétaire . . .

CASE 70

D 41.1.36 (Iulianus libro tertio decimo digestorum)

Cum in corpus quidem quod traditur consentiamus, in causis vero dissentiamus, non animadverto, cur inefficax sit traditio, veluti si ego credam me ex testamento tibi obligatum esse, ut fundum tradam, tu existimes ex stipulatu tibi eum deberi. Nam et si pecuniam numeratam tibi tradam donandi gratia, tu eam quasi creditam accipias, constat proprietatem ad te transire nec impedimento esse, quod circa causam dandi atque accipiendi dissenserimus.

Translation: (Julian in the 13th book of his *Digesta*)[11]

If we agree about the object to be transferred but have different understandings of the legal basis for the transfer, I do not see why the transfer should be invalid—for example, if I believe that I have an obligation under a will to deliver a piece of land to you, and you think the property is owed to you because of a *stipulatio*.[12] For if I deliver to you a fixed some of money with the understanding that it is a gift, and you accept it, thinking it is a loan, it is certain that the ownership transfers, and there is no impediment in the fact that we have not agreed on the grounds for giving and receiving.

Discussion Questions:

1) Can Julian, on the basis of this text, be seen simply as advocating an abstract understanding of *traditio* (i.e., waiving the [requirement of a] *iusta causa traditionis* ["legitimate reason for the delivery"])? Cf. on this point under Case 71.
2) With the understanding that Julian is here making an exception to the rule of D 41.1.31 pr. (Case 69: "causal" *traditio*), try to find the most explicit possible legal justifications for the transfer of ownership in the two fact-situations of the Julian passage.

---

[11] P. Salvius Julianus was a pupil of Javolenus and had an illustrious career under the emperors Hadrian, Antoninus Pius, and Marcus Aurelius, to all of whose *consilia* he belonged. When Julian was a young quaestor, Hadrian doubled his salary *propter insignem doctrinam* ["for his remarkable learning"], and later entrusted to him the final redaction of the praetorian edict. Julian attained the consulship (148 CE) and served as governor of Germania inferior, Hispania citerior, and Africa. In addition to his chief work, the *Digesta* in 90 books, there were transmitted four books *ad Urseium Ferocem* and six books *ex Minicio*. Since antiquity Julian counts as the most important of the Roman jurists. His fame rests chiefly on his clarity, elegance and intuition, and the fundamental insight and essential persuasiveness of his opinions. He rarely cites others, frequently bases his judgment on masterful "reasoning from case to case," and does not hesitate to step over dogmatic boundaries on the basis of considerations of justice. The late classical jurists, especially Ulpian, cite him as the most outstanding authority. Justinian took more than 450 direct excerpts of Julian's work into the Digest.

[12] Translator's note: A *stipulatio* is an enforceable oral promise.

3) Evaluate Julian's argumentation with the assumption that the compilers have substituted *traditio* for *mancipatio* in the land example.

Literature:

Kaser, Max. "Das Geld im römischen Sachenrecht," *RHD* 29 (1961) 169–229, at 225 ff.
Flume (Case 36) 53 ff.
Evans-Jones, R. and G. D. MacCormack. "Iusta causa traditionis," in *New Perspectives in the Roman Law of Property: Essays for Barry Nicholas.* New York: Oxford University Press, 1989, 99–109, at 102 ff.
Schermaier, Martin J. "Auslegung und Konsensbestimmung: Sachmängelhaftung, irrtum und anfängliche Unmöglichkeit nach römischem Kaufrecht," *ZRG* 115 (1998) 235–288, at 254 ff.

CASE 71

D 12.1.18 pr. (Ulpianus libro septimo disputationum)

Si ego pecuniam tibi quasi donaturus dedero, tu quasi mutuam accipias, Iulianus scribit donationem non esse: sed an mutua sit, videndum. Et puto nec mutuam esse magisque nummos accipientis non fieri, cum alia opinione acceperit. Quare si eos consumpserit, licet condictione teneatur, tamen doli exceptione uti poterit, quia secundum voluntatem dantis nummi sunt consumpti.

Translation: (Ulpian in the seventh book of his *Disputations*)[13]

If I turn over money to you with the intention of making a gift of it, but you accept it as if it is a loan, Julian writes that the gift is not valid: but we must examine whether the loan is.[14] And I think the loan too is not valid, and the money is not the property of the transferee, since he accepted it with a different understanding. Consequently, if he spends the money, although he is liable to a *condictio*, he can nevertheless use the *exceptio doli*, since the money was spent with the giver's consent.

Note on the Text:

The rule *in maiore minus inest* ("the smaller is contained in the larger"), cf. Labeo D 32.29.1, or *in eo quod plus sit semper inest et minus* ["in that which is more, less is always contained"], Paul D 50.17.110 pr., is applied to a variety of factual contexts in order to maintain a party's intention that has been defectively manifested: for example, if someone wishes to bequeath one-fourth of his property, but in his will erroneously writes "one-half" (Proculus, at Paul D 31.15 pr.), a valid bequest of one-fourth will exist. Or if Smith lets a piece of land for 5, but Jones thinks he is taking a lease for 10, the lease is not invalid for want of agreement: it takes effect at a payment of 5 (Pomponius D 19.2.52). Consider whether Julian could have used this rule in Case 71.

Discussion Questions:

1) Do you think that in Julian's view a loan has been made (cf. on this point D 41.1.36 [Case 70])?
2) On what grounds does Ulpian deny the existence of a loan?
3) Why does Ulpian grant a *condictio* [an *in personam* action for damages] rather than a *rei vindicatio* [an owner's *in rem* action for possession of property] against the transferee? (cf. Case 119)

---

[13] On Ulpian, see Case 11 (D 18.6.1.2); on his *Disputations*, see Case 44 (D 41.2.34 pr.); on Julian, see Case 70 (D 41.1.36).

[14] Translator's note: The issues raised by this and the preceding case will be clarified by referring back to Case 13 and the footnotes thereto.

4) How is the *exceptio doli* for the transferee to be explained? (cf. Case 68)
5) Smith wishes to make a deposit of money. Jones thinks he is accepting this money as a loan. Explain the legal situation.

Literature:

Backhaus, R. "In maiore minus est. Eine iustinianische regula iuris in den klassischen Rechtsquellen. Herkunft, Anwendungsbereich und Funktion." *ZRG* 100 (1983) 136–184, at 164 ff.
Flume (Case 36) 53 ff.
Evans-Jones/MacCormack (Case 70) 102 ff.

B. *Usucapio*

a. *Reversio in potestatem* (interpretation of the *lex Atinia*)

CASE 72

D 41.3.4.6 (Paulus libro quinquagensimo quarto ad edictum)

Quod autem dicit lex Atinia, ut res furtiva non usucapiatur, nisi in potestatem eius, cui subrepta est, revertatur, sic acceptum est, ut in domini potestatem debeat reverti, non in eius utique, cui subreptum est. igitur creditori subrepta et ei, cui commodata est, in potestatem domini redire debet.

Translation: (Paul in the 54th book of his *Commentary on the Praetor's Edict*)[15]

But what the *lex Atinia* ["Atilian Statute"] says, that stolen property cannot be usucapted unless it is returned to him from whom it was stolen, is understood as follows: that it must be returned to the control of the owner, not merely to the control of him from whom it was stolen. Therefore, property that has been stolen from a creditor or someone to whom it has been lent must return to the control of the owner.

Notes on the Text:

The Roman author, Aulus Gellius, states in his work, *Noctes Atticae* 17.7.1: *Legis veteris Atiniae verba sunt "Quod subruptum erit, <nisi in potestate eius, cui subruptum est, revertatur> eius rei aeterna auctoritas esto."* ("The ancient *lex Atinia* contains the following words: 'the *auctoritas* ['ownership interest'] over property that has been stolen will last for ever, <as long as it has not been returned to the *potestas* ["power/control"] of the person from whom it was stolen>.'")

   This means that a seller, who normally must "guarantee" (*auctoritatem praestare*) mancipated property until the purchaser has acquired it by usucapion, remains liable for the purchaser's eviction from *res furtivae* ["stolen property"] indefinitely.

   With usages like *sic acceptum* (or *sic accipiendum*) *est* ("is understood as") the jurists communicate an interpretation of language. Since they equate the understood content with the language of a law or legal rule, one refers to such a statement as an "expository" interpretation. This extremely common practice also takes the form of expressions like *intellegi, esse, videri, (appellatione) contineri* ["is understood, is, is seen as, is included (within the term)"]. The jurists also use these formulations in their interpretation of legal concepts, of the meaning of expressions of intent, and of the factual conduct of persons.

---

[15] On author and work, see Case 1 (D 41.2.3.1).

Discussion Questions:

1) [Referring to the "Notes" on Case 68] what sort of "construction" of the *lex* ["statute"] is set forth in this case?
2) Try to provide a rationale for this "construction."
3) Could it also be argued that with the return of the property to the deposi- tary or the borrower a *reversio ad dominum* ["return to the owner"] has taken place?
4) Is there a *reversio ad dominum* if the property reaches the owner's slave?

Literature:

Thomas, J. A. C. "The Theftuous Pledger and the Lex Atinia," in *Studi in Onore Di Gaetano Scherillo* 1. Milano: Cisalpino - La Goliardica, 1972, 395–404, at 396 ff.

CASE 73

D 41.3.41 (Neratius libro septimo membranarum)

Si rem subreptam mihi procurator meus adprehendit, quamvis per procuratorem pos-sessionem apisci nos iam fere conveniat, nihilo magis eam in potestatem meam redisse usuque capi posse existimandum est, quia contra statui captiosum erit.

Translation: (Neratius in the seventh book of his *Legal Notes*)[16]

If my procurator recovers a piece of property that was stolen from me, although it is now generally recognized that we can acquire possession through a procurator, it is not to be thought that the property has returned to my control and can be usucapted, because it would be harmful to decide otherwise.

Discussion Questions:

1) How might Neratius and Paul at D 41.3.4.6 (Case 72) have distinguished between *possessio* ["legal possession"] and *potestas* ["legal power/control"]?

2) In what might Neratius have detected the harmfulness of a contrary decision?

3) What would you expect the jurists' decision to be if the stolen property is returned without the knowledge of the *dominus* to his slave (with or without *peculium*)?

Literature:

Watson (Case 32) 22 ff. (reprinted in *Studies* 64 f.).
Honoré, A. M. "A Study of Neratius and a Reflection on Method," *RHD* 63 (1975) 223–240, at 231 ff.
Claus (Case 35) 125 ff.
Krenz (Case 33) 346 ff.

---

[16] Lucius Neratius Priscus (consul 87 CE, later legate of Pannonia) followed Celsus *pater* [the elder Celsus] as the head of the Proculian school and was a member of the *consilium* of Trajan and Hadrian. His works include collections of case law (*responsa*, letters, *regulae* ["rules" or "maxims"]). The *membranae* (literally "parchments" but, by metonymy, "legal notes") contained *responsa* and *quaestiones* ["legal questions"] in seven books.

CASE 74

D 41.3.4.21 (Paulus libro quinquagensimo quarto ad edictum)

Si rem pignori datam debitor subripuerit et vendiderit, usucapi eam posse Cassius scribit, quia in potestatem domini videtur pervenisse, qui pignori dederit, quamvis cum eo furti agi potest: quod puto rectius dici.

Translation: (Paul in the 54th book of his *Commentary on the Praetor's Edict*)[17]

If the debtor turns over property on pledge [i.e., as security] and then steals it back and sells it, Cassius writes that it can be usucapted, since it counts as having returned to the control of the owner who pledged it—although he can be sued for theft. I consider this decision to be better.

Note on the Text:

On *videtur* ("counts as"), see under Case 72.

Discussion Questions:

1) On what grounds could Cassius and Paul have based their decision?
2) "*Quod puto rectius dici*" ("I consider this decision to be better") alludes to a juristic controversy (cf. *verius* in Case 8). How might the contrary view be argued?

Literature:

Thomas (Case 72) 397.
Kaser (Case 159) 272.

---

[17] On author and work, see Case 1 (D 41.2.3.1); on Cassius, see Case 19 (D 41.2.21.3).

CASE 75

D 41.3.49 (Labeo libro quinto pithanon a Paulo epitomatorum)

Si quid est subreptum, id usucapi non potest, antequam in domini potestatem pervenerit. Paulus: immo forsitan et contra: nam si id, quod mihi pignori dederis, subripueris, erit ea res furtiva facta: sed simul atque in meam potestatem venerit, usucapi poterit.

Translation: (Labeo in the fifth book of Paul's Epitome of his *Pithana*)[18]

If something is stolen, it cannot be usucapted, as long as it has not returned to the *potestas* of the owner. Paul: perhaps also the opposite, since, if you have pledged something to me and then you steal it, it has become *res furtiva* ["stolen property"], yet as soon as it comes back into my control, it can be usucapted.

Discussion Questions:

Discuss the relationship of this text to Paul at D 41.3.4.6 (Case 72) and D 41.3.4.21 (Case 74).

Literature:

Thomas (Case 72) 396 ff.

---

[18] On author and work, see Case 37 (D 41.1.65 pr.).

CASE 76

D 41.3.4.10 (Paulus libro quinquagensimo quarto ad edictum)

Si rem, quam apud te deposueram, lucri faciendi causa vendideris, deinde ex paenitentia redemeris et eodem statu habeas: sive ignorante me sive sciente ea gesta sint, videri in potestatem meam redisse secundum Proculi sententiam, quae et vera est.

Translation: (Paul in the 54th book of his *Commentary on the Praetor's Edict*)[19]

If, with the intention of making a profit, you sell property that I have deposited with you, and then from regret you buy it back and keep it in the same condition as before, it counts as having returned to my control, whether I had knowledge of these events or not. That is the view of Proculus, which is also the correct view.

Note on the Text:

On *videri* ("counts as"), see under Case 72.

Discussion Questions:

1) The depositary sells the deposited property and later buys it back from regret. After his death his heir sells it to a good-faith acquirer. Can it be usucapted?
2) Compare the decision of Proculus and Paul with Paul at D 41.3.4.6 (Case 72). Can one resolve the contradiction by reference to the different subject matter, or only by assuming an interpolation?

---

[19] On author and work, see Case 1 (D 41.2.3.1); on Proculus, see Case 9 (D 41.1.55).

CASE 77

D 41.3.4.12 (Paulus libro quinquagensimo quarto ad edictum)

Tunc in potestatem domini redisse dicendum est, cum possessionem eius nactus sit iuste, ut avelli non possit, sed et tamquam suae rei: nam si ignorans rem mihi subreptam emam, non videri in potestatem meam reversam.

Translation: (Paul in the 54th book of his *Commentary on the Praetor's Edict*)[20]

It is to be said that property returns to the control of its owner if he obtains the defect-free possession in such a manner that he cannot be separated from it. However, he must have obtained it also with the knowledge that it involves his own property. So, if I unwittingly buy property that has been stolen from me, it does not count as returned to my control.

Note on the Text:

On *videri* ("counts as"), see under Case 72.

Discussion Questions:

1) What kind of interpretation does Paul prefer here? [See "Note on the Text" under Case 68].
2) Compare the requirement here of a defect-free *reversio* ["return"] with Cassius/Paul at D 41.3.4.25 (Case 78) and D 41.3.4.21 (Case 74), and with Paul at D 41.3.49 (Case 75).

---

[20] On author and work, see Case 1 (D 41.2.3.1).

CASE 78

D 41.3.4.25 (Paulus libro quinquagensimo quarto ad edictum)

Si dominus fundi possessorem vi deiecerit, Cassius ait non videri in potestatem eius redisse, quando interdicto unde vi restituturus sit possessionem.

Translation: (Paul in the 54th book of his *Commentary on the Praetor's Edict*)[21]

If the owner of a plot of land ousts the possessor with force, Cassius says the land does not count as returned to his control, since he must restore the possession under the *interdictum unde vi*.[22]

Note on the Text:

On *videri* ("counts as"), see under Case 72.

Discussion Questions:

1) Does this fact-situation fall within the application of the *lex Atinia*?
2) Consider and explain the relationship of this decision to Cassius/Paulus at D 41.3.4.21 (Case 74).
3) The owner, Smith, has lost the possession of his land to the intruder, Jones. After some time the current possessor, Jones, is forcibly driven off by Smith. Thereafter a bad-faith third party, Brown, enters the property and sells and delivers it to a good-faith acquirer, Green. Can Green usucapt?
4) The owner, Smith, is driven off his land by Jones. Jones gives the possession to Brown. Smith then ousts Brown. Has there been a *reversio ad dominum* ["return to the owner"]?

Literature:

Thomas (Case 72) 397 ff.
Manthe (Case 19) 94 ff.

---

[21] On author and work, see Case 1 (D 41.2.3.1).

[22] Translator's note: on the content of the *interdictum unde vi*, see the "Note on the Text" to Case 56.

CASE 79

D 41.2.3.13 and **14** (Paulus libro quinquagensimo quarto ad edictum)

13) *Sed et si vindicavero rem mihi subreptam et litis aestimationem accepero, licet corporaliter eius non sim nactus possessionem, usucapietur.*

14) *Idem dicendum est etiam, si voluntate mea alii tradita sit.*

Translation: (Paul in the 54th book of his *Commentary on the Praetor's Edict*)[23]

13) But if I vindicate property stolen from me and accept the judicial valuation in money,[24] the property can be usucapted, although I have not physically recovered its possession.

14) The same can be said if the property is transferred to another with my consent.

Discussion Questions:

1) Who is understood to acquire by usucapion in the first case?
2) Create a concrete example to clarify the second case.
3) How does Paul interpret the concept of *reversio* ["return"] in both cases?

---

[23] On author and work, see Case 1 (D 41.2.3.1).

[24] Translator's note: To expand upon the details for the sake of clarity, this case assumes that an owner has brought a successful *in rem* action against the defendant for recovery of possession. In lieu of restoring possession to the owner, however, the defendant has paid the owner damages equal to a judge's valuation of the property. The issue is whether acceptance of that payment counts as "return of the property to the owner's control" as required by the Atilian statute.

b. *Bona fides*

CASE 80

D 50.16.109 (Modestinus libro quinto pandectarum)

'Bonae fidei emptor' esse videtur, qui ignoravit eam rem alienam esse, aut putavit eum qui vendidit ius vendendi habere, puta procuratorem aut tutorem esse.

Translation: (Modestinus in the fifth book of his *Pandects*)[25]

Someone is deemed a "good-faith buyer" if he did not know that someone else's property was involved in the transaction, or he believed the seller had the right to sell it—e.g., he was a procurator or a guardian.

Note on the Text:

On *videtur* ("is deemed"), see under Case 72.

Discussion Questions:

1) Gaius Inst. 2.43 understands *bona fides* as belief that the transferor is the owner. How far beyond this "normal case" does the definition of Modestinus go?
2) According to Modestinus, is a buyer *bona fide* if he doubts the ownership of the seller?

Compare with this Case:

§ 1460 Austrian Civil Code:

For acquisition by prescription, in addition to the capacity of the person and the object, it is necessary that someone actually possesses the property or the right that is supposed to be acquired in this manner; that his possession is legally valid, reasonable, and true, and is continuous through the entire time specified by law (§§ 309, 316, 326, and 345).[26]

---

[25] Herennius Modestinus was a pupil of Ulpian and the last famous classical jurist. Around 240 CE he attained the office of *praefectus vigilum* in Rome. In addition to collections of cases (12 *libri pandectarum*, 19 *libri responsorum*) Modestinus wrote didactic literature (10 books of *regulae*, 9 books of *differentiae*) and a series of monographs.

[26] § 1460 ABGB: Zur Ersitzung wird nebst der Fähigkeit der Person und des Gegenstandes erfordert: daß jemand die Sache oder das Recht, die auf diese Art erworben werden sollen, wirklich besitze; daß sein Besitz rechtmäßig, redlich und echt sei, und durch die ganze von dem Gesetze bestimmte Zeit fortgesetzt werde (§§ 309, 316, 326 und 345).

§ 326 Austrian Civil Code:

He who on plausible grounds considers as his own the property that he possesses is a reasonable possessor. An unreasonable possessor is that person who knows, or from the circumstances must suspect, that the property in his possession belongs to another. From an error of fact or ignorance of the legal provisions someone can be a legally invalid (§ 316) but still reasonable possessor.[27]

§ 937 German Civil Code:

I   He who holds movable property for 10 years in proprietary possession acquires the ownership (prescription).[28]

II   Prescription is excluded if the acquirer at the time of acquiring his possession is not in good faith or if he later learns that the ownership does not belong to him.

§ 932 II German Civil Code:

The acquirer is not in good faith, if it is known by him, or unknown as a result of gross negligence, that the property does not belong to the transferor.[29]

---

[27] **§ 326 ABGB:** Wer aus wahrscheinlichen Gründen die Sache, die er besitzt, für die seinige hält, ist ein redlicher Besitzer. Ein unredlicher Besitzer ist derjenige, welcher weiß oder aus den Umständen vermuten muß, daß die in seinem Besitze befindliche Sache einem andern zugehöre. Aus Irrtum in Tatsachen oder aus Unwissenheit der gesetzlichen Vorschriften kann man ein unrechtmäßiger (§ 316) und doch ein redlicher Besitzer sein.

[28] **§ 937 BGB:**
  I Wer eine bewegliche Sache zehn Jahre im Eigenbesitze hat, erwirbt das Eigentum (Ersitzung).
  II Die Ersitzung is ausgeschlossen, wenn der Erwerber bei dem Erwerbe des Eigenbesitzes nicht in gutem Glauben ist oder wenn er später erfährt, daß ihm das Eigentum nicht zusteht.

[29] **§ 932 II BGB:** Der Erwerber ist nicht in gutem Glauben, wenn ihm bekannt oder infolge grober Fahrlässigkeit unbekannt ist, daß die Sache nicht dem Veräußerer gehört.

CASE 81

D 41.3.24 pr. (Pomponius libro vicensimo quarto ad Quintum Mucium)

Ubi lex inhibet usucapionem, bona fides possidenti nihil prodest.

Translation: (Pomponius in the 24th book of his *Commentary on the* Ius Civile *of Quintus Mucius*)[30]

Where a statute prohibits usucapion, the *bona fides* of the possessor is of no advantage.

Discussion Questions:

1) What statute could be meant here?
2) The thief, Smith, sells to a good-faith Jones, and Jones sells to the good-faith Brown. Can Brown usucapt?

Literature:

Mayer-Maly, Theo. *Das Putativtitelproblem bei der Usucapio,* Graz; Köln: Böhlaus, 1962, 143.

---

[30] On author and work, see Case 29 (D 41.1.21 pr.).

CASE 82

D 41.3.12 (Paulus libro vicensimo primo ad edictum)

Si ab eo emas, quem praetor vetuit alienare, idque tu scias, usucapere non potes.

Translation: (Paul in the 21st book of his *Commentary on the Praetor's Edict*)[31]

If you buy from someone on whom the Praetor has imposed a ban against alienating property, and you know it, you cannot usucapt.

Discussion Questions:

1) The Praetor has imposed a ban on alienating property against a spendthrift or a contingent heir in order to protect the dependents or creditors. Someone who is unaware of the ban buys property from this person. What are the legal consequences?
2) Titius without knowledge of the *lex Atinia* buys a stolen thing that he regards as the seller's property. Legal consequences?
3) What considerations could you offer to justify the decisions under "1" and "2"?

Literature:

Hausmaninger, H. Die bona fides des Ersitzungsbesitzers im klassischen römischen Recht, Wien: Herold, 1964, 38 ff.

---

[31] On author and work, see Case 1 (D 41.2.3.1).

CASE 83

D 22.6.9.4 (Paulus libro singulari de iuris et facti ignorantia)

Qui ignoravit dominum esse rei venditorem, plus in re est, quam in existimatione mentis: et ideo, tametsi existimet se non a domino emere, tamen, si a domino ei tradatur, dominus efficitur.

Translation: (Paul in his monograph on *Errors of Fact and of Law*)[32]

If someone does not know that the seller of a thing is the owner, the objective condition of the thing matters more than the subjective opinion. Therefore, even if he believes he is not buying from the owner, he nevertheless becomes the owner, if the property is in fact transferred by the owner.

Note on the Text:

Si emptor ["if a buyer"] would fit the context better than *qui* ["if someone"].

Discussion Questions:

Create a plausible fact situation and illustrate the decision.

Literature:

Hausmaninger (Case 82) 79 ff.
Wacke, Andreas. "Plus est in re quam in existimatione," *RHD* 64 (1996) 309–357, at 315 ff.

---

[32] On Paul, see Case 1 (D 41.2.3.1). His numerous small treatises are in part later excerpts from more comprehensive works, especially from his *Commentary on the Praetor's Edict*. Only a single fragment is preserved from the here cited monograph on *Errors of Fact and of Law*.

CASE 84

D 41.3.32.1 (Pomponius libro trigensimo secundo ad Sabinum)

Si quis id, quod possidet, non putat sibi per leges licere usucapere, dicendum est, etiamsi erret, non procedere tamen eius usucapionem, vel quia non bona fide videatur possidere vel quia in iure erranti non procedat usucapio.

Translation: (Pomponius in the 32nd book of his *Commentary on the* Ius Civile *of Sabinus*)[33]

If someone believes that under the statutes he may not usucapt the property he possesses, then it must be said that he cannot usucapt, even if he is wrong in his belief—either because he does not count as a good-faith possessor, or because there is no usucapion where there is an error of law.

Note on the Text:

While an error of fact (*error facti*) can sometimes be forgivable and work in favor of the person in error, a defective knowledge of law (error of law) is fundamentally no basis for excuse: *error iuris nocet* ("an error of law causes harm [to the party in error]"): cf. Paul D 22.6.9 pr. *regula est iuris quidem ignorantiam cuique nocere, facti vero ignorantiam non nocere*... ("the rule exists that ignorance of law causes harm, but error of fact does not cause harm"). In post-classical law the strict rule was relaxed in favor of certain groups of persons, of whom a complete knowledge of the law was not presumed (e.g., juveniles, women, peasants, soldiers).

Discussion Questions:

1) Could Pomponius be thinking of the case in which the possessor erroneously considers the property stolen?
2) How does Pomponius stand in relation to the statement *plus est in re quam in existimatione* ["the objective condition of the thing matters more than the subjective opinion "] at D 22.6.9.4 (Case 83). Describe his understanding of *bona fides*.

Literature:

Hausmaninger (Case 82) 72 ff.
Bauer, Karen. Ersitzung und Bereicherung im klassischen römischen Recht: und die Ersitzung im BGB, n.F., Bd. 11. Berlin: Duncker & Humblot, 1988, 58 ff.
Wacke (Case 83) 334 ff.

---

[33] On author and work, see Case 29 (D 41.1.21 pr.).

CASE 85

D 41.4.8 (Iulianus libro secundo ex Minicio)

Si quis, cum sciret venditorem pecuniam statim consumpturum, servos ab eo emisset, plerique responderunt eum nihilo minus bona fide emptorem esse, idque verius est: quomodo enim mala fide emisse videtur, qui a domino emit? Nisi forte et is, qui a luxurioso et protinus scorto daturo pecuniam servos emit, non usucapiet.

Translation: (Julian in the second book on *Minicius*)[34]

If someone, although he knows that the seller will immediately spend the money, buys slaves from this person, most jurists have decided that he is nevertheless a good-faith buyer, and that is the better opinion. For why should someone who has bought from the owner be seen as a bad-faith buyer? Unless it is the case that someone who buys slaves from a dissolute person, who is going to give the money to a prostitute, will not acquire by usucapion.

Discussion Questions [with model answers]:

1) Julian's presentation of the fact-situation is incomplete. Do you think that the buyer wrongly takes the seller for a *prodigus* ("spendthrift"), or that the seller is in fact a spendthrift under interdict but the buyer is not aware of this condition? [cf. Case 82]
2) *Plerique* ["most jurists"] and *verius est* ["better opinion"] (see Case 8) signal a controversy. Concerning what might the jurists be in disagreement?
3) Provide an interpretation of the question: "*quomodo enim mala fide emisse videtur, qui a domino emit?*" ["For why should someone who has bought from the owner be seen as a bad-faith buyer?"]
4) How should one understand Julian's *argumentum ad absurdum* (see Case 34): "*nisi forte et is . . .*" ["Unless it is the case . . ."]?
5) Compare Julian's conception of *bona fides* with that of the other jurists.

Answers:

1) The first. An interdicted spendthrift lacks capacity to alienate his property. Julian would not have referred to him simply as *dominus*.
2) Whether the subjective understanding of the acquirer (v. Pomponius at D 41.3.32.1 [Case 84]) or the objective circumstances (*plus in re quam in existimatione*: see Paul at D 22.6.9.4 [Case 83]) should be determinative.
3) The question of *bona fides* becomes irrelevant if the latter is not required in order to cure certain defects of acquisition.

---

[34] On author and work, see Case 70 (D 41.1.36).

4) Clearly no one will deny the usucapion if the buyer knows that the seller will apply the sales price to immoral purposes. Therefore in the present case also a moralizing treatment of *bona fides* would be irrelevant.

5) It is a functional concept of *bona fides*, like that of Paul (Case 83) but different from Pomponius (Case 84).

CASE 86

D 41.4.2.15 (Paulus libro quinquagensimo quarto ad edictum)

Si a pupillo emero sine tutoris auctoritate, quem puberem esse putem, dicimus usucapi-onem sequi, ut hic plus sit in re quam in existimatione: quod si scias pupillum esse, putes tamen pupillis licere res suas sine tutoris auctoritate administrare, non capies usu, quia iuris error nulli prodest.

Translation: (Paul in the 54th book of his *Commentary on the Praetor's Edict*)[35]

If I buy from a ward, whom I take for an adult, without the *auctoritas tutoris*, we say that there can be usucapion, on the grounds that here the (objective) fact is more at issue than the (subjective) opinion. But if you know that he is a ward and never-theless believe that a ward can manage his own affairs without the *auctoritas tutoris*, you cannot usucapt, since an error of law benefits no one.

Notes on the Text:

On *error iuris* ["mistake of law"] see on Case 84 .

Age and legal capacity:

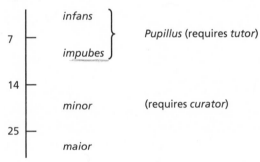

Discussion Questions:

1) The formulation *plus in re est, quam in existimatione* ["the (objective) fact is more at issue than the (subjective) opinion"] does not apply to Paul's deci-sion. Probably some text has fallen out between *sequi* and *ut* [i.e., just prior to the English clause beginning "on the grounds that . . ."]. Do you think it possible that the compilers omitted a case (*item si a minore emero, quem pupillum esse putem* [i.e., "likewise if I buy from a minor whom I take to be a ward"])?

---

[35] On author and work, see Case 1 (D 41.2.3.1).

2) Someone buys a thing from a 13-year-old *pupillus* ["ward"]. He thinks at the time: "The seller seems somewhat young to me: certainly I shall not ask about his age." Can the buyer usucapt?

3) What arguments speak in favor of and against allowing *usucapio* by a good-faith purchaser from someone who lacks legal capacity (esp. *pupillus* and *furiosus* ["insane person"])?

Literature:

Hausmaninger (Case 82) 29 ff.
Bauer (Case 84) 136 ff.
Mayer-Maly (Case 81) 103 ff.
Wacke (Case 83) 333 ff.

c. Putative Title

CASE 87

D 41.10.5 (Neratius libro quinto membranarum)

(pr.) *Usucapio rerum, etiam ex aliis causis concessa interim, propter ea, quae nostra existimantes possideremus, constituta est, ut aliquis litium finis esset.*

(1) *Sed id, quod quis, cum suum esse existimaret, possederit, usucapiet, etiamsi falso fuerit eius existimatio. Quod tamen ita interpretandum est, ut probabilis error possidentis usucapioni non obstet, veluti si ob id aliquid possideam, quod servum meum aut eius, cuius in locum hereditario iure successi, emisse id falso existimem, qui in alieni facti ignorantia tolerabilis error est.*

Translation: (Neratius in the fifth book of his *Legal Notes*)[36]

(pr.) Usucapion, which is allowed also for other reasons nowadays, was established with regard to those things that we possess in the belief that they belong to us, in order that there be some end to litigation.

(1) But someone can usucapt the thing he possesses in the belief that it is his property, even if his belief is incorrect. This should be understood to mean that an excusable error of the possessor does not stand in the way of usucapion—for example, if I erroneously believe that my slave or a slave of someone to whose place I succeed by hereditary right, has bought the property. This is true because ignorance of another's conduct is an excusable error.

Discussion Questions:

1) Neratius attempts to provide a historical perspective. Which cases of usucapion does he see as emerging earlier (and when?) and which later?
2) Do you think the formulation of Neratius is correct? How is the historical development of acquiring of ownership through use (usucapion) explained today?
3) As to what condition of acquiring ownership is the adverse possessor in error under the facts of this case?
4) Is Neratius saying that only an excusable error could count as *bona fides*?

Literature:

Mayer-Maly (Case81) 54 ff.

Hausmaninger (Case 82) 44 ff.

Greiner, Reinhold. *Opera Neratii; drei Textgeschichten*, Bd. 37. Karlsruhe: C. F. Müller, 1973, 41 ff.

Bauer (Case 84) 80 ff.

---

[36] On author and work, see Case 73 (D 41.3.41).

CASE 88

D 41.10.3 (Pomponius libro vicensimo secundo ad Sabinum)

Hominem, quem ex stipulatione te mihi debere falso existimabas, tradidisti mihi: si scis-sem mihi nihil debere, usu eum non capiam: quod si nescio, verius est, ut usucapiam, quia ipsa traditio ex causa, quam veram esse existimo, sufficit ad efficiendum, ut id quod mihi traditum est pro meo possideam. Et ita Neratius scripsit idque verum puto.

Translation: (Pomponius in the 22nd book of his *Commentary on the* Ius Civile *of Sabinus*)[37]

You have transferred to me a slave that you erroneously think you owe me on the basis of a *stipulatio* [i.e., a legally enforceable oral promise]. If I had known that nothing was owed to me, I would not acquire it by use [i.e., usucapt it]. If I do not know, it is more correct that I do usucapt, because the *traditio*, on a basis that I take for a valid *causa*, suffices to bring about that I possess *pro meo* ["as if mine"] what has been transferred to me. So writes Neratius, and I consider it correct.

Discussion Questions:

1) *Verius est* ["it is more correct"] could signal a controversy (see Case 8). How would the opposing view have been explained?
2) Discuss the relationship of this text to Neratius at D 41.10.5.1 (Case 87).

Literature:

Mayer-Maly (Case 81) 62 ff.
Hausmaninger (Case 82) 46 ff.
Bauer (Case 84) 126 ff.

---

[37] On author and work, see Case 29 (D 41.1.21 pr.); on Neratius, see Case 73 (D 41.3.41).

CASE 89

D 41.4.2.6 (Paulus libro quinquagensimo quarto ad edictum)

Cum Stichum emissem, Dama per ignorantiam mihi pro eo traditus est. Priscus ait usu me eum non capturum, quia id, quod emptum non sit, pro emptore usucapi non potest: sed si fundus emptus sit et ampliores fines possessi sint, totum longo tempore capi, quoniam universitas eius possideatur, non singulae partes.

Translation: (Paul in the 54th book of his *Commentary on the Praetor's Edict*)[38]

When I had bought Stichus, Dama was mistakenly transferred to me in his place. Priscus says I could not usucapt him, because that which has not been bought also cannot be usucapted *pro emptore* ["by someone acting in the good faith belief that he is a purchaser"]. If, however, a piece of land is purchased and a larger plot has been taken into possession, one can usucapt the entire plot, since it is possessed as a whole, not in its various parts.

Discussion Questions:

1) Can the jurist Neratius Priscus (see Case 87 [D 41.10.5.1] and Case 88 [D 41.10.3]) be meant?
2) Does Paul recognize usucapion of a putative title in land?

Literature:

Mayer-Maly, Th. "Der Ersitzungsbesitz am Sachbestandteil," *SDHI* 26 (1960) 176–189, at 187.

---

[38] On author and work, see Case 1 (D 41.2.3.1).

CASE 90

D 41.4.11 (Africanus libro septimo quaestionum)

Quod volgo traditum est eum, qui existimat se quid emisse nec emerit, non posse pro emptore usucapere, hactenus verum esse ait, si nullam iustam causam eius erroris emptor habeat: nam si forte servus vel procurator, qui emendam rem mandasset, persuaserit ei se emisse atque ita tradiderit, magis esse, ut usucapio sequatur.

Translation: (Africanus in the seventh book of his *Legal Questions*)[39]

According to Julian, what is commonly said—that the person who only thinks he has bought something but has not actually bought it cannot usucapt it *pro emptore*—is correct only if the buyer has no legally valid reason (*iusta causa*) for his error. If, for example, a slave or a procurator, whom he has assigned to purchase the property, reports that he has purchased it and then hands it over, it would instead be decided that usucapion is permissible.

Note on the Text:

On *vulgo traditum* see the note on *vulgo dictum* under Case 32.

Discussion Questions:

1) Formulate the fact-situation and legal issue.
2) How does Africanus explain his granting of usucapion? Was his opinion uncontested?
3) Consider what can be concluded from the texts discussed so far regarding the permissibility and interpretation of usucapting putative title. What new viewpoint does this case (D 41.4.11) provide?

Literature:

> Hausmaninger (Case 82) 66 ff.
> Mayer-Maly (Case 81) 30 ff.

---

[39] Sextus Caecilius Africanus was a pupil of Julian's and may have broadly reproduced decisions of Julian in his nine books of *Quaestiones* (131 excerpts in the Digest).

CASE 91

D 41.3.27 (Ulpianus libro trigensimo primo ad Sabinum)

Celsus libro trigensimo quarto errare eos ait, qui existimarent, cuius rei quisque bona fide adeptus sit possessionem, pro suo usucapere eum posse nihil referre, emerit nec ne, donatum sit nec ne, si modo emptum vel donatum sibi existimaverit, quia neque pro legato neque pro donato neque pro dote usucapio valeat, si nulla donatio, nulla dos, nullum legatum sit. Idem et in litis aestimatione placet, ut, nisi vere quis litis aestimationem subierit, usucapere non possit.

Translation: (Ulpian in the 31st book of his *Commentary on the* Ius Civile *of Sabinus*)[40]

Celsus says in the 34th book that they are wrong who think that one can usucapt *pro suo* ["as one's own"] any property of which one has good-faith possession, and that it makes no difference whether one has bought it or not, whether it was given or not, provided only that one merely thinks it was bought or given. Because one could effectively usucapt neither *pro legato* ["in the capacity of a legatee"] nor *pro donato* ["in the capacity of a donee"] nor *pro dote* ["in the capacity of the recipient of a dowry"], if there has been no gift, no dowry, no legacy. The same applies to the *litis aestimatio*,[41] so that someone cannot usucapt [the contested property], if he has not in fact undergone the *litis aestimatio*.

Discussion Questions:

1) Do you think that Celsus is engaging in a polemic with Neratius at D 41.10.5 (Case 87) and D 41.10.3 (Case 88)?
2) Has Celsus expressed a general rejection of any putative title?

Literature:

Hausmaninger (Case 82) 48 ff.
Mayer-Maly (Case 81) 30 ff.

---

[40] On author and work, see Case 11 (D 18.6.1.2); on Celsus, see Case 2 (D 41.2.18.2).

[41] Translator's note: The *litis aestimatio* is a judicial valuation of the money-value of contested property. It was conducted in order to assess the money damages owed to a plaintiff who succeeds in proving ownership of property that is currently possessed by the defendant and that the defendant is unwilling to surrender. Following the assessment and payment thereof, the defendant could usucapt the contested property. See the Translator's note to Case 79.

CASE 92

D 41.5.1 (Pomponius libro trigensimo secundo ad Sabinum)

Pro herede ex vivi bonis nihil usucapi potest, etiamsi possessor mortui rem fuisse existi-maverit.

D 41.5.3 (Pomponius libro vicensimo tertio ad Quintum Mucium)

Plerique putaverunt, si heres sim et putem rem aliquam ex hereditate esse quae non sit, posse me usucapere.

Translation: (Pomponius in the 32nd book of his *Commentary on the* Ius Civile *of Sabinus*)[42]

One cannot usucapt *pro herede* ["in the capacity of an heir"] anything from the property of a living person, even if the possessor believes that the property belonged to a deceased person.

(Pomponius in the 23rd book of his *Commentary on the* Ius Civile *of Quintus Mucius*)[43]

Most [jurists] are of the opinion that I could usucapt, if I should be an heir and believe the property belongs to the inheritance, although in fact it does not.

Note on the Text:

On *plerique* ("most [jurists]"), see Case 8.

Discussion Questions:

1) Explain why Pomponius sometimes allows usucapion and sometimes does not. Make reference to Pomponius at D 41.10.3 (Case 88) and at D 41.10.4.2 (Case 93) in your arguments.
2) Can someone who knows that he is not an heir usucapt an item from the estate *pro herede*?

Literature:

Bauer (Case 84) 100 ff.
Mayer-Maly (Case 81) 71 ff.

---

[42] On author and work, see Case 29 (D 41.1.21 pr.).
[43] On Q. Mucius Scaevola, see Case 133 (D 43.24.1.5).

CASE 93

D 41.8.2 (Paulus libro quinquagensimo quarto ad edictum)

Si possideam aliquam rem, quam putabam mihi legatam, cum non esset, pro legato non usucapiam:

D 41.8.2 (Papinianus libro vicensimo tertio quaestionum)

Non magis quam si quis emptum existimet, quod non emerit.

D 41.10.4.2 (Pomponius libro trigensimo secundo ad Sabinum)

Quod legatum non sit, ab herede tamen perperam traditum sit, placet a legatario usucapi, qui pro suo possidet.

Translation: (Paulus in the 54th book of his *Commentary on the Praetor's Edict*)[44]

If I possess something that I believe has been bequeathed to me, although it has not been, I would not usucapt it *pro legato*.

(Papinian in the 23rd book of his *Legal Questions*)[45]

any more than if he thought something was purchased that had not been.

(Pomponius in the 32nd book of his *Commentary on the* Ius *Civile of Sabinus*)[46]

What has not been bequeathed but has nevertheless been mistakenly delivered by the heir, according to established doctrine can be usucapted by the legatee, since he possesses it *pro suo*.

Note on the Text:

On *placet* ("according to established doctrine"), see Case 36.

Discussion Questions:

Interpret the decisions of the three jurists in light of Cases 87 to 92.

Literature:

Bauer (Case 84) 94 ff., 131 ff.
Mayer-Maly (Case 81) 66 ff., 85.

---

[44] On author and work, see Case 1 (D 41.2.3.1).

[45] On author and work, see Case 5 (D 18.1.74).

[46] On author and work, see Case 29 (D 41.1.21 pr.).

CASE 94

D 41.1.1 (Gaius libro secundo rerum cottidianarum sive aureorum)

(pr.)   *Quarundam rerum dominium nanciscimur iure gentium, quod ratione natu-*
rali inter omnes homines peraeque servatur, quarundam iure civili, id est
iure proprio civitatis nostrae, et quia antiquius ius gentium cum ipso genere
humano proditum est, opus est ut de hoc prius referendum sit.

(1)   *Omnia igitur animalia, quae terra mari caelo capiuntur, id est ferae bestiae*
et volucres pisces, capientium fiunt.

D 41.1.2 (Florentinus libro sexto institutionum)

Vel quae ex his apud nos sunt edita.

D 41.1.3 (Gaius libro secundo rerum cottidianarum sive aureorum)

(pr.)   *Quod enim nullius est, id ratione naturali occupanti conceditur.*

(1)   *Nec interest quod ad feras bestias et volucres, utrum in suo fundo quisque*
capiat an in alieno, plane qui in alienum fundum ingreditur venandi aucupan-
dive gratia, potest a domino si is providerit, iure prohiberi, ne ingrederetur.

(2)   *Quidquid autem eorum ceperimus, eo usque nostrum esse intellegitur, donec*
nostra custodia coercetur: cum vero evaserit custodiam nostram et in natu-
ralem libertatem se receperit, nostrum esse desinit et rursus occupantis fit.

D 41.1.4 (Florentinus libro sexto institutionum)

nisi si mansuefacta emitti ac reverti solita sunt.

D 41.1.5 pr.-2 (Gaius libro secundo rerum cottidianarum sive aureorum)

(pr.)   *Naturalem autem libertatem recipere intellegitur, cum vel oculos nostros*
effugerit vel ita sit in conspectu nostro, ut difficilis sit eius persecutio.

(1)   *Illud quaesitum est, an fera bestia, quae ita vulnerata sit, ut capi possit, statim*
nostra esse intellegatur. Trebatio placuit statim nostram esse et eo usque nos-
tram videri, donec eam persequamur, quod si desierimus eam persequi, desi-
nere nostram esse et rursus fieri occupantis: itaque si per hoc tempus, quo eam
persequimur, alius eam ceperit eo animo, ut ipse lucrifaceret, furtum videri nobis
eum commisisse. Plerique non aliter putaverunt eam nostram esse, quam si eam
ceperimus, quia multa accidere possunt, ut eam non capiamus: quod verius est.

(2)   *Apium quoque natura fera est: itaque quae in arbore nostra consederint,*
antequam a nobis alveo concludantur, non magis nostrae esse intellegun-
tur quam volucres, quae in nostra arbore nidum fecerint. Ideo si alius eas
incluserit, earum dominus erit.

Translation: (Gaius in the second book of his *Jurisprudence of Daily Life*, also known as the *Golden Rules*)[47]

(pr.) Of some things we acquire ownership by means of the *ius gentium*, which on the basis of natural reason is observed equally by all peoples; of others, by means of the *ius civile*, which is the particular law of our people. And since the *ius gentium* along with the human race itself came into being first, it is appropriate that it be discussed first.

(1) All animals that are caught on the earth, in the sea or in the air—i.e., wild beasts, birds and fish—are the property of the person who catches them.

(Florentinus in the sixth book of his *Institutes*)[48]

as also their young that are born on our premises.

(Gaius in the second book of his *Jurisprudence of Daily Life*, also known as the *Golden Rules*)

(pr.) That which is the property of no one will, by natural reason, belong to the person who takes possession of it.

(1) And with regard to wild beasts and birds it makes no difference whether someone catches them on his own land or the land of another: recognizing, however, that anyone who enters another's land for the sake of hunting or fowling can be rightfully prevented from entering by the owner of the land, if the latter has foreseen it.

(2) Whichever of these animals we have caught counts as our property, as long as it is kept within our custody. But if the animal escapes our custody and returns to its natural state of freedom, it ceases to be our property and can be taken in ownership by an occupier.

(Florentinus in the sixth book of his *Institutes*)

unless [they are] tamed beasts who are accustomed to be sent out and to return.

(Gaius in the second book of his *Jurisprudence of Daily Life*, also known as the *Golden Rules*)

(pr.) It is to be understood that a wild animal has recovered its natural state of freedom if it has either fled from our view or can only be seen in a location where pursuit is difficult.

---

[47] On Gaius and this work see Case 6 (D 41.1.9.6).

[48] Florentinus, like Gaius and Marcian, had no imperial office nor the *ius respondendi*. He worked as a teacher of law.

(1) The question is asked whether a wild beast that has been wounded sufficiently that it can be caught should be understood as immediately becoming our property. Trebatius was of the opinion that it did and that it remained our property as long as we continued to pursue the beast. But if we desisted from pursuing it, the beast ceased to be ours and became once again the property of whoever takes it first. Therefore if, while we are pursuing the beast, another takes it with the intention of securing the profit of it, he is deemed to have committed a theft against us. Most jurists, however, hold that the beast does not become ours until we capture it, since many things can happen to prevent us from capturing it. This is the more correct opinion.

(2) The nature of bees is also wild. Consequently those that build a nest in our tree are no more our property before they can be enclosed in our beehive than birds who have built a nest in our tree. Therefore if some other person encloses them, he becomes the owner.

Notes on the Text:

The compilers have broken up the text of Gaius, which they are using as an introduction to Title 41.1 of the Digest, with expansions (not always substantive ones) taken from the schoolbook of Florentinus. On Gaius D 41.1.5.1, see Case 8, where it was discussed in the context of acquiring possession.

Discussion Questions:

1) The owner of land forbids entry into his forest. A hunter enters the forest anyway and captures a beast. Has he acquired ownership thereby?

2) What means can a landowner use against a hunter who enters the land despite the prohibition?

3) How can the hunter (or fisher) defend against interference with hunting (or fishing) by the landowner or a third party?

4) Distinguish between wild, tamed, and tame animals: when and how do possession and ownership end:

— of an escaped chicken?
— of a swarm of bees?
— of a stag that is accustomed to return to his enclosure each evening and now has stayed away for three days.

5) The tortoise belonging to Gaius has hidden itself in a thorn bush or walked around the corner of the house. Has Gaius lost ownership of it? How could one better formulate the statement: *vel oculos nostros effugerit vel ita sit in conspectu nostro, ut difficilis sit eius persecutio* ["if it has either fled from our view or can only be seen in a location where pursuit is difficult"]?

6) Smith's bees formed a swarm and settled in Jones' tree. Smith and Jones observed this event. Jones encloses Smith's bees in his own hive before Smith enters the tree. Has Jones acquired ownership of the bees?

7) Do you think it justified to treat a swarm of bees and birds in a nest in the same way with respect to acquiring ownership?

8) An animal that is destined for the beast-fights in the arena escapes. Titius captures him. Has Titius acquired ownership?

9) Formulate as precisely as possible a legal maxim that expresses your own understanding of the acquisition of ownership of wild animals.

Compare with this Case:

§ 381 Austrian Civil Code:

Title to ownerless property exists in the natural freedom of taking it into possession. The way of acquiring possession is occupation, through which one gets control over ownerless property with the intent of treating it as one's own.[49]

§ 384 Austrian Civil Code:

Domestic bee-swarms and other tame or tamed animals are not subject to free capture; on the contrary, the owner has the right to pursue them on another's land, although he must compensate the landowner for any damage that is caused. If the owner of the parent stock does not pursue the swarm within two days; or if a tamed animal remains by itself for forty-two days, anyone on common land, or the landowner on his own land, can take and keep them.[50]

§ 958 I German Civil Code:

Whoever takes ownerless movable property into his proprietary possession, acquires ownership of the property."[51]

---

[49] **§ 381 ABGB:** Bei freistehende Sachen besteht der Titel in der angebornen Freiheit, sie in Besitz zu nehmen. Der Erwerbungsart ist die Zueignung, wodurch man sich einer freistehenden Sache bemächtigt, in der Absicht, sie als die seinige zu behandeln.

[50] **§ 384 ABGB:** Häusliche Bienenschwärme und andere zahme oder zahm gemachte Tiere sind kein Gegenstand des freien Tierfanges, vielmehr hat der Eigentümer das Recht, sie auf fremdem Grunde zu verfolgen; doch soll er dem Grundbesitzer den ihm etwa verursachten Schaden ersetzen. Im Falle, daß der Eigentümer des Mutterstockes den Schwarm durch zwei Tage nicht verfolgt hat; oder, daß ein zahm gemachtes Tier durch zweiundvierzig Tage von selbst ausgeblieben ist, kann sie auf gemeinem Grunde jedermann; auf dem seinigen der Grundeigentümer für sich nehmen, und behalten.

[51] **§ 958 I BGB:** Wer eine herrenlose bewegliche Sache in Eigenbesitz nimmt, erwirbt das Eigentum an der Sache.

§ 960 German Civil Code:

I Wild animals are ownerless, as long as they are free. Wild animals in zoological gardens and fish in ponds or other enclosed private water are not ownerless.

II If a captured wild animal recovers its freedom, it becomes ownerless, provided the owner fails to pursue it without delay, or if he abandons the pursuit.

III A tamed animal becomes ownerless, if it abandons its custom of returning to its particular place.[52]

§ 961 German Civil Code:

If a bee-swarm migrates, it becomes ownerless, provided the owner does not pursue it without delay, or if the owner abandons the pursuit.[53]

§ 962 German Civil Code:

The owner of a bee-swarm may go onto another's land in pursuit of the swarm]. If the swarm settles in an unoccupied hive belonging to another person, the owner of the swarm may open the hive to enter it and take the honeycomb away or break it out. He must pay compensation for the ensuing damage.[54]

§ Art. 718 Swiss Civil Code:

Ownerless property can be brought into ownership if someone takes possession of it with the intent of becoming its owner.[55]

§ Art. 719 Swiss Civil Code:

Captive animals become ownerless [718] if they gain their freedom again and their owner does not search for them without delay and without interruption and try to recapture them.

---

[52] **§ 960 BGB:**
  I Wilde Tiere sind herrenlos, solange sie sich in der Freiheit befinden. Wilde Tiere in Tiergärten und Fische in Teichen oder anderen geschlossenen Privatgewässern sind nicht herrenlos.
  II Erlangt ein gefangenes wildes Tier die Freiheit wieder, so wird es herrenlos, wenn nicht der Eigentümer das Tier unverzüglich verfolgt oder wenn er die Verfolgung aufgibt.
  III Ein gezähmtes Tier wird herrenlos, wenn es die Gewohnheit ablegt, an den ihm bestimmten Ort zurückzukehren.

[53] **§ 961 BGB:** Zieht ein Bienenschwarm aus, so wird er herrenlos, wenn nicht der Eigentümer ihn unverzüglich verfolgt oder wenn der Eigentümer die Verfolgung aufgibt.

[54] **§ 962 BGB:** Der Eigentümer des Bienenschwarmes darf bei der Verfolgung fremde Grundstücke betreten. Ist der Schwarm in eine fremde nicht besetzte Bienenwohnung eingezogen, so darf der Eigentümer des Schwarmes zum Zwecke des Eingangens die Wohnung öffnen und die Waben herausnehmen oder heraus brechen. Er hat den entstehenden Schaden zu ersetzen.

[55] **§ Art. 718 ZGB:** Eine herrenlose Sache wird dadurch zu Eigentum erworben, daß jemand sie mit dem Willen, ihr Eigentümer zu werden, in Besitz nimmt.

Tamed animals become ownerless as soon as they return to a condition of wildness and do not return to their owner any more.

Bee-swarms do not become ownerless just because they go to the land of another.[56]

Compare the following case with these statutes:

Ghen v Rich, 8 Fed. 159 (D. Mass. 1881).

Ghen, a whale-hunter, killed a whale near Cape Cod on April 9. The whale washed up onto the beach 17 miles away on April 12. The finder, Ellis, sold the whale to Rich, the defendant.

The plaintiff relied on the long-standing custom of hunting whales with "bomb-lances fired from guns made expressly for the purpose." (Because of the fleetness of the type of whale concerned, a hunt with harpoons would not have come into question.) The whale is "instantly killed" and sinks "immediately" to the floor of the sea and within three days floats back to the surface, where it is towed off by boats or washes up onto the shore. The finder informs the owner, who is recognizable by the lance; and the owner retrieves the whale and pays the finder a small fee.

The judge awarded damages to the plaintiff on the basis of the custom, since he was considered to have acquired possession and ownership of the whale. He added that even without the existence of a custom, the Common Law would have led to the same result: "If the fisherman does all that is possible to do to make the animal his own, that would seem to be sufficient. Such a rule might well be applied in the interest of trade, there being no usage or custom to the contrary."

Literature:

Daube D. "Doves and bees," in *Droits de l'antiquité et sociologie juridique. Mélanges H. Lévy-Bruhl*. Paris: Sirey, 1959, 63–75. (reprinted in Daube, D. *Collected Studies in Roman Law*, David Cohen and Simon Dieter eds. Frankfurt/Main: Klostermann, 1991, at 899 ff.

Filip-Fröschl, Johanna. "Cervi, qui in silvas ire et redire solent," in *Iurisprudentia Universalis: Festschrift Th. Mayer-Maly*, Martin Josef Schermaier, Johannes Michael Rainer, and Laurens Winkel, eds. Köln: Böhlau, 2002, 191–213, at 198 ff.

Frier, B. W. "Bees and Lawyers," *CJ* 78 (1982) 105–114, at 108.

Knütel (Case 8).

McCleod, Grant. "Wild and Tame Animals and Birds in Roman Law," in *New Perspectives in the Roman Law of Property: Essays for Barry Nicholas*. New York: Oxford University Press, 1989, 169–176, at 169 ff.

Weiss. *Das Willensmoment bei der occupatio* (diss. 1955) 13 ff., 22 ff.

---

[56] **§ Art. 719:** Gefangene Tiere werden herrenlos [**718**], wenn sie die Freiheit wieder erlangen und ihr Eigentümer ihnen nicht unverzüglich und ununterbrochen nachforscht und sie wieder einzufangen bemüht ist.

Gezähmte Tiere werden herrenlos, so bald sie wieder in den Zustand der Wildheit geraten und nicht mehr zu ihrem Herrn zurückkehren.

Bienenschwärme werden dadurch, daß sie auf fremden Boden gelangen, nicht herrenlos [**700, 705**].

CASE 95

D 41.2.3.14-16 (Paulus libro quinquagensimo quarto ad edictum)

(14) *Item feras bestias, quas vivariis incluserimus, et pisces, quos in piscinas coieceri-mus, a nobis possideri. Sed eos pisces, qui in stagno sint, aut feras, quae in silvis circumseptis vagantur, a nobis non possideri, quoniam relictae sint in libertate naturali: alioquin etiam si quis silvam emerit, videri eum omnes feras possidere, quod falsum est.*

(15) *Aves autem possidemus, quas inclusas habemus, aut si quae mansuetae factae custodiae nostrae subiectae sunt.*

(16) *Quidam recte putant columbas quoque, quae ab aedificiis nostris volant, item apes, quae ex alveis nostris evolant et secundum consuetudinem redeunt, a nobis possideri.*

Translation: (Paul in the 54th book of his *Commentary on the Praetor's Edict*)[57]

(14) Likewise it is understood that we possess the wild animals that we have in enclosures and the fish that we have thrown into man-made pools, but those fish that are in a pond or wild animals that wander about in fenced woods are not possessed by us, since they have been left in their state of natural freedom. Otherwise if someone should buy the forest he would be deemed to possess all of the animals, which is incorrect.

(15) We possess birds that we hold in enclosures or that have been tamed and remain in our control.

(16) Some [jurists] have correctly thought that we also possess pigeons that fly out from our buildings, and bees that fly out from our hives and custom-arily return to them.

Note on the Text:

On the *argumentum ad absurdum*—"*alioquin* . . ." ("otherwise . . .")—see on Case 34.

Discussion Questions:

1) Do you think the decision makes sense in denying possession of stags in fenced woods while affirming it of pigeons in a loft?

2) Is the similar treatment of pigeons and bees illuminating?

3) Compare to this the bee-swarms and birds-in-a-nest at D 41.5.2. (Case 94).

---

[57] On author and work, see Case 1 (D 41.2.3.1).

CASE 96

D 41.1.44 (Ulpianus libro nono decimo ad edictum)

Pomponius tractat: cum pastori meo lupi porcos eriperent, hos vicinae villae colonus cum robustis canibus et fortibus, quos pecoris sui gratia pascebat, consecutus lupis eripuit aut canes extorserunt: et cum pastor meus peteret porcos, quaerebatur, utrum eius facti sint porci, qui eripuit, an nostri maneant: nam genere quodam venandi id erant nancti. Cogitabat tamen, quemadmodum terra marique capta, cum in suam naturalem laxitatem pervenerant, desinerent eorum esse qui ceperunt, ita ex bonis quoque nostris capta a bestiis marinis et terrestribus desinant nostra esse, cum effugerunt bestiae nostram perse- cutionem. Quis denique manere nostrum dicit, quod avis transvolans ex area aut ex agro nostro transtulit aut quod nobis eripuit? Si igitur desinit, si fuerit ore bestiae liberatum, occupantis erit, quemadmodum piscis vel aper vel avis, qui potestatem nostram evasit, si ab alio capiatur, ipsius fit. Sed putat potius nostrum manere tamdiu quamdiu reciperari possit: licet in avibus et piscibus et feris verum sit quod scribit. Idem ait, etsi naufragio quid amissum sit, non statim nostrum esse desinere: denique quadruplo teneri eum qui rapuit. Et sane melius est dicere te quod a lupo eripitur, nostrum manere, quamdiu recipi possit id quod ereptum est.

Translation: (Ulpian in the 19th book of his *Commentary on the Praetor's Edict*)[58]

Pomponius discusses the following case. When wolves snatched some pigs from my herder, the tenant of a neighboring farm pursued them with strong and cou- rageous dogs that he kept for protecting his cows, and he snatched them back or the dogs wrested them from the wolves. And when my herder asked for the pigs back, the question arose whether they had become the property of the man who had recovered them (because they had been obtained through a kind of hunting) or remained our property.

Pomponius considered whether, just like wild animals that have been cap- tured on land or sea cease to be the property of the person who captured them once they have recovered their natural state of freedom, so also those goods that are taken from our property by wild sea or land animals cease to be our property once the animals have escaped our pursuit. For who would say that what an over- flying bird carries across or snatches from our threshing floor or field remains our property? If it therefore ceases to be our property, it becomes the property of the person who seizes it, as soon as it is taken from the mouth of the animal. Likewise the fish or the boar or the bird that has escaped from our control and is caught by another will become the property of that person.

But Pomponius means that it remains our property as long as it can be recov- ered, even if what he writes may be true of birds and fish and wild animals. He also says that even if something is lost in a shipwreck, it does not cease to be ours: in

---

[58] On author and work, see Case 11 (D 18.6.1.2); on Pomponius, see Case 29 (D 41.1.21.pr.).

fact he who steals such property is liable for four times its value. And so it is better for you to say that what a wolf steals remains our property for as long as the thing he stole can be recovered.

Note on the Text:

This exhaustive report of Ulpian's shows evidence of numerous textual omissions, but they have not impaired the substantive content. On the meaning of *melius est* ("it is better to say") see on Case 107.

Discussion Questions:

1) Can pigs be treated as the spoils of hunting?
2) What arguments speak for and against the loss of ownership in property that is carried off by wild animals?
3) A ring falls into the sea and is swallowed by a fish. Would Pomponius decide that ownership has been lost?
4) Do you think that Pomponius would consider that ownership of everything that is lost in a shipwreck remains intact? How long would he let the ownership last? Compare Case 97 on this issue.

D. Abandonment and Finding

CASE 97

D 41.1.58 (Javolenus libro undecimo ex Cassio)

Quaecumque res ex mari extracta est, non ante eius incipit esse qui extraxit, quam dominus eam pro derelicto habere coepit.

Translation: (Javolenus in the eleventh book of his *Abridgement of Cassius*)[59]

Property that is drawn out from the sea does not belong to the person who drew it out until the owner considers it to be abandoned.

Discussion Questions:

1) Someone thinks the property is abandoned. Can he usucapt it?
2) Someone throws away another's property. Can it be usucapted?
3) In an emergency at sea the passengers throw their luggage overboard in order to lighten the boat. Can the finder acquire ownership of the luggage?

Compare with this Case:

§ 386 Austrian Civil Code:

Any citizen of the country can assume ownership of movable property that the owner no longer wishes to keep as his own and therefore abandons. In cases of doubt, it is not to be supposed that someone wished to give up his ownership; therefore no finder may consider found property to be abandoned and claim it as his own.[60]

§ 959 German Civil Code:

A movable piece of property becomes ownerless, if the owner abandons possession of the property with the intention of renouncing ownership.[61]

Literature:

Manthe (Case 19) 144 f.

---

[59] On Javolenus, see Case 3 (D 46.3.79); on Cassius, see Case 19 (D 41.2.21.3).

[60] § **386 ABGB:** Bewegliche Sachen, welche der Eigentümer nicht mehr als die seinigen behalten will, und daher verläßt, kann sich jedes Mitglied des Staates eigen machen. Im Zweifel is nicht zu vermuten, dass jemand sein Eigentum aufgeben wolle; daher darf kein Finder eine gefundene Sache für verlassen ansehen und sich diese zueignen.

[61] § **959 BGB:** Eine bewegliche Sache wird herrenlos, wenn der Eigentümer in der Absicht, auf das Eigentum zu verzichten, den Besitz der Sache aufgibt.

CASE 98

D 47.2.43.8–9 (Ulpianus libro quadragensimo primo ad Sabinum)

(8) *Proinde videamus, si nescit cuius esset, sic tamen tulit quasi redditurus ei qui desid-erasset vel qui ostendisset rem suam, an furti obligetur. Et non puto obligari eum. Solent plerique etiam hoc facere, ut libellum proponant continentem invenisse se et redditurum ei qui desideraverit: hi ergo ostendunt non furandi animo se fecisse.*

(9) *Quid ergo, si* εὕρετρα *quae dicunt petat? Nec hic videtur furtum facere, etsi non probe petat aliquid.*

Translation: (Ulpian in the 41st book of his *Commentary on the* Ius Civile *of Sabinus*)[62]

(8) Let us therefore consider whether the finder, who does not know to whom the property belongs, but has taken it up, as if to return it to the person who should seek it or show that it is his, is liable for theft. I do not believe that he is liable. Many people are accustomed to posting a notice that they have found property and will turn it over on request. This therefore shows that they have not handled it with theftuous intent.

(9) But what if someone requests a so-called finder's fee? Also here he does not count as a thief, even if he asks for something, contrary to good manners.

Note on the Text:

On *videtur* ("counts as"), see on Case 72.

Discussion Questions:

1) Is the honest finder a possessor?
2) Is the dishonest finder a possessor?
3) Is the finder in Rome obliged to give notice?
4) Is theft to be inferred, if the finding is not reported?
5) Under what circumstances can the finder acquire ownership?

Compare with this Case:

§ 390 Austrian Civil Code:

The finder must immediately notify the appropriate person responsible for found property (Subsec. 5 Security Police Ordinance), surrendering the property that was found, and providing information about all the circumstances that are pertinent for discovery of the person who has lost the property.[63]

---

[62] On author and work, see Case 11 (D 18.6.1.2).

[63] § 390 ABGB: Der Finder hat den Fund unverzüglich der zuständigen Fundbehörder (§ Abs. 5 SPG) unter Angabe der gefundene Sache anzuzeigen und über alle für die Ausforschung eines Verlustträgers maßgeblichen Umstände Auskunft zu geben.

§ 391 Austrian Civil Code:

The obligations under **§ 390** do not apply, if

1) the finder delivers the found property to the person who lost the property prior to making the report, or
2) the customary value of the found property does not exceed 10 Euros, unless it can be recognized that the recovery of the property is of importance to the person who lost it.[64]

§ 395 Austrian Civil Code:

If within one year the property is not claimed by the person who lost it, the finder acquires ownership of the property still in his custody at the expiration of the ·period, [and] in property that was surrendered, with its delivery to him. The period begins in the case of **§ 391 subsec. 2** with the time of the finding, otherwise with the giving of notice (**§ 390**).[65]

§ 965 I German Civil Code:

He who finds and takes possession of lost property must immediately notify the person who lost it or the owner or an otherwise authorized recipient.[66]

§ 973 I German Civil Code:

After the expiration of one year from the time of notifying the police authority of the finding, the finder acquires ownership of the property ... [67]

n.b. : The BGB devotes no fewer than 19 paragraphs (**§§ 965–983**) to the topic of "finding" (exclusive of treasure-trove).

---

[64] **§ 391 ABGB:** Die Pflichten nach **§ 390** bestehen nicht, wenn

1. der Finder die gefundene Sache einem Verlustträger vor der Anzeige-erstattung ausfolgt oder.

2. der gemeine Wert der gefundenen Sache 10 Euro nicht übersteigt, es sei denn erkennbar, dass die Wiedererlangung der Sache für einen Verlustträger von erheblicher Bedeutung ist.

[65] **§ 395 ABGB:** Wird die Sache innerhalb eines Jahres von keinem Verlustträger angesprochen, so erwirbt der Finder das Eigentum an der in seiner Gewahrsame befindlichen Sache mit Ablauf der Frist, an der abgegebenen Sache mit ihrer Ausfolgung an ihn. Die Frist beginnt im Fall des **§ 391 Z 2** mit dem Zeitpunkt des Findens, sonst mit der Erstattung der Anzeige (**§ 390**).

[66] **§ 965 I BGB:** Wer eine verlorene Sache findet und an sich nimmt, hat dem Verlierer oder dem Eigentümer oder einem sonstigen Empfangsberechtigteten unverzüglich Anzeige zu machen.

[67] **§ 973 I BGB:** Mit dem Ablauf eines Jahres nach der Anzeige des Fundes bei der Polizeibehörde erwirbt der Finder das Eigentum an der Sache ...

Art. 720 Swiss Civil Code:

He who finds lost property must tell the owner of it and, if he does not know who the owner is, either notify the police of the find, or himself take care to make inquiry and publication in a manner appropriate to the circumstances . . . [68]

Art. 722 Swiss Civil Code:

He who fulfills his obligations as finder [**720/1**], acquires ownership of the property, if for a period of five years following the publication or notice [**720**] the owner cannot be identified.

If the property is returned, the finder has a claim for indemnification of all expenses, as well as an appropriate finder's fee . . . [69]

Literature:

Düll, R. "Äuslobung und Fund im antiken Recht." *ZSS* 61 (1941) 19–43, at 41 ff.

---

[68] **Art. 720 ZGB:** Wer eine verlorene Sache findet, hat den Eigentümer davon zu benachrichtigen und, wenn er ihn nicht kennt, entweder der Polizei den Fund anzuzeigen oder selbst für eine den Umständen angemessene Bekanntmachung und Nachfrage zu sorgen . . .

[69] **Art. 722 ZGB:** Wer seinen Pflichten als Finder nachkommt [**720/1**], erwirbt, wenn während fünf Jahren von der Bekanntmachung oder Anzeige [**720**] an der Eigentümer nicht festgestellt werden kann, die Sache zu Eigentum.

Wird die Sache zurückgegeben, so hat der Finder Anspruch auf Ersatz aller Auslagen, sowei auf einen angemessenen Finderlohn . . .

E. Treasure-trove

CASE 99

D 41.1.31.1 (Paulus libro trigensimo primo ad edictum)

Thensaurus est vetus quaedam depositio pecuniae, cuius non exstat memoria, ut iam dominum non habeat: sic enim fit eius qui invenerit, quod non alterius sit. Alioquin si quis aliquid vel lucri causa vel metus vel custodiae condiderit sub terra, non est thensaurus: cuius etiam furtum fit.

Translation: (Paul in the 31st book of his *Commentary on the Praetor's Edict*)[70]

A treasure-trove is an old deposit of money (valuables), of which no memory exists, so that it no longer has any owner. So something that belongs to no one else becomes the property of the person who finds it. If, however, someone hides something in the ground to seek profit or from fear or for protection, it is not treasure-trove: and it is subject to theft.

Discussion Questions:

1) Does a deposit of money become treasure-trove as soon as someone forgets where he buried it? (see Case 47a)
2) Does buried money become treasure-trove with the death of the owner?
3) When is possession and when is ownership of concealed valuables extinguished?

Compare with this Case:

§ 397 Subsec. 1 Austrian Civil Code:

If buried, walled-in, or otherwise concealed property of an unknown owner is uncovered, the rules that apply are analogous to those that are specified for lost property.[71]

---

[70] On author and work, see Case 1 (D 41.2.3.1).

[71] **§ 397 Abs. 1 ABGB:** Werden vergrabene, eingemauerte oder sonst verborgene Sachen eines unbekannten Eigentümers entdeckt, so gilt sinngemäß das, was für di verlorenen Sachen bestimmt ist.

§ 398 Austrian Civil Code:

If the discovered property consists of money, jewelry, or other precious material, which has been concealed so long that its erstwhile owner can no longer be determined, then it is called a treasure-trove . . .[72]

See also **§ 399 ABGB, § 984 BGB, Art. 723 f. ZGB** (reproduced under Case 100).

Literature:

Hill, George F. *Treasure Trove in Law and Practice from the Earliest Time to the Present Day.* Oxford: Clarendon Press, 1936; reprint Aalen: Scientia Verlag, 1980, 5ff.

Knütel (Case 8) 573 ff.

Mayer-Maly (Case 47a) 283 ff.

---

[72] **§ 398 ABGB:** Bestehen die entdeckten Sachen in Geld, Schmuck oder andern Kostbarkeiten, die so lange im Verborgenen gelegen haben, daß man ihren vorigen Eigentümer nicht mehr erfahren kann, dann heißen sie ein Schatz . . .

CASE 100

D 41.2.3.3 (Paulus libro quinquagensimo quarto ad edictum)

*Neratius et Proculus et solo animo [non] posse nos adquirere possessionem, si non ante-
cedat naturalis possessio. Ideoque si thensaurum in fundo meo positum sciam, continuo
me possidere, simul atque possidendi affectum habuero, quia quod desit naturali possessioni, id animus implet. Ceterum quod Brutus et Manilius putant eum, qui fundum
longa possessione cepit, etiam thensaurum cepisse, quamvis nesciat in fundo esse, non est
verum: is enim qui nescit non possidet thensaurum, quamvis fundum possideat. Sed et si
sciat, non capiet longa possessione, quia scit alienum esse. Quidam putant Sabini sententiam veriorem esse nec alias eum qui scit possidere, nisi si loco motus sit, quia non sit sub
custodia nostra: quibus consentio.*

Translation: (Paul in the 54th book of his *Commentary on the Praetor's Edict*)[73]

Neratius and Proculus say that one could [not][74] also acquire possession *solo animo*,
if there should be no *naturalis possessio* beforehand. Therefore, if I know that a treasure is buried on my land, I immediately begin to possess it as soon as I conceive
the possessory intent, since the intent satisfies what is lacking from the *naturalis
possessio*.

Now what Brutus and Manilius think, that someone who has acquired a plot
by prescription also has acquired the treasure, even if he does not know that the
treasure is buried on his land, is not correct. He who knows nothing of the treasure does not possess it, even if he does possess the land. In fact, even if he does
know, he will still not acquire by prescription, since he knows it is another's
property.

Many consider the opinion of Sabinus to be sounder. According to it, someone who has obtained knowledge of the treasure first acquires possession of it by
moving it from its place, since before that we do not have it in our custody. I agree
with this position.

Notes on the Text:

As transmitted, the introductory statement—i.e., one could not acquire possession *solo animo* unless one were already the *naturalis possessor*—does not fit the

---

[73] On author and work, see Case 1 (D 41.2.3.1); on Neratius, see Case 73 (D 41.3.41); on
Proculus, see Case 9 (D 41.1.55). M. Iunius Brutus (*praetor* 142 BCE) and Manlius Manilius
(*consul* 149 BCE), along with P. Mucius Scaevola, were described by Pomponius as the founders of
the *ius civile* (D 1.2.2.39 *qui fundaverunt ius civile*). On Sabinus, see Case 11 (D 18.6.1.2).

[74] Translator's note: On the editorial convention regarding the use of square brackets in the case
texts and the corresponding translations, see fn. 38 on Case 57. In the present case, the square brackets
around the Latin word *non*, English "not," signal that the editors feel the word does not belong in the
original text. An explanation is provided under the "Notes on the Text" section of this case.

accompanying case description and its abstract reasoning: *quia quod desit naturali possessioni, id animus implet* [= "since the intent satisfies what is lacking from the *naturalis possessio*"]. Neratius and Proculus, making an exception, have waived *naturalis possessio* as a requirement in the case of treasure-trove. A later editor, however, under the influence of the proposition *apiscimur possessionem corpore et animo, neque per se animo . . .* ["we acquire possession *corpore et animo*, not *animo* alone . . ."] Paul D 41.2.3.1 [Case 1]) has introduced *non* ["not"]. On *veriorem* ("sounder"), see on Case 8 .

Discussion Questions:

1) Are Brutus and Manilius treating the *thensaurus* like part of the land?
2) Under *thensaurus* [with the meaning of "treasure-trove"] is understood some valuable property that has been hidden for so long that its owner can no longer be determined (cf. Paul D 41.1.31.1 = Case 99). The Latin word is also used for any valuable property that belongs to another: e.g., for jewelry or coins that the owner buried on his own or another's land from fear of passing robbers. Of which kind of *thensaurus* are Brutus and Manilius speaking?
3) Do you think *sed et si sciat . . . quia scit alienum esse* ["even if he does know . . . since he knows it is another's property"] is the legal view of Paul, or the gloss of a later editor?
4) Explain the controversy between Proculus and Sabinus regarding treasure-trove.

Compare with this Case:

Inst. Just. 2.1.38

Hadrian grants half the trove to the finder and half to the land-owner.

§ 399 Austrian Civil Code:

Of a treasure-trove, the finder and the owner of the ground each receive half.[75]

§ 984 German Civil Code:

If a piece of property, which has been concealed for so long that the owner is no longer able to be found (treasure-trove), is found and, following the discovery,

---

[75] **§ 399 ABGB:** Von einem Schatz erhalten der Finder und der Eigentümer des Grundes je die Hälfte.

taken into possession, then the ownership of half the property is acquired by the discoverer and half by the owner of the property in which the treasure-trove was concealed.[76]

§ 723 Swiss Civil Code:

If a valuable object is found, concerning which it can be understood with certainty under the circumstances that it was concealed or buried for a long time and no longer has an owner, then it is considered to be treasure-trove.

The treasure-trove, except for objects that are determined to be of scientific value [724], passes to the owner of the land or movable property in which it was found.

The finder has a claim for reasonable remuneration, which, however, may not exceed half the value of the treasure-trove.[77]

§ 724 Swiss Civil Code:

If a natural body or an antiquity of high scientific value is found, then the ownership is obtained by the canton of the territory in which it was found.

The owner, in whose land such objects are found, is obliged to permit excavation in return for indemnification of damage caused thereby.

The finder and, in the case of treasure-trove [723] also the owner have a claim for a reasonable remuneration, which, however, must not exceed the value of the objects.[78]

---

[76] § 984 BGB: Wird eine Sache, die so lange verborgen gelegen hat, daß der Eigentümer nicht mehr zu ermitteln ist (Schatz), entdeckt und infolge der Entdeckung in Besitz genommen, so wird das Eigentum zur Hälfte von dem Entdecker, zur Hälfte von dem Eigentümer der Sache erworben, in welcher der Schatz verborgen war.

[77] § 723 ZGB:
Wird ein Wertgegenstand aufgefunden, von dem nach den Umständen mit Sicherheit anzunehmen ist, daß er seit langer Zeit vergraben oder verborgen war und keinen Eigentümer mehr hat, so wird er als Schatz angesehen.

Der Schatz fällt unter Vorbehalt der Bestimmung über Gegenstände von wissenschaftlichem Wert [724] an den Eigentümer des Grundstückes oder der beweglichen Sache, in der er aufgefunden worden ist.

Der Finder hat Anspruch auf eine angemessene Vergütung, die jedoch die Hälfte des Wertes des Schatzes nicht übersteigen darf.

[78] § 724 ZGB: Werden herrenlose Naturkörper oder Altertümer von erheblichem wissenscaftlichem Wert aufgefunden, so gelangen sie in das Eigentum des Kantons, in dessen Gebiet sie gefunden worden sind.

Der Eigentümer, in dessen Grundstück solche Gegenstände aufgefunden werden, ist verpflichtet, ihre Ausgrabung zu gestatten gegen Ersatz des dadurch veursachten Schadens.

Der Finder und im Falle des Schatzes [723] auch der Eigentümer haben Anspruch auf eine angemessene Vergütung, die jedoch den Wert der Gegenstände nicht übersteigen soll.

Literature:

Backhaus, Ralph. Casus perplexus: die Lösung in sich widersprüchlicher Rechtsfälle durch die klassische römische Jurisprudenz. München: Beck, 1981, 146 ff.

Hausmaninger (Case 10) 113 ff.

Hill (Case 99) 36 ff.

Knütel (Case 8) 571 ff.

CASE 101

D 6.1.67 (Scaevola libro primo responsorum)

A tutore pupilli domum mercatus ad eius refectionem fabrum induxit: is pecuniam invenit: quaeritur ad quem pertineat. Respondi, si non thensauri fuerunt, sed pecunia forte perdita vel per errorem ab eo ad quem pertinebat non ablata, nihilo minus eius eam esse, cuius fuerat.

Translation: (Scaevola in the first book of his *Opinions*)[79]

Someone has purchased a house from the guardian of a ward and, for the purpose of renovation, has brought in a craftsman. This one found money there. It was asked to whom the money belonged. I answered: if it was not treasure-trove, but was money that was lost or mistakenly not taken by the owner, it belonged, even as before, to the erstwhile owner.

Discussion Questions:

1) What is meant here by *pecunia perdita* ["money that was lost"]? Can one "lose" property in one's own house? Cf. Case 46 on this question.
2) Who acquires ownership if the money is a true *thensaurus*?
3) What significance does the factual detail *a tutore pupilli* ["from the guardian of a ward"] have?
4) Before a trip, someone buried his valuables in another's land. After his return, he has clearly forgotten the place. Has he lost the possession and the ownership? (See Case 47a on this). What can he do if the landowner prevents his entry and himself starts to look for the "treasure?" *Rei vindicatio*? *Actio ad exhibendum*?[80] Self-help?

---

[79] Q. Cervidius Scaevola was a teacher of Paul and an adviser of Marcus Aurelius. His works (six books of *responsa*, 20 books of *quaestiones*, 40 books of *digesta*) contain terse, precise case decisions, often without reasoning. They are strongly represented in the Digest with 306 excerpts.

[80] Translator's note: The *rei vindicatio* is an *in rem* action by which an owner sues for recovery of possession of his property. It is discussed in detail in Section "A" of Chapter 4. The *actio ad exhibendum* is an *in personam*" action to compel production" in court of property that the defendant has in his possession. Failure to produce the property can result in a judgment for damages equal to the property's value. The action can serve as the prelude to a *rei vindicatio* by the owner.

Compare with this Case:

§ 401 Austrian Civil Code:

If workmen find a treasure-trove in an accidental manner, then a [third] part of it belongs to them as finders. If, however, they were hired expressly to search for the treasure-trove, then they must content themselves with their ordinary pay.[81]

Literature:

Mayer-Maly (Case 47a) 285.
Hill (Case 99) 14.

---

[81] **§ 401 ABGB:** Finden Arbeitsleute zufälliger Weise einen Schatz, so gebührt ihnen as Findern ein [Dritt] teil davon. Sind sie aber von dem Eigentümer ausdücklich zur Aufsuchung eines Schatzes gedungen worden, so müssen sie sich mit ihrem ordentlichen Lohne begnügen.

F. Acquiring Fruits

CASE 102

D 22.1.25.2 (Iulianus libro septimo digestorum)

Bonae fidei emptor sevit et antequam fructus perciperet, cognovit fundum alienum esse: an perceptione fructus suos faciat, quaeritur. Respondi: bonae fidei emptor quod ad percipiendos fructus intellegi debet, quamdiu evictus fundus non fuerit: nam et servus alienus quem bona fide emero tamdiu mihi ex re mea vel ex operis suis adquiret, quamdiu a me evictus non fuerit.

Translation: (Julian in the seventh book of his *Digesta*)[82]

A good faith buyer has sown seed. Before he harvested the fruit he learned that the land was the property of another. The question was posed whether he acquired ownership of the fruits by harvesting them. I replied: with regard to the harvesting of fruits, the buyer must be considered to be of good faith for as long as he has not been evicted from the farm. For even another's slave, if I have bought in good faith, will acquire for me, provided he does so with my money or his own labor, for as long as I have not been evicted from the possession of him.

Note on the Text:

On *intellegi* ["be understood"] see on Case 72.

Discussion Questions:

1) Can the buyer of the land usucapt it, although he has learned that it is owned by another?
2) At what point in time is *bona fides* required for acquiring the fruits? Cf. also under Case 103.
3) Who, in the above described case, will have acquired ownership, if the fruits of the field or tree are stolen?
4) What legal assistance is available to a tenant whose fruits of the tree or field are stolen?
5) Try to clarify the distinction between acquisition by severance and acquisition by collection.

---

[82] On author and work, see Case 70 (D 41.1.36).

Compare with this Case:

§ 330 Austrian Civil Code:

To the reasonable possessor belong all the fruits of the property, as soon as they have been severed from the property . . .[83]

§ 955 I German Civil Code:

He who holds property in proprietary possession acquires the ownership of the products and other objects pertaining to the fruits of the property. . . upon the separation.[84]

---

[83] **§ 330 ABGB:** Dem redlichen Besitzer gehören alle aus der Sache entspringende Früchte, sobald sie von der Sache abgesondert worden sind . . .

[84] **§ 955 I BGB:** Wer eine Sache im Eigenbesitze hat, erwirbt das Eigentum an den Erzeugnissen und sonstigen zu den Früchten der Sache gehörenden Bestandteilen . . . mit der Trennung.

CASE 103

D 41.1.48.1 (Paulus libro septimo ad Plautium)

In contrarium quaeritur, si eo tempore, quo mihi res traditur, putem vendentis esse, deinde cognovero alienam esse, quia perseverat per longum tempus capio, an fructus meos faciam. Pomponius verendum, ne non sit bonae fidei possessor, quamvis capiat: hoc enim ad ius, id est capionem, illud ad factum pertinere, ut quis bona aut mala fide possideat: nec contrarium est, quod longum tempus currit, nam e contrario is, qui non potest capere propter rei vitium, fructus suos facit.

Translation: (Paul in the seventh book of his *Commentary on Plautius*)[85]

Conversely it is asked whether I acquire ownership of the fruits—if I think the property belongs to the seller at the time it is turned over to me, but later learn it is another's—inasmuch as the possession continues for a long time [i.e., the requisite period of prescription]. Pomponius says one should beware that he is not a good faith possessor, even though he holds the property. For one must distinguish between the question of law—i.e., the possession—and the question of fact—i.e., whether someone possesses in good or bad faith. And it makes no difference that a long time [i.e., the period of prescription] is running, because, to the contrary, he who cannot usucapt the property because of a defect nevertheless does acquire ownership of the fruits.

Note on the Text:

In reference to prescription there was a principle of Roman law: *mala fides superveniens non nocet* ("supervening bad faith causes no harm"). The issue of good faith applies only at the time of acquiring possession.

---

[85] On Paul, see Case 1 (D 41.2.3.1); on his *Commentary on Plautius,* see under Case 130 (D 21.3.2); on Pomponius, see Case 29 (D 41.1.21 pr.).

Discussion Questions:

Analyze the positions, including those of Julian at D 22.2.25.2 (Case 102).

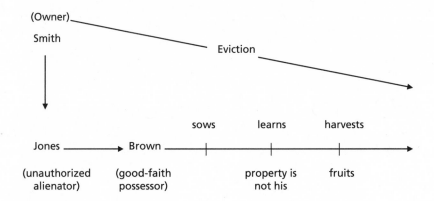

CASE 104

D 41.2.4.19 (Paulus libro quinquagensimo quarto ad edictum)

Lana ovium furtivarum si quidem apud furem detonsa est, usucapi non potest, si vero apud bonae fidei emptorem, contra: quoniam in fructu est, nec usucapi debet, sed statim emptoris fit . . .

Translation: (Paul in the 54th book of his *Commentary on the Praetor's Edict*)[86]

If the wool of stolen sheep is shorn by the thief, it cannot be usucapted, but if it is shorn by a good faith buyer, the opposite is true: since it is among the fruits, it does not need to be usucapted, but it becomes the buyer's property immediately . . .

Discussion Questions:

1) Who is the owner of the wool that has been shorn by the thief?
2) Can the wool shorn by the thief be usucapted by the good faith buyer?
3) When must the buyer of the sheep be of good faith, in order to acquire ownership of the wool shorn by himself? Cf. Cases 102 and 103.

Literature:

Thielmann G. "Produktion als Grundlage des Fruchterwerbs." *ZRG* 94 (1977) 76–100, at 87 ff.

Filip-Fröschl, Johanna. "Partus et fetus et fructus: Bemerkungen zur rechtlichen Behandlung der Tierjungen bei den Römern," in *Fest-Schr. W. Waldstein*, Wolfgang Waldstein and Martin Josef Schermaier eds., Stuttgart: Steiner, 1993, 99–121, at 115 ff.

---

[86] On author and work, see Case 1 (D 41.2.3.1).

G. Accession, Blending, and Mixing

a. Accession of Movables to Land

CASE 105

D 41.1.7.13 (Gaius libro secundo rerum cottidianarum sive aureorum)

Si alienam plantam in meo solo posuero, mea erit: ex diverso si meam plantam in alieno solo posuero, illius erit: si modo utroque casu radices egerit: antequam enim radices ageret, illius permanet, cuius et fuit. His conveniens est, quod, si vicini arborem ita terra presserim, ut in meum fundum radices egerit, meam effici arborem: rationem enim non permittere, ut alterius arbor intellegatur, quam cuius fundo radices egisset. Et ideo prope confinium arbor posita, si etiam in vicinum fundum radices egerit, communis est.

Translation: (Gaius in the second book of his *Jurisprudence of Daily Life*, also known as the *Golden Rules*)[87]

If I plant another's plant in my ground, it becomes my property. Correspondingly, if I plant my plant in another's ground, it becomes the property of the other land-owner. In both cases it is understood that the plant has taken root; since, as long as it has not taken root, it belongs to the erstwhile owner. Likewise I acquire owner-ship of a neighbor's tree, if I cover it with earth in such a way that it drives its roots into my land. For logic will not tolerate treating as the tree's owner someone who is not the owner of the land into which the tree has put down its roots. If, therefore, a tree that is planted near a boundary should drive its roots into a neighbor's land too, it is co-owned.

Discussion Questions:

1) Someone steals a tree and plants it on his land. Has he acquired ownership?
2) A tree is transferred to another's land and drives down roots there. Does it fall back into the ownership of the original owner, if he later digs it out of the new ground?

Compare with this Case:

Gaius Inst. 2.73

Praeterea id quod in solo nostro ab aliquo aedificatum est, quamvis ille suo nomine aedificaverit, iure naturali nostrum fit, quia superficies solo cedit.

---

[87] On author and work, see Case 6 (D 41.9.6).

Translation: (Gaius in the second book of his *Institutes*)[88]

Moreover, that which is built by another on our land becomes ours by *ius naturale* ["natural law"], even if he built it in his own name, because the building above yields to the ground below.

Notes on the Text:

The rule *superficies solo cedit* (the building above shares the same legal status as the ground beneath it) applies to those structures that are firmly attached to the ground: a house erected on another's land passes into the ownership of the landowner as part of the property. Compare with this the still more broadly framed principle *accessio cedit principali* ("an addition yields to the principal property") under Case 110.

Compare with this Text:

§ 420 Austrian Civil Code:

What has been provided up to this point in regard to buildings that are erected with another's materials applies also to the cases when a field is sown with another's seed or occupied with another's plants. Such an addition belongs to the owner of the land, provided the plants have already put down their roots.[89]

Literature:

Daube, D. "Implantatio and satio," in *Collected Studies in Roman law*, II, David Cohen and Simon Dieter, eds. Frankfurt/Main:Klostermann, 1991, 739–743, at 739 ff.
Knütel (Case 8) 556 ff.

---

[88] On author and work, see Case 6 (D 41.9.6).
[89] **§ 420 ABGB:** Was bisher wegen der mit fremden Materialien aufgeführten Gebäude bestimmt worden ist, gilt auch für die Fälle, wenn ein Feld mit fremden Samen besät, oder mit fremden Pflanzen besetzt worden ist. Ein solcher Zuwachs gehört dem Eigentümer des Grundes, wenn anders die Planzen schon Wurzel geschlagen haben.

CASE 106

D 41.1.60 (Scaevola libro primo responsorum)

Titius horreum frumentarium novum ex tabulis ligneis factum mobile in Seii praedio posuit: quaeritur, uter horrei dominus sit. Respondit secundum quae proponerentur non esse factum Seii.

Translation: (Scaevola in the first book of his *Opinions*)[90]

Titius placed a new, movable grain-bin that was made with wooden panels on a field belonging to Seius. It was asked which of the two was the owner of the bin. Scaevola replied that according to the facts as presented Seius was not the owner.

Discussion Questions:

Justify Scaevola's opinion.

Compare with this Case:

§ 297 Austrian Civil Code:

Likewise there belong to immovable property those things that have been put on the ground or the surface with the intention that they should remain there always...[91]

§ 946 German Civil Code:

If a movable thing is attached to land in such a way that it becomes an essential part of the land, then the ownership of the land extends to this thing.[92]

§ 93 German Civil Code:

Constituents of a thing that cannot be separated from each other without the one or the other being changed in its essential character (essential constituents) cannot in themselves be objects of rights.[93]

---

[90] On author and work, see Case 101 (D 6.1.67).

[91] **§ 297 ABGB:** Ebenso gehören zu den unbeweglichen Sachen diejenigen, welche auf Grund und Boden in der Absicht aufgeführt werden, daß sie stets darauf bleiben sollen . . .

[92] **§ 946 BGB:** Wird eine bewegliche Sache mit einem Grundstücke dergestalt verbunden, daß sie wesentlicher Bestandteil des Grundstücks wird, so erstreckt sich das Eigentum an dem Grundstück auf diese Sache.

[93] **§ 93 BGB:** Bestandteile einer Sache, die voneinander nicht getrennt werden können, ohne daß der eine oder der andere zerstört oder in seinem Wesen verändert wird (wesentliche Bestandteile), können nicht Gegenstand besonderer Rechte sein.

§ 94 German Civil Code:

I To the essential constituents of a piece of land belong the things which are firmly attached to the land or the surface, especially buildings, just as [do] the products of the land, as long as they are united with the ground. Seed with the sowing, a plant with the planting, becomes an essential constituent of the land.

II To the essential constituents of a building belong the things joined together for the creation of the building.[94]

§ 95 German Civil Code:

To the constituents of a piece of land do not belong such things as are attached to the ground or surface only for a transitory purpose . . .[95]

Literature:

Meincke J. P. "Superficies solo cedit," *ZRG* 88 (1971) 136–183, at 144 ff.

---

[94] § 94 BGB:

I Zu den wesentlichen Bestandteilen eines Grundstücks gehören die mit dem Grund und Boden fest verbundenen Sachen, inbesondere Gebäude, sowie die Erzeugnisse des Grundstücks, solange sie mit dem Boden zusammenhängen. Samen wird mit dem Aussäen, eine Pflanze wird mit dem Einpflanzen wesentlicher Bestandteil des Grundstücks.

II Zu den wesentlichen Bestandteilen eines Gebäudes gehören die zur Herstellung des Gebäudes eingefügten Sachen.

[95] § 95 BGB: Zu den Bestandteilen eines Grundstücks gehören solche Sachen nicht, die nur zu einem vorübergehenden Zwecke mit dem Grund und Boden verbunden sind . . .

CASE 107

D 6.1.38 (Celsus libro tertio digestorum)

In fundo alieno, quem imprudens emeras, aedificasti aut conseruisti, deinde evincitur: bonus iudex varie ex personis causisque constituet. finge et dominum eadem facturum fuisse: reddat impensam, ut fundum recipiat, usque eo dumtaxat, quo pretiosior factus est, et si plus pretio fundi accessit, solum quod impensum est. finge pauperem, qui si reddere id cogatur, laribus sepulchris avitis carendum habeat: sufficit tibi permitti tollere ex his rebus quae possis, dum ita ne deterior sit fundus, quam si initio non foret aedificatum. constituimus vero, ut, si paratus est dominus tantum dare, quantum habiturus est possessor his rebus ablatis, fiat ei potestas: neque malitiis indulgendum est, si tectorium puta, quod induxeris, picturasque corradere velis, nihil laturus nisi ut officias. finge eam personam esse domini, quae receptum fundum mox venditura sit: nisi reddit, quantum prima parte reddi oportere diximus, eo deducto tu condemnandus es.

Translation: (Celsus in the third book of his *Digesta*)[96]

On another's farm that you imprudently purchased you built or sowed, then you were evicted from it. A good judge will decide differently according to the individuals and the circumstances.

Suppose the owner would have done the same thing [that you did]: if he wishes to regain his property, he should repay the cost [of your outlay], but only up to the value that has been added to the property; and if more value than the expenditure was added, then only the amount that was spent.

Suppose the owner is a poor man who, if he has to repay the cost, must give up his ancestors' graves and house-gods: in that case it is sufficient to permit you to take away what you can from your additions, provided that the farm does not become worse than if there had not been any building in the first place. But we decide that if the owner is prepared to give the possessor the value he would if the property were removed, he should have the power to do so. And there is to be no tolerance of malice—for example, if you wanted to scrape off stucco that you had brought in, or frescoes, which you would not take except to cause annoyance.

Suppose the owner had the intention of immediately selling the farm once it was recovered: in that case, unless he pays what we stated he had to pay in the first part [above], that sum will be deducted from the award against you.

Notes on the Text:

With the expression *bonus iudex* ("a good judge") the adjective *bonus* expresses a behavioral standard of honesty and care that is exemplary and binding: cf. also the

---

[96] On author and work, see Case 2 (D 41.2.18.2).

bonus pater familias ["good father of the family"], the *bonus vir* ["good man"]—Case 151), and the definition given by Celsus in Ulpian D.1.1 pr. *ius est ars boni et aequi* ("Law is the art of realizing the good and the fair"). Also the comparative *melius* ["better"] in Case 96 is used in this sense.

The principle *malitiis non est indulgendum* ("there is to be no tolerance of malice") is directed against abuse of legal process. Compare the modern prohibition against chicanery: § 1295 (2) ABGB and § 226 BGB [below].

Discussion Questions:

1) The worth of unimproved land is 100, the cost of a house that is built is 50. What amount must the landowner repay to the person who paid for the building, if this person has built it well or ill, and thereby the worth of the land with the building has increased to 130? to 170?

2) To what extent is the person who built the building placed in a worse position by the *ius tollendi* ["right of removal"] than by compensation?

3) Does the poor owner have a choice between granting a *ius tollendi* or paying the cost of the materials?

4) How does the prohibition against chicanery fit in the sequence of thought in this case?

5) Does the last opinion (owners' plan to sell the property) contemplate a well-off owner, or a poor one?

6) Do you think that Celsus has drawn a distinction between a knowing and an unknowing act of building on another's land? Cf. on this point Julian/Ulpian at D 6.1.37 (Case 129).

7) Titius in good faith builds a house with his own materials on land belonging to Seius. After he learns that Seius is the landowner, he pulls the house down and carries off the material. Can Seius sue?

Compare with this Case:

§ 331 Austrian Civil Code:

If the reasonable possessor of property has incurred an expense that either was necessary for the continuous possession of the substance or was useful for increasing its still enduring uses, then he is entitled to compensation according to its present worth, insofar as it does not exceed the expense actually incurred.[97]

---

[97] **§ 331 ABGB:** Hat der redliche Besitzer an die Sache entweder zur fortwährenden Erhaltung der Substanz einen notwendigen, oder, zur Vermehrung noch fortdauernder Nutzungen einen nützlichen Aufwand gemacht, so gebührt ihm der Ersatz nach dem gegenwärtigen Werte, insofern er den wirklich gemachten Aufwand nicht übersteigt.

§ 332 Austrian Civil Code:

Of the expense that was incurred only for enjoyment or embellishment, compensation will be limited to the amount in general value that the property actually increased; however, the erstwhile possessor has the choice of taking away everything that can be removed without damage to the substance.[98]

§ 1295 (2) Austrian Civil Code:

Additionally, whoever intentionally causes damage in a manner contrary to good behavior, is liable for it; although, if this occurs by means of using legal process, [there is liability] only if the use of process clearly had the goal of injuring the other party.[99]

§ 226 German Civil Code:

The exercise of a right is not permissible, if it only has the goal of causing injury to another.[100]

Literature:

MacCormack G. "Ius tollendi." *BIDR* 85 (1982) 77–99, at 78 ff.

Bürge A. *Retentio im römischen Sachen- und Obligationenrecht*, Zürich: Schulthess, 1979, 59 ff.

·   Frier, Bruce W. *Landlords and Tenants in Imperial Rome*. Princeton: Princeton University Press, 1980, 182 ff.

Liebs, Detlef. *Römisches Recht: ein Studienbuch*, 4th ed. Göttingen: Vandenhoeck & Ruprecht, 1993, 182 ff.

---

[98] **§ 332 ABGB:** Von dem Aufwande, welcher nur zum Vergnügen und zur Verschönerung gemacht worden ist, wird nur so viel ersetzt, als die Sache dem gemeinen Werte nach wirklich dadurch gewonnen hat; doch hat der vorige Besitzer die Wahl, alles für sich wegzunehmen, was davon ohne Schaden der Sustanz weggenommen werden kann.

[99] **§ 1295 (2) ABGB:** Auch wer in einer gegen die guten Sitten verstoßenden Weise absichtlich Schaden zufügt, ist dafür verantwortlich, jedoch falls dies in Ausübung eines Rechtes geschah, nur dann, wenn die Ausübung des Rechtes offenbar den Zweck hatte, den anderen zu schädigen.

[100] **§ 62 BGB:** Die Ausübung eines Rechtes ist unzulässig, wenn sie nur den Zweck haben kann, einem anderen Schaden zuzufügen.

CASE 108

D 41.1.7.10 (Gaius libro secundo rerum cottidianarum sive aureorum)

Cum in suo loco aliquis aliena materia aedificaverit, ipse dominus intellegitur aedificii, quia omne quod inaedificatur solo cedit. nec tamen ideo is qui materiae dominus fuit desiit eius dominus esse: sed tantisper neque vindicare eam potest neque ad exhibendum de ea agere propter legem duodecim tabularum, qua cavetur, ne quis tignum alienum aedibus suis iunctum eximere cogatur, sed duplum pro eo praestet. appellatione autem tigni omnes materiae significantur, ex quibus aedificia fiunt. ergo si aliqua ex causa dirutum sit aedificium, poterit materiae dominus nunc eam vindicare et ad exhibendum agere.

Translation: (Gaius in the second book of his *Jurisprudence of Daily Life*, also known as the *Golden Rules*)[101]

If someone builds on his land with another's materials, he is treated as the owner of the building, since everything that is built thereon goes with the land. However, the former owner of the materials does not lose his ownership: he merely, for the time being, can neither vindicate the property nor make use of the *actio ad exhibendum*.[102] Indeed the Law of the Twelve Tables provides that someone who has joined another's timber to his property cannot be compelled to take it out, but he is liable for compensation [to the owner] of double its value. With the word "timber" is understood all forms of material used in buildings. Therefore, if for some reason the building should be torn down, the owner of the materials can vindicate them or bring the *actio ad exhibendum*.

Note on the Text:

On *intellegitur* ("he is treated"), see on Case 72 .

Discussion Questions:

1) Can the owner of the house usucapt roof-tiles that he used in good faith, though they belonged to someone else?
2) Must the builder also pay double the value of another's materials, if he used them in good faith?
3) Can someone, if he has brought the *actio de tigno iuncto*[103] successfully, vindicate his materials upon disassembly of the house?

Literature:

Bürge (Case 107) 18 ff.
Hinker, Hannes. "Tignum iunctum." *ZRG* 108 (1991) 94–122, at 115, 121 ff.

---

[101] On author and work, see Case 6 (D 41.1.9.6).

[102] Translator's note: On the *actio ad exhibendum*, see fn. 82 on Case 101.

[103] Translator's note: The *actio de tigno iuncto* ("action on timber that has been joined") is the suit for double damages for use of one's materials in another's building.

CASE 109

D 6.1.59 (Iulianus libro sexto ex Minicio)

Habitator in aliena aedificia fenestras et ostia imposuit, eadem post annum dominus aedificiorum dempsit: quaero, is qui imposuerat possetne ea vindicare. respondit posse: nam quae alienis aedificiis conexa essent, ea quam diu iuncta manerent, eorundem aedificiorum esse; simul atque inde dempta essent, continuo in pristinam causam reverti.

Translation: (Julian in the sixth book *On Minicius*)[104]

The inhabitant of another's building installed windows and doors in it. After one year the building's owner took them out. I ask whether the person who installed them can vindicate them. He replied that he can, since what is joined to another's building remains a part of the building as long as it is joined to it. But as soon as it has been removed, it immediately returns to its previous legal condition.

Discussion Questions:

1) Is the *actio de tigno iuncto* available in this case?
2) Is the rule *superficies solo cedit* applicable?
3) May the inhabitant who installed the door take it with him when he leaves the house?

Compare with this Case:

D 19.2.19.4 (Ulpianus libro trigensimo secundo ad edictum)

Si inquilinus ostium vel quaedam alia aedificio adiecerit, quae actio locum habeat? Et est verius quod Labeo scripsit competere ex conducto actionem, ut ei tollere liceat, sic tamen, ut damni infecti caveat, ne in aliquo dum aufert deteriorem causam aedium faceret, sed ut pristinam faciem aedibus reddat.

Translation: (Ulpian in the 32nd book of his *Commentary on the Praetor's Edict*)[105]

If a renter installs a door or other thing in the building, what is the action that lies? What Labeo wrote is correct: that an action on the rental contract lies; so [the renter] may remove the property, but, executing the *cautio damni infecti* ["guarantee

---

[104] On Julian, see Case 70 (D 41.1.36). Minicius, a member of the Sabinian school, is known to us only through the work of Julian, who published six books of the legal cases of Minicius, adding his own annotations.

[105] On author and work, see Case 11 (D 18.6.1.2).

that no damage will be caused"] he must do so only in a manner that the removal causes no damage to the building, but restores it to its original condition.

Literature:

> Frier (Case 107) 158 ff.
> Hinker (Case 108) 109 ff.

b. Accession of Movables to Movables

CASE 110

D 41.1.9.1 (Gaius libro secundo rerum cottidianarum sive aureorum)

Litterae quoque licet aureae sint, perinde chartis membranisque cedunt, ac solo cedere solent ea quae aedificantur aut seruntur. ideoque si in chartis membranisve tuis carmen vel historiam vel orationem scripsero, huius corporis non ego, sed tu dominus esse intellegeris. sed si a me petas tuos libros tuasve membranas nec impensas scripturae solvere velis, potero me defendere per exceptionem doli mali, utique si bona fide eorum possessionem nanctus sim.

Translation: (Gaius in the second book of his *Jurisprudence of Daily Life*, also known as the *Golden Rules*)[106]

The ownership of written letters, even if they be of gold, follows the ownership of the papyrus or parchment, like the ownership of buildings or sown seed follows the land. If, therefore, I write a poem or a history or a speech on your papyrus or parchment, you, not I, count as the owner of the work. If you, however, ask me for your papyrus or parchment, and are not willing to pay the cost of the writing, I can defend the suit with the *exceptio doli*—provided that I have obtained the possession in good faith.

Note on the Text:

[The rule of] *accessio cedit principali* ("an addition yields to the main thing"—i.e., as regards its legal condition) [means]: when two movables are joined together, the owner of the subsidiary property loses his ownership to the owner of the main property. Compare the more narrowly formulated rule: *superficies solo cedit* (Case 105).

Discussion Questions:

1) Gaius applies the principle of *superficies solo cedit* (cf. Case 105) to the joining of two pieces of movable property into a unified thing. Does consideration of the relative value of the two things play a role?
2) Formulate the principal consideration that accounts for awarding to the owner of paper, wood, or wool the ownership of a new thing created by writing on the paper, painting on the wood, or dyeing of the wool.
3) What measures can be taken against the bad-faith possessor of the paper?
4) Do you think the solution of Gaius would be practical in application? Can you propose other solutions?

---

[106] On author and work, see Case 6 (D 41.1.9.6).

Compare with this Text:

§§ 414–416 Austrian Civil Code (quoted under Case 120)

§ 947 German Civil Code:

I   If movable things are joined to each other in such a way that they become essential parts of a single unified thing, then the erstwhile owners become co-owners of this thing; their [respective] shares are determined according to the relationship of the values which the constituent things had at the time of the joining.[107]

II   If one of the things is to be understood as the main thing, then its owner acquires the sole ownership.

Art. 727 Swiss Civil Code:

If movable things of different owners are mixed with or joined to each other such that they cannot be separated without essential damage or disproportionate work and expense, then co-ownership of the new thing by the persons concerned comes about [646/51], and it is proportional to the values that the individual parts had at the time of the joining.

If a movable thing is mixed or joined with another such that it appears as a subsidiary part of it, the whole thing belongs to the owner of the chief part.

Claims of compensation for damages **[OR 41/61]** and [unjust] enrichment **[OR 42/9]** remain available.[108]

---

[107] § 947 BGB:

I   Werden bewegliche Sachen miteinander dergestalt verbunden, daß sie wesentliche Bestandteile einer einheitlichen Sache werden, so werden die bisherigen Eigentümer Miteigentümer dieser Sache; die Anteile bestimmen sich nach dem Verhältnisse des Wertes, den die Sachen zur Zeit der Verbindung haben.

II   Ist eine der Sachen als die Hauptsache anzusehen, so erwirbt ihr Eigentümer das Alleineigtum.

[108] Art. 727 ZGB:

Werden bewegliche Sachen verschiedener Eigentümer so miteinander vermischt oder verbunden, daß sie ohne wesentliche Beschädigung oder unverhältnismäßige Arbeit und Auslagen nicht mehr getrennt werden können, so entsteht für die Beteiligten Miteigentum [646/51] an der neuen Sache, und zwar nach dem Werte, den die einzelnen Teile zur Zeit der Verbindung haben.

Wird eine bewegliche Sache mit einer andern derart vermischt oder verbunden, daß sie als deren nebensächlicher Bestandteil erscheint, so gehört die ganze Sache dem Eigentümer des Hauptbestandteiles.

Vorbehalten bleiben die Ansprüche auf Schadenersatz **[OR 41/61]** und aus Bereicherung [OR 42/9].

CASE 111

Gai. Inst. 2.78

Sed si in tabula mea aliquis pinxerit veluti imaginem, contra probatur: magis enim dicitur tabulam picturae cedere. cuius diversitatis vix idonea ratio redditur. certe secundum hanc regulam si me possidente petas imaginem tuam esse nec solvas pretium tabulae, poteris per exceptionem doli mali summoveri; at si tu possideas, consequens est, utilis mihi actio adversum te dari debeat; quo casu nisi solvam inpensam picturae, poteris me per exceptionem doli mali repellere, utique si bonae fidei possessor fueris. illud palam est, quod sive tu subripueris tabulam sive alius, conpetit mihi furti actio.

Translation: (Gaius in the second book of his *Institutes*)[109]

But if someone paints, for example, a picture on my panel, the opposite result is approved, for in that case the ownership of the panel yields to the painting. A satisfactory explanation of this difference is not given. If, according to this rule, you demand a painting of yours that I possess, but you are not willing to pay the price of the panel, I will certainly be able to block you with the *exceptio doli*. If, on the other hand, you are in possession of it, then logically an *actio utilis* ["analogous action based on the same policy"] should be given to me against you. If in this case I do not pay the cost of the painting, provided you are a good-faith possessor, you can defend against me with the *exceptio doli*. This much is clear: I have an *actio furti* ["action for theft"], if you or someone else steals the painting [from me].

Note on the Text:

Observe the legal criticism that is expressed in the formulation *vix idonea ratio redditur* ("A satisfactory explanation of this difference is not given"). As an academic teacher without the *ius respondendi*[110] Gaius could only present the applicable law, but he could not contribute to its development through his own decisions.

Discussion Questions:

1) From what point of view does Gaius support treating a picture and a literary work in the same way?
2) What justification(s) can be produced for making a distinction?
3) Does Gaius preserve for the erstwhile owner of the panel a right of recovery of the picture in response to a *rei vindicatio* by the painter?

---

[109] On author and work, see Case 6 (D 41.1.9.6).

[110] Translator's note: The *ius respondendi* ("right of giving *responsa*") refers to an imperially recognized right of giving presumptively authoritative legal opinions.

4) To what extent can the erstwhile owner of the panel get compensation by means of the *exceptio doli* or the *actio utilis*?

5) Do you think that the *actio utilis* mentioned here is an action *in rem*?[111]

Literature:

Kaser M. "Tabula picta." *RHD* 36 (1968) 31–56, at 31 ff.

Behrends, O. "Die Spezifikationslehre, ihre Gegner und die media sententia in der Geschichte der römischen Jurisprudenz." *ZRG* 112 (1995) 195–238, at 207 ff.

---

[111] Translator's note: Roman legal procedure divided lawsuits into actions *in rem* ("against the property") and actions *in personam* ("against the person"). The former involved a claim for property in the possession of the defendant. The latter involved a claim for compensation based on a personal obligation arising from a contract or a delict (the causing of loss, damage, or injury). The *rei vindicatio* was an action *in rem*.

CASE 112

D 6.1.23.3 (Paulus libro vicensimo primo ad edictum)

Sed et id, quod in charta mea scribitur aut in tabula pingitur, statim meum fit: licet de pictura quidam contra senserint propter pretium picturae: sed necesse est ei rei cedi, quod sine illa esse non potest.

Translation: (Paul in the 21st book of his *Commentary on the Praetor's Edict*)[112]

But that which is written on my paper or painted on my panel becomes mine at once. Granted that some feel differently on account of the value of the picture, but it must yield to the thing (i.e., the panel), since it cannot exist without it.

Discussion Questions:

Explain this text in relation to Gaius Inst. 2.78 (Case 111) and Inst. Iust. 2.1.34 (quoted below).

Compare with this Text:

Inst. Iust. 2.3.34

Si quis in aliena tabula pinxerit, quidam putant tabulam picturae cedere: aliis videtur picturam, qualiscumque sit, tabulae cedere. Sed nobis videtur melius esse tabulam picturae cedere: ridiculum est enim picturam Apellis vel Parrhasii in accessionem vilissimae tabulae cedere . . .

Translation:

If someone has painted a picture on another's panel, many [jurists] think the ownership of the panel yields to the picture. Others think that the picture, whatever may be its quality, yields to the panel. But it seems better to us that the panel yields to the picture: for it is ridiculous that a painting by Apelles or Parrhasius should yield to an extremely cheap panel . . .

Note on the Text:

On *videtur melius* ("it seems better to us"), see on Case 107.

Literature:

    Kaser (Case 111) 37.
    Behrends (Casd 111) 207 ff.

---

[112] On author and work, see Case 1 (D 41.2.3.1).

CASE 113

D 6.1.23.5 (Paulus libro vicensimo primo ad edictum)

Item quaecumque aliis iuncta sive adiecta accessionis loco cedunt, ea quamdiu cohaerent dominus vindicare non potest, sed ad exhibendum agere potest, ut separentur et tunc vindicentur: scilicet excepto eo, quod Cassius de ferruminatione scribit. dicit enim, si statuae suae ferruminatione iunctum bracchium sit, unitate maioris partis consumi et quod semel alienum factum sit, etiamsi inde abruptum sit, redire ad priorem dominum non posse. non idem in eo quod adplumbatum sit, quia ferruminatio per eandem materiam facit confusionem, plumbatura non idem efficit. ideoque in omnibus his casibus, in quibus neque ad exhibendum neque in rem locum habet, in factum actio necessaria est. at in his coporibus, quae ex distantibus corporibus essent, constat singulas partes retinere suam propriam speciem, ut singuli homines, singulae oves: ideoque posse me gregem vindicare, quamvis aries tuus sit immixtus, sed et te arietem vindicare posse. quod non idem in cohaerentibus corporibus evenire: nam si statuae meae bracchium alienae statuae addideris, non posse dici bracchium tuum esse, quia tota statua uno spiritu continetur.

Translation: (Paul in the 21st book of his *Commentary on the Praetor's Edict*)[113]

Likewise in the case of things that are joined or added to other things and yield [their identity] in the accession, as long as they cohere, the owner cannot vindicate them, but he can bring an *actio ad exhibendum*, with a view to their separation and subsequent vindication—with the exception, however, of what Cassius writes in reference to welding. He says that if an arm is welded onto his statue, the ownership of it is lost because of its unity with the larger part, and what has once become something else cannot return to its former owner, even if it should be broken off. This does not, however, apply to things that are soldered, since welding creates a merger of the same material, but soldering does not do the same. Therefore in all these cases, in which neither the *actio ad exhibendum* nor the *actio in rem* is available, an *actio in factum* is possible. But in the case of collections of things that consist of separate parts it is clear that the individual parts retain their identity, like slaves or single sheep. Therefore I can vindicate my herd, even though a ram belonging to you is mixed in it, and you also can vindicate your ram. That does not apply, however, to entities that consist of cohering parts: for if you add the arm from another statue to my statue, it cannot be said that the arm is your property, since the entire statue is a unified whole.

---

[113] On author and work, see Case 1 (D 41.2.3.1); on Cassius, see Case 19 (D 41.2.21.3).

Discussion Questions:

1) How does Paul justify loss of ownership in the case of welding but preservation of ownership in the case of soldering?
2) Paul distinguishes between unified things and collective things and, regarding the latter, between a totality of *rerum cohaerentium* ["cohering parts"] and *rerum distantium* ["separate parts"]. What is a house? How about a statue with an arm that is soldered on rather than welded on?
3) How does the former owner of the welded arm make his claim effective?
4) Can the *actio ad exhibendum* be used in reference to a tree that has been planted on another's property? On this, see Case 108.

CASE 114

D 41.1.27.2 (Pomponius libro trigensimo ad Sabinum)

Cum partes duorum dominorum ferrumine cohaereant, hae cum quaereretur utri cedant, Cassius ait pro portione rei aestimandum vel pro pretio cuiusque partis. sed si neutra alteri accessioni est, videamus, ne aut utriusque esse dicenda sit, sicuti massa confusa, aut eius, cuius nomine ferruminanta est. sed Proculus et Pegasus existimant suam cuiusque rem manere.

Translation: (Pomponius in the 30th book of his *Commentary on the* Ius Civile *of Sabinus*)[114]

If parts that belong to two owners are joined together by welding, and if it is asked to whom the ownership falls, Cassius says one must decide according to the respective shares of the property or according to the value of each part. But if neither part is an accession to the other, we must examine whether one should say that the ownership belongs to both, as in the case of a mass of metal that has melted together, or to that person in whose name the welding took place. But Proculus and Pegasus think that each retains the ownership of his property.

Discussion Questions:

What new viewpoint emerges from this text as compared with Paul D 6.1.23.5 (Case 113)?

Literature:

Schermaier, Martin Josef. "Teilvindikation oder Teilungsklage?" *ZRG* 110 (1993) 124–183, at 146 ff.

---

[114] On author and work, see Case 29 (D 41.1.21 pr.); on Cassius, see Case 19 (D 41.2.21.3); on Proculus, see Case 9 (D 41.1.55). Pegasus succeeded Proculus as head of the legal school. He was a consul under Vespasian and *praefectus urbi* ["City Prefect"] under Vespasian and Domitian.

c. Blending (*confusio*) and Mixing

CASE 115

D 6.1.5 pr. (Ulpianus libro sexto decimo ad edictum)

Idem Pomponius scribit: si frumentum duorum non voluntate eorum confusum sit, competit singulis in rem actio in id, in quantum paret in illo acervo suum cuiusque esse: quod si voluntate eorum commixta sunt, tunc communicata videbuntur et erit communi dividundo actio.

Translation: (Ulpian in the 16th book of his *Commentary on the Praetor's Edict*)[115]

The same Pomponius writes: if grain belonging to two owners is mixed together without their consent, each has an *actio in rem* for that portion of the whole which appears to belong to him. If, however, the grain was mixed with their consent, then it is a matter of co-ownership and there will be an *actio communi dividundo*.[116]

Discussion Questions:

Explain the decision of Pomponius.

Compare with this Case:

§§ 414–416 ABGB (quoted under Case 120); **§ 947 BGB** (quoted under Case 110)

§ 948 German Civil Code:

I If movable things are inseparably blended or mixed together, the provisions of **§947** are correspondingly applicable.

II The inseparability is the same, if the separation of the mixed or blended things would be accomplished at disproportionate cost.[117]

Literature:

Kaser (Case 70) 186 ff.

Cromme, Ingrid. Vindicatio incertae partis: ihre Bedeutung für die Erkenntnis der geschichtlichen Entwicklung des klassischen dinglichen Verfahrens, diss. University of Heidelberg (1971) 56 ff.

Schermaier, Martin J. Materia: Beiträge zur Frage der Naturphilosophie im klassischen römischen Recht. Wien: Böhlau, 1992, 164 ff.

Schermaier (Case 114) 170 f.

Behrends (Case 111) 229 ff.

---

[115]On author and work, see Case 11 (D 18.6.1.2); on Pomponius, see Case 29 (D 41.1.21.pr.).

[116]Translator's note: The *actio communi dividundo* was a partition action among co-owners for the division of property owned in common.

[117]§ 948 BGB:

I Werden bewegliche Sachen miteinander untrennbar vermischt oder vermengt, so finden die Vorschriften des § 947 entsprechende Andwendung.

II Der Untrennbarkeit steht es gleich, wenn die Trennung der vermischten oder vermengten Sachen mit unverhältnismäßigen Kosten verbunden sein würde.

CASE 116

D 6.1.3.2 (Ulpianus libro sexto decimo ad edictum)

Pomponius scribit, si quid quod eiusdem naturae est ita confusum est atque commixtum, ut deduci et separari non possint, non totum, sed pro parte esse vindicandum. ut puta meum et tuum argentum in massam redactum est: erit nobis commune, et unusquisque pro rata ponderis quod in massa habemus vindicabimus, etsi incertum sit, quantum quisque ponderis in massa habet.

Translation: (Ulpian in the 16th book of his *Commentary on the Praetor's Edict*)[118]

Pomponius writes: if quantities of the same nature are so blended or mixed together that they cannot be drawn apart or separated, the vindication must not be of the whole, but *pro parte* ["proportionally"]. If, for example, my silver and your silver are melted together into a clump, it belongs to us in common, and we will vindicate it in proportion to the weight of our shares, even if it is uncertain how much weight each of us has in the share.

Discussion Questions:

1) Is Pomponius thinking here of a mixing with, or without, the consent of the owners? (cf. D 6.1.5 pr. [Case 115]).
2) Do you think that Pomponius reached the same decision in the case of a blending of copper and gold, of lead and silver, or with a mixture of wine and honey (cf. D 6.1.5.1 [Case 118])?

Literature:

Kaser (Case 70) 186 ff.
Cromme (Case 115) 54 ff.
Schermaier (Case 115) 164 ff.
Schermaier (Case 114) 135 ff.

---

[118] On author and work, see Case 11 (D 18.6.1.2); on Pomponius, see Case 29 (D 41.1.21 pr.).

CASE 117

D 41.1.7.8 (Gaius libro secundo rerum cottidianarum sive aureorum)

Voluntas duorum dominorum miscentium materias commune totum corpus efficit, sive eiusdem generis sint materiae, veluti vina miscuerunt vel argentum conflaverunt, sive diversae, veluti si alius vinum contulerit alius mel, vel alius aurum alius argentum: quamvis et mulsi et electri novi corporis sit species.

Translation: (Gaius in the second book of his *Jurisprudence of Daily Life*, also known as the *Golden Rules*)[119]

The intent of two owners, who have mixed their materials, makes the whole object owned in common. [This is true] whether the materials are of the same kind—as when they have mixed wine or melted silver—or are of different kinds—as when one has contributed the wine and the other the honey; or one, the gold, and the other, silver. [And this is true] even though the honeyed wine and the electrum are forms of a new substance.

Discussion Questions:

Explain this text in connection with Pomponius/Ulpian at D 6.1.3.2 (Case 116).

Literature:

> Kaser (Case 70) 186 ff.
> Cromme (Case 115) 61 ff.
> Schermaier (Case 115) 166 ff.
> Schermaier (Case 114) 137 f.

---

[119] On author and work, see Case 6 (D 41.1.9.6).

CASE 118

D 6.1.5.1 (Ulpianus libro sexto decimo ad edictum)

Idem scribit, si ex melle meo, vino tuo factum sit mulsum, quosdam existimasse id quoque communicari: sed puto verius, ut et ipse significat, eius potius esse qui fecit, quoniam suam speciem pristinam non continet. sed si plumbum cum argento mixtum sit, quia deduci possit, nec communicabitur nec communi dividundo agetur, quia separari potest: agetur autem in rem actio. sed si deduci, inquit, non possit, ut puta si aes et aurum mixtum fuerit, pro parte esse vindicandum: nec quaquam erit dicendum, quod in mulso dictum est, quia utraque materia etsi confusa manet tamen.

Translation: (Ulpian in the 16th book of his *Commentary on the Praetor's Edict*)[120]

The same (Pomponius) writes: if honeyed-wine is made out of my honey and your wine, some jurists think a joint ownership arises from that. I consider more accurate, however, what Pomponius himself also expresses: that the new thing belongs to the person who made it, since it does not retain its earlier identity (*speciem*). If, however, lead is mixed with silver, a joint ownership does not occur, since the result is separable, and therefore will be sued on not by means of the *actio communi dividundo*, but with the *actio in rem*. Yet if one cannot make the separation, for example in the case of copper and gold, he says one must vindicate *pro parte* ["proportionally"], and the decision would in no way be the same as with honeyed wine, since both substances remain separate, in spite of the mixture.

Notes on the Text:

Observe the melting points of the named metals: copper 1083° (Celsius), gold 1063°, silver 960.5°, lead 327.4°. On *verius* ("more accurate"), see on Case 8.

Discussion Questions:

1) Does the example concern an agreed upon mixing (i.e., with the owners' mutual consent), or does the mixing take place without an agreement?
2) Justify the decision as regards the ownership of the metal mixtures.
3) What is the justification for a joint ownership arising from a mixture of wine and honey?

---

[120] On author and work, see Case 11 (D 18.6.1.2); on Pomponius, see Case 29 (D 41.1.21 pr.).

Literature:

Thielmann, G. "Zum Eigentumserwerb durch Verarbeitung im römischen Recht," in *Sein und Werden im Recht : Festgabe für Ulrich von Lübtow zum 70. Geburtstag am 21. August 1970*, Walter G. Becker and Manfred Herder eds. Berlin: Duncker & Humblot, 1970, 187–232, at 205 ff.

Cromme (Case 115) 57 ff.

Schermaier, Martin J. "D. 41,1,24 und 26 pr. Ein Versuch zur Verarbeitungslehre des Paulus," *ZRG* 105 (1988) 436-487, 436 ff.

Schermaier (Case 115) 164 ff.

Schermaier (Case 114) 140 ff.

Behrends (Case 111) 229 ff.

d. The Special Case of Money

CASE 119

D 46.3.78 (Iavolenus libro undecimo ex Cassio)

Si alieni nummi inscio vel invito domino soluti sunt, manent eius cuius fuerunt: si mixti essent, ita ut discerni non possent, eius fieri qui accepit in libris Gaii scriptum est, ita ut actio domino cum eo, qui dedisset, furti competeret.

Translation: (Javolenus in the eleventh book of his *Abridgement of Cassius*)[121]

If another's coins are spent without the knowledge or against the wishes of the owner, they remain the property of the person to whom they belonged. If they have been mixed with others, such that one can no longer distinguish them, it is written in the books of Gaius (Cassius) that they are the property of the person who received them, with the result that the erstwhile owner has an *actio furti* [i.e., "action for theft"] against the person who spent the coins.

Discussion Questions:

1) Does the text presume the good faith of the payee who mixes the coins with his own? Are there different legal consequences depending upon his good or bad faith?
2) Does the text presume the bad faith of the payor?
3) In the case of inseparable mixing of other solid materials (e.g., grain) without the consent of both owners, according to Pomponius/Ulpian (D 6.1.3.5 pr.), the erstwhile ownership interests remain intact and can be made operative through a vindication of the respective amounts. What supports the use of this same rule also in the case of money?
4) What arguments speak in favor of a special rule for money in property law?
5) Jones, who is keeping money for Smith, mistakenly uses the money to pay a debt to Brown. Has Brown thereby become the owner of the money? Is Jones' debt satisfied? How does Smith get his money back?
6) In the previous question are you assuming the bad faith of Jones?

Compare with this Text:

§ 370 Austrian Civil Code:

A person who sues for the return of movable property must describe the property with characteristics by which it can be distinguished from all similar property of the same type.[122]

---

[121] On Javolenus, see Case 3 (D 46.3.79); on Cassius, see Case 19 (D 41.2.21.3).

[122] § 370 ABGB: Wer eine bewegliche Sache gerichtlich zurückfordert, muß sie durch Merkmale beschreiben, wodurch sie von allen ähnlichen Sachen gleicher Gattung ausgezeichnet wird.

§ 371 Austrian Civil Code:

Things which in this manner cannot be distinguished, such as cash mixed with other cash,... are therefore generally not the objects of *in rem* lawsuits...[123]

Literature:

Manthe (Case 19) 45 ff.

Wacke A. "Die Zahlung mit fremden Geld. Zum Begriff des pecuniam consumere." *BIDR* 79 (1976) 49–144, at 114 ff.

Kaser (Case 70) 183 ff.

Bauer (Case 84) 153 ff.

Schermaier (Case 114) 149 ff.

Gamauf, Richard. "Eigentumserwerb an Geld durch Vermengung im römischen Recht (D 46.3.78) und in § 371 ABGB," Part 1 in *JAP* (1997/98) 154 ff.

---

[123] **§ 371 ABGB:** Sachen, die sich auf diese Art nicht unterscheiden lassen, wie bares Geld mit anderm baren Geld vermengt, . . . sind also in der Regel kein Gegenstand der Eigentumsklage . . .

H.   Transformation (Specification)

CASE 120

D 41.1.7.7 (Gaius libro secundo rerum cottidianarum sive aureorum)

*Cum quis ex aliena materia speciem aliquam suo nomine fecerit, Nerva et Proculus
putant hunc dominum esse qui fecerit, qui quod factum est, antea nullius fuerat. Sabinus
et Cassius magis naturalem rationem efficere putant, ut qui materiae dominus fuerit,
idem eius quoque, quod ex eadem materia factum sit, dominus esset, quia sine materia
nulla species effici possit: veluti si ex auro vel argento vel aere vas aliquod fecero, vel ex
tabulis tuis navem aut armarium aut subsellia fecero, vel ex lana tua vestimentum, vel ex
vino et melle tuo mulsum, vel ex medicamentis tuis emplastrum aut collyrium, vel ex uvis
aut olivis aut spicis tuis vinum vel oleum vel frumentum. est tamen etiam media sententia
recte existimantium, si species ad materiam reverti possit, verius esse, quod et Sabinus
et Cassius senserunt, si non possit reverti, verius esse, quod Nervae et Proculo placuit.
ut ecce vas conflatum ad rudem massam auri vel argenti vel aeris reverti potest, vinum
vero vel oleum vel frumentum ad uvas et olivas et spicas reverti non potest: ac ne mulsum
quidem ad mel et vinum vel emplastrum aut collyria ad medicamenta reverti possunt.
videntur tamen mihi recte quidam dixisse non debere dubitari, quin alienis spicis excus-
sum frumentum eius sit, cuius et spicae fuerunt: cum enim grana, quae spicis continentur,
perfectam habeant suam speciem, qui excussit spicas, non novam speciem facit, sed eam
quae est detegit.*

Translation: (Gaius in the second book of his *Jurisprudence of Daily Life*, also known
as the *Golden Rules*)[124]

If someone makes something new in his own name out of another's materials,
Nerva and Proculus think that the person who makes it is the owner, because the
thing that is made previously belonged to no one. Sabinus and Cassius think that
natural reason leads to the conclusion that the owner of the materials is also the
owner of the object that is made from them, since without the material no new
thing could be created. So, for example, if I make a vase out of your gold or silver
or copper, or I make a ship or a box or a chair with your lumber, or a garment
from your wool, or honeyed wine with your wine and honey, or a plaster or salve
from your medicaments, wine from your grapes, oil from your olives, or grain from
your ears [of wheat]. But there is also the middle view of those who rightly think
that if the manufactured thing can be returned to its original rough condition, the
opinion of Sabinus and Cassius is more correct; but if that is not possible, then
the opinion of Nerva and Proculus is. So, for example, a vase can be melted and
made back into its original material of gold, silver or copper. The wine or the oil or
the grain cannot be remade into grapes or olives or ears of wheat. Honeyed wine

---

[124]On author and work, see Case 6 (D 41.1.9.6); on Nerva, see Case 13 (D 12.1.9.9); on
Proculus, see Case 9 (D 41.1.55); on Sabinus, see Case 11 (D 18.6.1.2); on Cassius, see Case 19
(D 41.2.21.3).

too cannot become honey and wine again, or a plaster or salve cannot be brought back to the original medicaments. Still, those are correct who have said that one cannot doubt that grain winnowed from another's ears of wheat belongs to the owner of the ears: because the grain that is contained in the ears already has its finished form. The person who winnowed it has not created a new thing, but merely uncovered an existing one.

Discussion Questions:

1) How do "the Proculians" and "the Sabinians" justify their different viewpoints?
2) Gaius names six chief types of material-processing (metal, wood, textiles, brewing, medicine, and agriculture). To which of them is the *media sententia* ["middle view"] applicable?
3) Who acquires ownership if the reprocessing takes place at the order of the owner of the materials or a third party?
4) Applying the Proculian doctrine, what is the legal consequence, if a thief makes stolen gold into rings?
5) What claims does an owner of materials have, if he has lost his ownership according to the Proculian doctrine?
6) What claims does a producer have, if he must surrender the product to the owner of the materials according to the Sabinian doctrine?

Compare with this Case:

§ 414 Austrian Civil Code:

Whoever reprocesses the property of another; whoever unites, blends, or mixes it with his own, acquires thereby no claim to the other's property.[125]

§ 415 Austrian Civil Code:

If such reprocessed property can be brought back to its previous condition; if the united or blended or mixed property can be separated again, then to each owner his own is returned, and liability for damage is imposed on the person responsible. If a return to the previous condition or a separation is not possible, then the property is owned in common by those who have a share of it; although the person whose property was by the other wrongfully taken into the combination has the choice of whether he wishes to keep the object and pay the other party for its increase in value, or to receive compensation himself and let the other party have the object.

---

[125] § 414 ABGB: Wer fremde Sachen verarbeitet; wer sie mit den seinigen vereinigt, vermengt, oder vermischt, erhält dadurch noch keinen Anspruch auf das fremde Eigentum.

The share-holder who bears the fault will be treated according to the nature of his reasonable or unreasonable intent. If, however, neither party is deemed to be at fault, the choice belongs to the person whose share is of greater worth.[126]

§ 416 Austrian Civil Code:

If another's materials are used to improve a property, the other's materials pass to the owner of the principal thing [that is improved], and he is required, according to nature of his reasonable or unreasonable behavior, to compensate the former owner for the value of the materials that were used.[127]

§ 950 I German Civil Code:

Whoever produces a new piece of movable property by means of processing or transforming one or multiple materials acquires the ownership of the new property, provided the worth of the processing or transformation is not substantially less than the worth of the material. Writings, signs, paintings, printings, engravings or similar reworkings of the surface count as processed products.[128]

§ 951 I German Civil Code:

Whoever suffers a loss of rights pursuant to the provisions of §§ 946 to 950 can... claim monetary compensation. The re-establishment of the earlier condition cannot be claimed...[129]

---

[126] § 415 ABGB: Können dergleichen verarbeitete Sachen in ihren vorigen Stand zurückgebracht; vereinigte, vermengte oder vermischte Sachen wieder abgesondert werden; so wird einem jeden Eigentümer das Seinige zurückgestellt, und demjenigen Schadloshaltung geleistet, dem sie gebührt. Ist die Zurücksetzung, in den vorigen Stand, oder die Absonderung nicht möglich, so wird die Sache den Teilnehmern gemein; doch steht demjenigen, mit dessen Sache der andere durch Verschulden die Vereinigung vorgenommen hat, die Wahl frei, ob er den ganzen Gegenstand gegen Ersatz der Verbesserung behalten, oder ihn dem andern ebenfalls gegen Vergütung überlassen wolle. Der Schuld tragende Teilnehmer wird nach Beschaffenheit seiner redlichen oder unredlichen Absicht behandelt. Kann aber keinem Teile ein Verschulden beigemessen werden, so bleibt dem, dessen Anteil mehr wert ist, dei Auswahl vorbehalten.

[127] § 416 ABGB: Werden fremde Materialien nur zur Ausbesserung einer Sache verwendet, so fällt die fremde Materie dem Eigentümer der Hauptsache zu, und dieser ist verbunden, nach Beschaffenheit seines redlichen oder unredlichen Verfahrens, dem vorigen Eigentümer der verbrauchten Materialien den Wert derselben zu bezahlen.

[128] § 950 I BGB: Wer durch Verarbeitung oder Umbildung eines oder mehrer Stoffe eine neue bewegliche Sache herstellt, erwirbt das Eigentum an der neuen Sache, sofern nicht der Wert der Verarbeitung oder der Umbildung erheblich geringer ist als der Wert des Stoffes. Als Verarbeitung gilt auch das Schreiben, Zeichen, Malen, Drucken, Gravieren oder eine ähnliche Bearbeitung der Oberfläche.

[129] § 951 I BGB: Wer infolge der Vorschriften der §§ 946 bis 950 einen Rechtsverlust erleidet, kann ... Vergütung in Geld ... fordern. Die Wiederherstellung des früheren Zustandes kann nicht verlangt werden.

Art. 726 Swiss Civil Code:

If someone has processed or transformed the property of another, the new product belongs to the producer, if the work is more valuable than the material, otherwise to the owner [of the material].

If the producer has not acted in good faith, the judge can award the new product to the owner of the materials, even if the work is valuable.

Claims for compensation of damage (**OR 41/6**) and [unjust] enrichment (**OR 62/9**) remain available.[130]

Literature:

Mayer-Maly, Th. "Spezifikation. Leitfälle, Begriffsbildung, Rechtsinstitut." *ZRG* 73 (1956) 120–154, at 120 ff.

Schermaier (Case 115) 98 ff.

Stoop, B. C. "Non solet locatio dominium mutare. Some Remarks on *specificatio* in Classical Roman Law." *RHD* 66 (1998) 3–24, at 5 ff.

---

[130] **Art. 726 ZGB:**

Hat jemand eine fremde Sache verarbeitet oder umgebildet, so gehört die neue Sache, wenn die Arbeit kostbarer ist als der Stoff, dem Verarbeiter, andernfalls dem Eigentümer.

Hat der Verarbeiter nicht in gutem Glauben gehandelt, so kann der Richter, auch wenn die Arbeit kostbarer ist, die neue Sache dem Eigentümer des Stoffes zusprechen.

Vorbehalten bleiben die Ansprüche auf Schadenerstatz [OR 41/61] und aus Bereicherung [OR 62/9].

CHAPTER IV

Protection and Limitations of Ownership

Introduction

This chapter aims to present some examples of how and to what extent the owner can legally pursue his rights.

The *rei vindicatio* ["vindication of property"] is the suit of a civil-law owner[1] to assert his rights and recover possession of his property. Two aspects are here presented for discussion: the establishment of the defendant's liability to suit, and the extent of the defendant's obligation to make restitution (fruits, compensation for damage, expenses).

The *actio publiciana* ["Publician action"] is modeled on the *rei vindicatio*. It gives the usucapting possessor legal protection against third parties with a lesser claim to it. The Publician action is also available to the "bonitary owner" (i.e., someone to whom a civil-law owner has transferred *res mancipi* by *traditio* [with *iusta causa*, but not by the formal procedure of *mancipatio* or *in iure cessio*, with the result that the conveyance is technically defective]. The bonitary owner can use the *actio publiciana* against the civil-law owner whose *rei vindicatio*, or *exceptio dominii* ["affirmative defense of ownership"] when defending a suit, can be defeated by the bonitary owner's use of *exceptiones* or *replicationes rei venditae et traditae* or *doli*.[2]

The suit to clear title is called the *actio negatoria* ["denial action"]. It served to defend against claims of servitudes, "immisions" [i.e., the commission of what at common law would be called nuisance or trespass], and other impairments of ownership.

In addition to all of these, the owner could, under certain conditions, make use of the possessory interdicts and a series of special legal remedies involving relations with neighbors. As an especially effective and illustrative legal remedy in this connection the *interdictum quod vi aut clam* [i.e., interdict of the form that begins: "What by force or stealth . . . "] will be discussed. It will provide a glance at how Roman jurists interpreted the Praetor's edict.

---

[1] Translator's note: A "civil-law owner" is an owner whose ownership rights are established by the Roman *ius civile*.

[2] Translator's note: The *exceptio* or *replicatio* ("reply to an affirmative defense") *rei venditae et traditae* consisted of proving that the "property had been sold and delivered." The *exceptio* or *replicatio doli* required proof of fraud, deceit, or bad faith.

Literature:

Kaser, Max. *Restituere als Prozessgegenstand: ein Beitrag zur Lehre von der materiellrechtlichen Beschaffenheit der in iudicium deduzierten Ansprüche im klassischen römischen Recht,* 2nd ed. München: C. H. Beck, 1968.

———. "Nochmals über Besitz und Verschulden bei den actiones in rem." *ZRG* 98 (1981) 77–146.

Wimmer, Markus. *Besitz und Haftung des Vindikationsbeklagten.* Köln: Böhlau, 1995.

Kaser, M. "In bonis esse." *ZRG* 78 (1961) 173–220.

Apathy, P. "Die actio Publiciana beim Doppelkauf vom Nichteigentümer." *ZRG* 99 (1982) 158–187.

Maifeld, Jan. *Die aequitas bei L. Neratius Priscus.* Trier: WVT Wissenschaftlicher Verlag, 1991.

Watson, Alan. *The Law of Property in the Later Roman Republic.* Oxford: Clarendon, 1968, 176 ff. (*actio negatoria*), 222 ff. (*quod vi aut clam*).

Thielmann, Georg. "Nochmals: Doppelveräusserung durch Nichtberechtigte: D. 19, 1, 31, 2 und D. 6, 2, 9, 4." *ZRG* 111 (1994) 197–241.

Wesener, Gunter. "Die Immissionen: Zur Entstehungsgeschichte des § 906 BGB," in *Vestigia iuris Romani : Festschrift für Gunter Wesener zum 60. Geburtstag am 3. Juni 1992,* Gunter Wesener, Georg Klingenberg, Michael J. Rainer, and Herwig Stiegler, eds. Graz: Leykam, 1992, 351 ff.

A. The *rei vindicatio*

Si paret rem, qua de agitur *ex iure Quiritium Auli Agerii*[3] *esse,*	⎤ *intentio* ["*charge*"]
neque ea res restituetur,	⎤ *clausula arbitraria* [defendant's response to interlocutory order]
quanti ea res erit, tantam pecuniam *iudex Numerium Negidium Aulo Agerio condemnato,* *si non paret, absolvito.*	⎫ ⎬ *condemnatio* ["*judgment*"] ⎭

Translation:

If it appears that the property, which this suit concerns,
by Quiritary law belongs to the plaintiff,

and this property will not be restored [by the defendant],

then the judge must give judgment that the defendant pay as much money
as the property is worth.

If it does not so appear, then he must absolve the defendant.

Notes on the Text:

The pleading-formula of the *rei vindicatio* is comprised of three clausulae:

> The *intentio* [= "statement of the charge"] indentifies the basis of the suit, the law on which the plaintiff bases his legal claim. It is expressed as a condition of the *condemnatio* [= "judgment"] (*si paret . . . condemnato*) ["if it so appears . . . pass judgment against the defendant"].
>
> The *condemnatio* instructs the judge to condemn or absolve (in modern terminology of civil procedure, to award judgment to the plaintiff or the defendant); *quanti ea res erit* ["as much as the property is worth"] refers to the property's worth at the time of the judgment.
>
> The *clausula arbitraria* [coming between the *intentio* and *condemnatio*] makes possible (provisionally compels) actual restitution of the property in place of compensation in money. The *iudex* (judge) evaluates the plaintiff's claim; if he finds it justified, he makes an initial ruling on the claim (*pronuntiatio*) and instructs the defendant to restore the property (*iussum de restituendo* ["order of restitution"]). According to the defendant's response to this ruling, there then follows the judge's final acquittal or imposition of an (increased) money judgment on the defendant.

---

[3] Translator's note: *Aulus Agerius* is a fictive name that signifies "the plaintiff;" *Numerius Negidius* is a fictive name signifying "the defendant." The names are alliterative mnemonics for, respectively, the party *qui agit* ("one who brings a lawsuit:" i.e., the plaintiff) and the party *qui negat* ("one who denies the claims:" i.e., the defendant).

a. Defendant's Liability to Suit

CASE 121

D 6.1.9 (Ulpianus libro sexto decimo ad edictum)

Officium autem iudicis in hac actione in hoc erit, ut iudex inspiciat, an reus possideat: nec ad rem pertinebit, ex qua causa possideat: ubi enim probavi rem meam esse, necesse habebit possessor restituere, qui non obiecit aliquam exceptionem. quidam tamen, ut Pegasus, eam solam possessionem putaverunt hanc actionem complecti, quae locum habet in interdicto uti possidetis vel utrubi. denique ait ab eo, apud quem deposita est vel commodata vel qui conduxerit aut qui legatorum servandorum causa vel dotis ventrisve nomine in possessione esset vel cui damni infecti nomine non cavebatur, quia hi omnes non possident, vindicari non posse. puto autem ab omnibus, qui tenent et habent restituendi facultatem, peti posse.

Translation: (Ulpian in the 16th book of his *Commentary on the Praetor's Edict*)[4]

The duty of the judge in this kind of suit [the *rei vindicatio*] will consist of this: that the judge investigates whether the defendant has possession; and regarding this question it will not be relevant on what grounds he has possession. For when I have proven that the property is mine, the possessor must make restitution, unless he has some defense.

Some jurists, however, like Pegasus, think that this action applies only to the possession which is the subject of an *interdictum uti possidetis* or *utrubi*.[5] Therefore, he claims, one cannot vindicate property from a depositary, or from someone to whom it has been given in loan [*commodatum*], or from someone who has rented it, or who holds it in order to preserve a legacy, or holds it in the name of a dowry or unborn child, or someone to whom the *cautio damni infecti* ["guarantee that no damage will be caused"] has not been given—since all of these are not possessors.

But I believe that anyone can be sued, if he holds the property and has the capacity to return it.

Discussion Questions:

1) What defenses can the defendant make against a *rei vindicatio* by the plaintiff?
2) What speaks in favor of the opinion of Pegasus (limitations on the defendant's liability to suit)?
3) What arguments can be given in support of Ulpian's decision?

---

[4] On author and work, see Case 11 (D 18.6.1.2); on Pegasus, see Case 114 (D 41.1.27.2).

[5] Translator's note: On these two interdicts, see the Excursus following Case 55.

Compare with this Case:

§ 985 German Civil Code:

The owner can demand surrender of the property from the possessor.[6]

§ 366 Austrian Civil Code (quoted under Case 131)

§ 369 Austrian Civil Code:

The plaintiff who brings an ownership suit must produce proof that the defendant has in his possession the property that is the subject of the suit, and that this property is the plaintiff's.[7]

§ 375 Austrian Civil Code:

The person who possesses property in another's name can protect himself against an ownership suit by identifying the person in whose name he holds the property and proving his own role in the matter.[8]

Literature:

Kaser, M. "Nochmals über Besitz und Verschulden bei den actiones in rem," *ZRG* 98 (1981) 77–146, at 90 ff.

---

[6] **§ 985 BGB:** Der Eigentümer kann von dem Besitzer die Herausgabe der Sache verlangen.

[7] **§ 369 ABGB:** Wer die Eigentumsklage übernimmt, muß den Beweis führen, daß der Geklagte die eingeklagte Sache in seiner Macht habe, und daß diese Sache sein Eigentum sei.

[8] **§ 375 ABGB:** Wer eine Sache in fremdem Namen besitzt, kann sich gegen die Eigentumsklage dadurch schützen, daß er seinen Vormann namhaft macht, und sich darüber ausweist.

CASE 122

D 6.1.27.1 (Paulus libro vicensimo primo ad edictum)

Possidere autem aliquis debet utique et litis contestatae tempore et quo res iudicatur. quod si litis contestationis tempore possedit, cum autem res iudicatur sine dolo malo amisit possessionem, absolvendus est possessor. item si litis contestatae tempore non possedit, quo autem iudicatur possidet, probanda est Proculi sententia, ut omnimodo condemnetur: ergo et fructuum nomine ex quo coepit possidere damnabitur.

Translation: (Paul in the 21st book of his *Commentary on the Praetor's Edict*)[9]

In principle one must be in possession both at the time of the *litis contestatio* ["joinder of issue"][10] and when the judgment is made. If, however, someone was in possession at the time of the *litis contestatio*, but has lost possession without *dolus malus* ["fraud, deceit"] at the time of the judgment, then the possessor should be absolved. Contrariwise, if he was not in possession at the time of the *litis contestatio* but did possess at the time of the judgment, the view of Proculus is approved: namely that he should be condemned anyway. He will therefore also be condemned for the fruits that were acquired from the time of taking possession.

Note on the Text:

Clearly present in this text is an abbreviated report of a juristic controversy. While the first sentence states a fundamental principle, the second refers to an exception which was advanced by the (victorious) Sabinian school. The third sentence identifies an exception stemming from the Proculians. It too won out.

Discussion Questions:

1) Justify the exception of the Sabinians.
2) Explain the viewpoint of the Proculians.
3) Create an example of loss of possession without *dolus malus* after the *litis contestatio*.
4) Try to explain how the *litis contestatio* could come about, if the defendant were not the possessor. Why are the fruits awarded to the plaintiff not reckoned from the time of the *litis contestatio*?

---

[9] On author and work, see Case 1 (D 41.2.3.1); on Proculus, see Case 9 (D 41.1.55).

[10] Translator's note: The *litis contestatio* was the conclusion of the first phase of proceedings in a private lawsuit—i.e., the proceedings before the magistrate who granted a trial. At the *litis contestatio*, the legal and factual issues relevant to the dispute were established and expressed in the applicable formula. It marked the point when *res judicata* would apply, thereby precluding another lawsuit between the same parties on the same matter. Trial of the factual issues in dispute would follow the *litis contestatio*.

Literature:

Kaser (Case 121) 97 ff.

Wimmer, Markus. *Besitz und Haftung des Vindikationsbeklagten.* Köln: Böhlau, 1995, 12 ff.

CASE 123

D 6.1.7 (Paulus libro undecimo ad edictum)

Si is, qui optulit se fundi vindicationi, damnatus est, nihilo minus a possessore recte petitur, sicut Pedius ait.

Translation: (Paul in the 11th book of his *Commentary on the Praetor's Edict*)[11]

If someone defends a *rei vindicatio* of land (without being in possession of it) and is condemned, recovery can still be sought from the possessor, just as Pedius said.

Discussion Questions:

    1) What might be the motive for a non-possessor to submit to a *rei vindicatio*?
    2) How can extending liability to suit to this non-possessor be justified?
    3) How can double recovery by the plaintiff be justified?

Compare with this Text:

§ 376 Austrian Civil Code:

A person who [fraudulently] denies possession of property before a court, and is shown to have done so, must already for this reason alone relinquish possession to the plaintiff; although he retains the right to advance his own claim of ownership subsequently.[12]

§ 377 Austrian Civil Code:

A person who claims to possess something that he does not possess and thereby deceives the plaintiff is liable for all damages arising therefrom.[13]

§ 378 Austrian Civil Code:

A person who had property in his possession and, after notice of a lawsuit, let it go, must at his own expense recover it for the plaintiff, if the latter does not wish

---

[11] On author and work, see Case 1 (D 41.2.3.1). Sextus Pedius is known only as someone cited by Paul and Ulpian. He wrote a comprehensive commentary on the praetorian edict and was probably a contemporary of Julian.

[12] § 376 ABGB: Wer den Besitz einer Sache vor Gericht leugnet und dessen überwiesen wird, muß dem Kläger deswegen allein schon den Besitz abtreten; doch behält er das Recht, in der Folge seine Eigentumsklage anzustellen.

[13] § 377 ABGB: Wer eine Sache, die er nicht besitzt, zu besitzen vorgibt, und den Kläger dadurch irreführt, haftet für allen daraus entstehenden Schaden.

to sue the actual detentor, or pay compensation for the extraordinary worth of the same.[14]

Literature:

>   Kaser (Case 121) 140 ff.

---

[14] **§ 378 ABGB:** Wer eine Sache im Besitze hatte, und nach zugestellter Klage fahren ließ, muß sie dem Kläger, wenn dieser sich nicht an den wirklichen Inhaber halten will, auf seine Kosten zurückverschaffen, oder den außerordentlichen Wert derselben ersetzen.

CASE 124

D 44/2/17 (Gaius libro trigensimo ad edictum provinciale)

Si rem meam at te petiero, tu autem ideo fueris absolutus, quod probaveris sine dolo malo te desisse possidere, deinde postea coeperis possidere et ego a te petam: non nocebit mihi exceptio rei iudicatae.

Translation: (Gaius in the 30th book of his *Commentary on the Provincial Edict*)[15]

If I have sued you for my property, and you have been absolved because you could prove that without *dolus* you had ceased to possess it, and you later begin to possess it again, and I bring a new suit against you, the defense of *res judicata* will not bar me.

Notes on the Text:

In modern civil procedure too the maxim *ne bis in idem* ["not twice against the same thing"] or *ne bis de eadem re sit actio* ("let there be no action twice in the same matter") is operative. This means that if an action on a matter is pending or has already been decided by legal process, the praetor grants no further suit on the same, or he grants to the defendant an *exceptio rei iudicatae vel in iudicium deductae* (defense of *res judicata* or pending litigation).

Discussion Questions:

Construct a concrete fact situation and explain the opinion of Gaius.

Literature:

> Kaser (Case 121) 139.
> Wimmer (Case 122) 18 ff.

---

[15] On Gaius, see Case 6 (D 41.1.9.6); on his *libri ad edictum provinciale* ["Books on the Provincial Edict"], see Case 64 (D 41.2.9).

b. Scope of the Defendant's Obligation of Restitution

CASE 125

D 6.1.33 (Paulus libro vicensimo primo ad edictum)

Fructus non modo percepti, sed et qui percipi honeste potuerunt aestimandi sunt: et ideo si dolo aut culpa possessoris res petita perierit, veriorem putat Pomponius Trebatii opinionem putantis eo usque fructuum rationem habendam, quo usque haberetur, si non perisset, id est ad rei iudicandae tempus: quod et Iuliano placet . . .

Translation: (Paul in the 21st book of his *Commentary on the Praetor's Edict*)[16]

Not only the actually harvested fruits are subject to valuation, but also those that could have been harvested lawfully. If, therefore, the property that is the subject of the suit is lost through the *dolus* or *culpa* of the possessor, Pomponius considers the opinion of Trebatius to be more correct: namely, that the fruits are reckoned up to the time they would have been reckoned if there had been no loss—i.e., up to the time when judgment is given. This opinion is also accepted by Julian. . . .

Note on the Text:

On *veriorem* ("more correct"), see on Case 8.

Discussion Questions:

1) Create a concrete fact situation to illustrate Paul's decision.
2) The plaintiff proves to the *iudex* ["judge"] that he would have drawn a greater quantity or higher quality of fruits if the field had been awarded to him at the time of the *litis contestatio*. Up to what point in time as regards the value of the fruits will the judge condemn the defendant?
3) The sued for slave dies during the ownership suit. How will the jurists decide regarding the value of the fruits (i.e., the value of the slave's labor)?
4) Does the plaintiff get compensation also for property that has perished?
5) What rule applies to the fruits that were harvested before the *litis contestatio*?

Compare with this Case:

D 6.1.79 (Labeo libro sexto pithanon a Paulo epitomatorum)

Si hominem a me petieris et is post litem contestatam mortuus sit, fructus quoad is vixerit aestimari oportet. Paulus: ita id verum esse puto, si non prius is homo in eam valetudinem inciderit, propter quam operae eius inutiles factae sunt: nam ne si vixisset quidem in ea valetudine, fructus eius temporis nomine aestimari conveniret.

---

[16] On author and work, see Case 1 (D 41.2.3.1); on Pomponius, see Case 29 (D 41.1.21 pr.); on Trebatius, see Case 8 (D 41.1.5.1); on Julian, see Case 70 (D 41.1.36).

Translation: (Labeo in the sixth book of Paul's epitome of his *Pithana*)[17]

If you have sued me for a slave and he dies after the *litis contestatio*, the value of the fruits must be reckoned [only] for the time when he was still alive. Paul: I consider that correct, provided the slave was not so ill beforehand that his work was worthless. Because if he had lived in this state of ill health, one could have placed no value on the fruits during that time.

Literature:

Kaser, Max. *Restituere als Prozessgegenstand: ein Beitrag zur Lehre von der materiellrechtlichen Beschaffenheit der in iudicium deduzierten Ansprüche im klassischen römischen Recht,* Hft. 16, 197. München: C. H. Beck, 1932, 192 ff.

Wimmer (Case 122) 77 ff.

---

[17] On author and work, see Case 37 (D 41.1.65 pr.).

CASE 126

D 6.1.16.1 (Paulus libro vicensimo primo ad edictum)

Culpa non intellegitur, si navem petitam tempore navigationis trans mare misit, licet ea perierit: nisi si minus idoneis hominibus eam commisit.

Translation: (Paul in the 21st book of his *Commentary on the Praetor's Edict*)[18]

It does not count as carelessness if someone sends a ship, which is the subject of a suit, out to sea during the time of navigation, even if it sinks—unless he entrusted it to men who were not suitable.

Note on the Text:

On *intellegitur* ("count as"), see on Case 72.

Discussion Questions:

1) Would the defendant not be obliged to keep the ship in harbor up to the conclusion of the trial?
2) What is the significance of the factual detail *tempore navigationis* ("the time of navigation")?
3) Can the owner sue the possessor who negligently let the ship sink prior to the *litis contestatio*?
4) Is the defendant liable for a runaway slave who is the subject of suit?

Literature:

Wacke, A. "Gefahrerhöhung als Besitzerverschuulden," in *Festschrift für Heinz Hübner zum 70. Geburtstag am 7. November 1984*, G. Baumgaertel et al. eds. Berlin, 1984, 673 ff.
Wimmer (Case 122) 48 ff.

---

[18] On author and work, see Case 1 (D 41.2.3.1).

CASE 127

D 6.1.15.3 (Ulpianus libro sexto decimo ad edictum)

Si servus petitus vel animal aliud demortuum sit sine dolo malo et culpa possessoris, pretium non esse praestandum plerique aiunt: sed est verius, si forte distracturus erat petitor si accepisset, moram passo debere praestari: nam si ei restituisset, distraxisset et pretium esset lucratus.

Translation: (Ulpian in the 16th book of his *Commentary on the Praetor's Edict*)[19]

If a slave or other animal that is the subject of an ownership suit should die without *dolus* ["deceit/fraud"] or *culpa* ["fault"] of the possessor, most jurists say that compensation for the value does not have to be paid. But it is more correct, if the plaintiff had intended to sell the slave or beast after recovering it, for compensation to be paid for the damage caused by delay. For if the possessor had restored the property to the owner, the latter would have sold it and obtained the sales price.

Notes on the Text:

The risk of accidental (caused by no one else) loss of property is normally borne by the owner: *casum sentit dominus* ["the owner feels the loss"]. Only in the case of wrongful damage or destruction through another's agency is compensation required. A basis for such liability can arise from the consequences of breach of contract or a delict: so the debtor responsible for delay is liable for *casus* ["accident"] as is the thief. With regard to thieves, the following rule was formulated: *fur semper in mora est* ("a thief is always in delay").

Discussion Questions:

1) How would *plerique* ["most jurists," as referred to in this case] have argued: i.e., those that would allow liability only for wrongful loss of property? On *plerique* and *verius* ["more correct"] see on Case 8.
2) Do you think that Ulpian would absolve the defendant if the latter can show that the property would have been lost in the plaintiff's possession too, or the defendant could show that the plaintiff had received no firm offer to purchase?
3) To what extent will the plaintiff's damages be compensated?
4) How would Ulpian and how would *plerique* probably have decided in regard to the fruits?

---

[19] On author and work, see Case 11 (D 18.6.1.2).

Compare with this Text:

D 5.3.40 pr. (Paulus libro vicesimo ad edictum)

Illud quoque quod in oratione divi Hadriani est, ut post acceptum iudicium id actori praestetur, quod habiturus esset, si eo tempore quo petit restituta esset hereditas, interdum durum est. quid enim, si post litem contestatam mancipia aut iumenta aut pecora deperierint? damnari debebit secundum verba orationis, quia potuit petitor restituta hereditate distraxisse ea. et hoc iustum esse in specialibus petitionibus Proculo placet: Casssius contra sensit. in praedonis persona Proculus recte existimat, in bonae fidei possessoribus Cassius. nec enim debet possessor aut mortalitatem praestare, aut propter metum huius periculi temere indefensum ius suum relinquere.

Translation: (Paul in the 20th book of his *Commentary on the Praetor's Edict*)[20]

That principle that is found in the *oratio* ["declaration"] of the deified [Emperor] Hadrian, namely, that after authorization to proceed with the lawsuit is granted, the plaintiff should be awarded what he would have had if the inheritance had been delivered to him at that time, often causes hardship. For example, what should happen if slaves or beasts of burden or heads of cattle should die after the *litis contestatio*? According to the words of the *oratio*, the defendant must be condemned [for the full value], since the plaintiff, upon delivery of the inheritance, could have sold the property. And Proculus considers this correct in suits for specific property: Cassius holds the opposite view. With regard to a bad-faith possessor Proculus is correct, and Cassius is correct in the case of a good-faith possessor. For the possessor should not be liable for damage without fault, nor should he rashly give up his rights from fear of this result.

Literature:

Müller-Ehlen, Martina. *Hereditatis petitio: Studien zur Leistung auf fremde Schuld und zur Bereicherungshaftung in der römischen Erbschaftsklage*. Köln: Böhlau, 1998, 376 ff.

Willvonseder, Reinhard. *Die Verwendung der Denkfigur der "condicio sine qua non" bei den römischen Juristen*. Wien: Böhlau, 1984, 125 ff.

Wimmer (Case 122) 58 ff, 68 ff.

---

[20] On author and work, see Case 1 (D 31.2.3.1).

CASE 128

D 6.1.17 pr. (Ulpianus libro sexto decimo ad edictum)

Iulianus libro sexto digestorum scribit, si hominem, qui Maevii erat, emero a Titio, deinde cum eum Maevius a me peteret, eundem vendidero eumque emptor occiderit, aequum esse me pretium Maevio restituere.

Translation: (Ulpian in the 16th book of his *Commentary on the Praetor's Edict*)[21]

Julian writes in the sixth book of his *Digesta*: if I have bought from Titius a slave who is the property of Maevius and, when Maevius seeks to recover him from me, I sell him to a buyer who kills him, it is fair that I pay the *pretium* ("price/value") to Maevius.

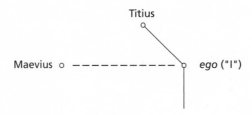

Discussion Questions:

1) Could Maevius make a valid claim against Titius?
2) Why does Maevius not turn to the last buyer?
3) What is the liability of *ego* to a *rei vindicatio*?
4) What conclusions do you draw from *aequum esse* ["it is fair"] as a basis for the decision? (On *aequitas* ["equity/fairness"] see under Case 130.)
5) Does *pretium restituere* ["pay the *pretium*"] mean payment of the price actually received by the seller, or payment of compensation for the value of the property?

Compare with this Case:

D 50.17.131 (Paulus libro vicesimo secundo ad edictum)

Qui dolo desierit possidere, pro possidente damnatur, quia pro possessione dolus est.

---

[21] On author and work, see Case 11 (D 18.6.1.2); on Julian, see Case 70 (D 41.1.36).

Translation: (Paul in the 22nd book of his *Commentary on the Praetor's Edict*)[22]

A person who surrenders possession with fraudulent intent is condemned as a possessor, since the fraud takes the place of the possession.

Literature:

Wimmer (Case 122) 94 ff.

---

[22] On author and work, see Case 1 (D 41.2.3.1).

CASE 129

D 6.1.37 (Ulpianus libro septimo decimo ad edictum)

Iulianus libro octavo digestorum scribit: si in aliena area aedificassem, cuius bonae fidei quidem emptor fui, verum eo tempore aedificavi, quo iam sciebam alienam, videamus, an nihil mihi exceptio prosit: < . . .> *nisi forte quis dicat prodesse de damno sollicito. puto autem huic exceptionem non prodesse: nec enim debuit iam alienam certus aedificium ponere: sed hoc ei concedendum est, ut sine dispendio domini areae tollat aedificium quod posuit.*

Translation: (Ulpian in the 17th book of his *Commentary on the Praetor's Edict*)[23]

Julian writes in the eighth book of his *Digesta*: if I have erected a building on another's land that I bought in good faith, but had already learned it was another's when I built, let us see whether any defense is available to me. < . . . > unless perhaps someone would say that there would be a defense on the basis of "self-inflicted loss." I believe, however, that there would be no defense for this defendant. For he ought not to have erected a building once he knew the land belonged to another. But this much can be granted to him: that he may, without damage to the owner of the property, remove the building he erected.

Note on the Text:

After Ulpian's *videamus, an mihi exceptio prosit* ("let us see whether any defense is available to me") there could have fallen out the report of a controversy, of which there survives only an *argumentum ad absurdum*: i.e., *nisi forte quis dicat . . . sollicito* ("unless perhaps . . . on the basis of self-inflicted loss"). For this formulation, see Case 85; on the *argumentum ad absurdum,* cf. Case 34.

Discussion Questions:

What claims can a good-faith builder validly make against the owner? On this question compare Celsus D 6.1.38 (Case 107). Should a bad-faith builder also be able to make valid claims against the owner?

Literature:

> Bürger (Case 107) 73 ff.
> MacCormack (Case 107) 83 ff.

---

[23] On author and work, see Case 11 (D 18.6.1.2); on Julian, see Case 70 (D 41.1.36).

B. The *actio publiciana* and Defenses

Actio Publiciana

Si quem hominem Aulus Agerius (bona fide) emit
et is ei traditus est, anno possedisset, tum si eum hominem,
de quo agitur, eius ex iure Quiritium esse oporteret,

si is homo Aulo Agerio non restituetur,

quanti ea res erit, tantam pecuniam
iudex Numerium Negidium Aulo Agerio condemnato,
si non paret absolvito.

Translation:

[Formula of] the Publician Action

If the plaintiff had possessed for a year the slave that he purchased in good faith, and that was delivered to him, then if this slave, about whom the action is, ought to be his [i.e., the plaintiff's] by Quiritian right [i.e., Roman civil law],

if he is not restored to the plaintiff

the judge must condemn the defendant to pay as much money as the property is worth. If it does not so appear, he must acquit.

Defenses to the Publician Action:

Exceptiones ["affirmative defenses"] were introduced before the *condemnatio* of the formula (*quanti ea res erit . . .*) in the form of negative conditional clauses; *replicationes* ["replies to affirmative defenses"] took the form of positive conditional clauses (*aut si . . .*) and were attached to the pertinent defenses.

Exceptio rei venditae et traditae ["defense of property sold and delivered"]:
    Si non Aulus Agerius fundum, quo de agitur, Numerio Negidio vendidit et tradidit.
    ("If the plaintiff did not sell and deliver the land, which is the subject of this suit, to the defendant.")

Exceptio doli ["defense of fraud"]:
    Si in ea re nihil dolo malo Auli Agerii factum sit neque fiat.
    ("If in this matter nothing has been or is being done with fraudulent intent by the plaintiff.")

Exceptio (iusti) dominii ["defense of valid ownership"]:
    Si ea res Numerii Negidii non sit.
    ("If this property is not owned by the defendant.")

Replicatio rei venditae et traditae [plaintiff's "reply of property sold and delivered"]:
    Aut si N^s N^s fundum, quo de agitur, A^o A^o vendidit et tradidit.
    ("Or if the defendant sold and delivered the land, which is the subject of this suit, to the plaintiff.")

CASE 130

D 21.3.2 (Pomponius libro secundo ex Plautio)

Si a Titio fundum emeris qui Sempronii erat isque tibi traditus fuerit, pretio autem soluto Titius Sempronio heres extiterit et eundem fundum Maevio vendiderit et tradiderit: Iulianus ait aequius esse priorem[24] te tueri, quia et si ipse Titius fundum a te peteret, exceptione summoveretur et si ipse Titius eum possideret, Publiciana peteres.

Translation: (Pomponius in the second book of his *Commentary on Plautius*)[25]

If you have bought from Titius a farm that belonged to Sempronius, and this farm has been delivered to you, but after payment of the price Titius has inherited the farm from Sempronius and sold and delivered the same farm to Maevius, Julian says it would be fairer to protect you as the prior transferee, since even Titius himself, if he should wish to recover the farm from you, would be blocked by means of an *exceptio*, and you, even if Titius himself were in possession of the farm, could sue him with the *actio publiciana*.

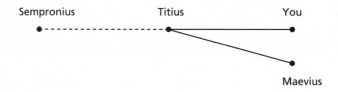

Notes on the Text:

While *bona fides* defines a standard of behavior as well as an issue to be decided by the *iudex*, who is given that charge in the formula issued by the Praetor, *aequitas* (fairness, justice, equity) is a consideration by which the Praetor lets himself be guided in granting actions, defenses, and other legal remedies. *Aequitas* thereby functions frequently as corrective of a *ius civile* that is perceived as rigid or imperfect.

    The jurists, however, also cite *aequitas* in other connections, if they wish to emphasize aspects like even-handedness, equal treatment, and balance.

---

[24] The word *priorem* could be a mistake for <*praetorem*>: cf. Case 131. [If the latter is correct,] the translation would be ". . . fairer that the Praetor protects you . . ."

[25] On Pomponius, see Case 29 (D 41.1.21 pr.). The work of the early classical Plautius was the subject of commentaries as numerous as the *Ius Civile* of Sabinus. Besides Pomponius (in seven books), Neratius, Javolenus, and especially Paul (18 books) wrote commentaries *ad Plautium*. On Julian, see Case 70 (D 41.1.36).

Discussion Questions:

1) What is your legal position relative to the property of Sempronius that Titius has sold and delivered?
2) Did the subsequent inheritance of Titius have an effect on your legal position?
3) What action could Titius bring against you? Which defenses could you make effectively? Cf. Ulp. D 44.4.4.32 (Case 131) .
4) What legal position does Maevius acquire in the land that Titius sold and delivered to him, although he had already sold and delivered the same land to you?

Literature:

Apathy, P. "Die actio Publiciana beim Doppelkauf vom Nichteigentümer," *ZRG* 99 (1982) 158–187, at 176 ff.

Thielmann, Georg. "Nochmals : Doppelveräusserung durch Nichtberechtigte : D. 19, 1, 31, 2 und D. 6, 2, 9, 4," *ZRG* 111 (1994) 197–241, 212 ff.

Ankum, Hans. *ZRG* 118 (2001) 442–462 (review of Potjewijd, G. H. *Beschikkingsbevoegdheid, bekrachtiging en convalescentie: een romanistische studie.* Dordrecht; Boston: Kluwer, 1998.

CASE 131

D 44.4.4.32 (Ulpianus libro septuagensimo sexto ad edictum)

Si a Titio fundum emeris qui Sempronii erat isque tibi traditus fuerit pretio soluto, deinde Titius Sempronio heres extiterit et eundem fundum Maevio vendiderit et tradiderit: Iulianus ait aequius esse praetorem te tueri, quia et, si ipse Titius fundum a te peteret, exceptione in factum comparata vel doli mali summoveretur et, si ipse eum possideret et Publiciana peteres, adversus excipientem 'si non suus est' replicatione utereris, ac per hoc intellegeretur eum fundum rursum vendidisse, quem in bonis non haberet.

Translation: (Ulpian in the 76th book of his *Commentary on the Praetor's Edict*)[26]

If you have bought from Titius a farm that belongs to Sempronius, and this farm has been delivered to you with payment of the price, and then Titius has inherited the farm from Sempronius and sold and delivered the same farm to Maevius, Julian says it would be fairer that the Praetor protect you, since even Titius himself, if he should wish to recover the farm from you, would be blocked by an *exceptio in factum* or *doli*. And if he himself were in possession of the farm and you sued him with the *actio Publiciana*, you could meet his *exceptio* "if the land was not in my ownership" with a *replicatio* [of "fraud"]; and thereby it would be clear that he had resold a farm that he did not have *in bonis* ["among his goods"].

Discussion Questions:

Examine the relationship of this text from Title 44.4 of the Digest *de doli mali et metus exceptione* ["on the defenses of 'fraud and fear'"] to D 21.3.2 (Case 130) from the Title entitled *de exceptione rei venditae et traditae* ["on the defense of 'property sold and delivered'"].

Compare with this Text:

§ 366 Austrian Civil Code:

With the right of the owner to exclude anyone else from possession of his property is also attached the right to obtain, through the legal process of an ownership suit, repossession of formerly held property from anyone who is in possession of it. However, this right does not exist for anyone who alienated the property in his own name during the time when he was not yet the owner of it, but only acquired the ownership of it afterward.[27]

---

[26] On author and work, see Case 11 (D 18.6.1.2); on Julian, see Case 70 (D 41.1.36).

[27] § 366 ABGB: Mit dem Rechte des Eigentümers, jeden andern von dem Besitze seiner Sache auszuschließen, ist auch das Recht verbunden, seine ihm vorenthaltene Sache von jedem Inhaber durch die Eigentumsklage gerichtlich zu fordern. Doch steht dieses Recht demjenigen nicht zu, welcher seine Sache zur zeit, da er noch nicht Eigentümer war, in seinem eigenen Namen veräußert, in der Folge aber das Eigentum derselben erlangt hat.

Literature:

Apathy (Case 130) 176 ff.
Thielmann (Case 130) 212 ff.
Wesener, Gunter. "Nichtediktale Einreden." *ZRG* 112 (1995) 109–150, at 145 ff.
Ankum (Case 130) 451 ff.

CASE 132

D 6.2.9.4 (Ulpianus libro sexto decimo ad edictum)

Si duobus quis separatim vendiderit bona fide ementibus, videamus, quis magis Publiciana uti possit, utrum is cui priori res tradita est an is qui [tantum]<prior> emit, et Iulianus libro septimo digestorum scripsit, ut, si quidem ab eodem non domino emerint, potior sit cui priori res tradita est, quodsi a diversis non dominis, melior causa sit possidentis quam petentis. quae sententia vera est.

Translation: (Ulpian in the 16th book of his *Commentary on the Praetor's Edict*)[28]

If someone has sold some property to two good faith purchasers separately, we must consider which of the two has a better claim to the *actio Publiciana*: the one to whom the property was transferred first, or the one who [only] <first> bought it.[29] Julian writes in the seventh book of his *Digesta*: if both have bought from the same non-owner, the stronger claim belongs to the one to whom it was first delivered; but if they have bought from different non-owners, the position of the possessor is more favorable than that of the claimant. And that decision is correct.

Notes on the Text:

Someone who only purchased but did not take delivery of the property cannot obtain the *actio Publiciana*, because of the formula's requirement *et is ei traditus est* ["and it was delivered to him"]. Therefore the text must refer to the person "who first bought it" [rather than "who only bought it"].

1. First fact-situation:

```
                              1. Sale
Owner -------- Non-owner ●──────────────────────► Possessor Smith
                              3. Delivery

                        2. Sale & delivery
                                          ──────► Possessor Jones
```

---

[28] On author and work see Case 11 (D 18.6.1.2); on Julian see Case 70 (D 41.1.36).

[29] Translator's note: To interpret the text of this case, it is necessary to know the editorial convention regarding the use of angled and square brackets: see fn. 38 on Case 57. Two words are bracketed in the Latin text of the present case and in the corresponding English translation. Square brackets enclose a word that is considered to be an "interpolation." Angled brackets enclose a word that is considered to have fallen out of the manuscript tradition. So, the Latin text as actually transmitted for this case would mean in English: " . . . the one to whom the property was transferred first, or the one who only bought it." But the editors believe the original text probably meant " . . . the one to whom the property was transferred first, or the one who first bought it." An explanation of why they think so is provided under the "Notes on the Text" section of this case.

2. Second fact-situation:

Non-owner Smith ●————————————→ Possessor Brown

1. Sale and delivery

Non-owner Jones ●————————————→ Possessor Green

1. Sale and delivery

In civil procedure generally the plaintiff must prove his right: *actori incumbit probatio* ["the burden of proof lies with the plaintiff"], and also *ei incumbit probatio, qui dicit, non qui negat* ("the burden of proof lies with the party that asserts, not with the party that denies")—Paul D 22.3.2. A plaintiff who demands the production of property will prevail only if his right is stronger than that of the defendant in possession: *in pari causa melior est condicio possidentis* ("in a case of equal claims, the position of the possessor is better"). On this point, see also the discussion under Cases 176 and 178a.

Discussion Questions:

Explain Julian's distinction and try to provide a justification for it.

Compare with this Case:

§ 372 Austrian Civil Code:

If the *plaintiff* does not succeed with the proof of having acquired ownership of property that is being withheld from him, but has established the valid title and the proper way by which he came into its possession, then he will be deemed the true owner as against any possessor who can produce no claim or only a weaker claim for possession.[30]

---

[30] **§ 372 ABGB:** Wenn der Kläger mit dem Beweise des erworbenen Eigentumes einer ihm vorenthaltenen Sache zwar nicht ausreicht, aber den gültigen Titel, und die echte Art, wodurch er zu ihrem Besitze gelangt ist, dargetan hat; so wird er doch in Rücksicht eines jeden Besitzers, der keinen, oder nur einen schwächeren Titel seines Besitzes anzugeben vermag, für den wahren Eigentümer gehalten.

§ 374 Austrian Civil Code:

If the defendant and the plaintiff have equal claims to good possession, then the preference is owed to the defendant in virtue of the possession.[31]

Literature:

> Apathy (Case 130) 161 ff.
> Thielmann (Case 130) 199 ff.

---

[31] **§ 374 ABGB:** Haben der Geklagte und der Kläger einen gleichen Titel ihres echten Besitzes, so gebührt dem Geklagten kraft des Besitzes der Vorzug.

CASE 133

D 19.1.31.2 (Neratius libro terio membranarum)

Uterque nostrum eandem rem emit a non domino, cum emptio venditioque sine dolo malo fieret, traditaque est: sive ab eodem emimus sive ab alio atque alio, is ex nobis tuendus est, qui prior ius eius adprehendit, hoc est, cui primum tradita est. si alter ex nobis a domino emisset, is omnimodo tuendus est.

Translation: (Neratius in the third book of his *Legal Notes*)[32]

Each of us two has bought the same thing from a non-owner. The purchase and sale took place without fraud, and the property was delivered. Whether we acquired from the same or different sellers, protection belongs to the one of us who first acquired a right in the property: that means the one to whom it was first delivered. If one of us bought from the owner, he should be protected in any case.[33]

Discussion Questions:

1) Annotate this case. What "right" is Neratius referring to?
2) How might Neratius have argued against Julian D 6.2.9.4 (Case 132)?

Literature:

Apathy (Case 130) 160 ff.
Maifeld, Jan. *Die aequitas bei L. Neratius Priscus.* Trier: WVT Wissenschaftlicher Verlag, 1991, 32 ff., 48 ff.
Thielmann (Case 130) 199 ff.

---

[32] On author and work, see Case 73 (D 41.3.41).

[33] Translator's note: To clarify the legal situation: this case concerns which of two potentially usucapting possessors has the better possessory right and will succeed against the other in a Publician action.

C.   The *actio negatoria*[34]

CASE 134

D 8.5.8.5 (Ulpianus libro septimo decimo ad edictum)

Aristo Cerellio Vitali respondit non putare se ex taberna casiaria fumum in superiora aedificia iure immitti posse, nisi ei rei servitutem talem admittit. idemque ait: et ex superiore in inferiora non aquam, non quid aliud immitti licet: in suo enim alii hactenus facere licet, quatenus nihil in alienum immittat, fumi autem sicut aquae esse immissionem: posse igitur superiorem cum inferiore agere ius illi non esse id ita facere. Alfenum denique scribere ait posse ita agi ius illi non esse in suo lapidem caedere, ut in meum fundum fragmenta cadant. dicit igitur Aristo eum, qui tabernam casiariam a Minturnensibus conduxit, a superiore prohiberi posse fumum immittere, sed Minturnenses ei ex conducto teneri: agique sic posse dicit cum eo, qui eum fumum immittat, ius ei non esse fumum immittere. ergo per contrarium agi poterit ius esse fumum immittere: quod et ipsum videtur Aristo probare. sed et interdictum uti possidetis poterit locum habere, si quis prohibeatur, qualiter velit, suo uti.

Translation: (Ulpian in the 70th book of his *Commentary on the Praetor's Edict*)[35]

Aristo, in an opinion to Cerellius Vitalis, stated that he did not believe that someone could lawfully send smoke from his cheese factory into higher buildings, unless a servitude to that effect permitted it. The same jurist also said that it was not permissible to let water or anything else fall from a higher floor onto a lower one: for people are free to act on their own premises only to the degree that they do not send anything into the premises of another, such as smoke or water. Therefore the inhabitant above could sue the one below, alleging that the latter did not have a right to act as he did. He further states, Alfenus writes, that one can sue on the charge that someone does not have the right to chip stone on his own property in such a way that the chips fall onto my property. So Aristo stated that someone who leased a cheese factory from the municipality of Minturnae could be sued by a neighbor who dwelt higher up for sending up smoke, but that the municipality of Minturnae was liable to him on the contract. And he says that in this way it is possible to sue the person who sends up the smoke on the grounds that he does not have a right to send it up. On the other hand, it will also be possible to sue on the charge that one does have the right to send up smoke: which Aristo also seems to have accepted. But the *interdictum uti possidetis*[36] will also be available if someone is kept from using his property as he wishes.

---

[34] Translator's note: The *actio negatoria* was an action brought by a landowner against a neighbor who used his own property as if it were benefited by a servitude that burdened the plaintiff's property. The purpose of the action was to establish that there was no such servitude. At common law the similar facts underlying facts might give rise to a suit in trespass or private nuisance as well as a petition for injunctive relief at equity.

[35] On author and work see Case 11 (D 18.6.1.2). Titius Aristo may have been a pupil of Cassius, to whose *Ius Civile* he provided annotations. Aristo did not have the *ius respondendi* by imperial authority, but he was an important jurist, who was consulted in writing by famous colleagues, like Neratius and Celsus. On Alfenus see Case 7 (D 18.6.15.1).

[36] Translator's note: The interdict *uti possidetis* is described in the Excursus following Case 55.

Discussion Questions:

3) What legal remedies are available to defend against discharges from a neighboring property into or onto one's own property? To what degree must such discharges be tolerated?

4) In which of the following situations can an affected neighbor get relief?

— Titius opens a smithy and hammers there all day long.

— Seius practices his trumpet every night.

— Maevius' rooster awakens the neighbors every day at sunrise.

Compare with this Text:

§ 364 Austrian Civil Code:

1) In general the exercise of one's ownership rights is valid only insofar as neither an interference with the rights of a third party occurs thereby, nor a violation of limitations that are prescribed in laws for the preservation and advancement of the general well-being.[37]

2) The owner of a piece of land can prohibit his neighbor from allowing the effects of waste water, smoke, gases, heat, odor, noise, trembling, and similar things that arise from the neighbor's land only insofar as they exceed the normal measure according to the local circumstances and they actually impair the use of the land that is customary in that place. Direct discharge [of such substances] without a special legal right is impermissible under all circumstances. . .

§ 523 Austrian Civil Code:

In reference to servitudes there is a double right of suit. One can assert the right of the servitude against the owner [of the servient property], or the owner can complain of the usurpation of a servitude . . .[38]

---

[37] **§ 364 ABGB:**

(1) Überhaupt findet die Ausübung des Eigentumrechtes nur insofern statt, als dadurch weder in die Rechte eines Dritten ein Eingriff geschieht, noch die in den Gesetzen zur Erhaltung und Beförderung des allgemeinen Wohles vorgeschriebenen Einschränkungen übertreten werden.

(2) Der Eigentümer eines Grundstückes kann dem Nachbarn die von dessen Grund ausgehenden Einwirkungen durch Abwässer, Rauch, Gase, Wärme, Geruch, Geräusch, Erschütterung und ähnliche insoweit untersagen, als sie das nach den örtlichen Verhältnissen gewöhnliche Maß überschreiten und die ortsübliche Benutzung des Grundstückes wesentlich beeinträchtigen. Unmittelbare Zuleitung ist ohne besonderen Rechtstitel unter allen Umständen unzulässig . . .

[38] **§ 523 ABGB:** In Ansehung der Servituten findet ein doppeltes Klagerecht statt. Man kann gegen den Eigentümer das Recht der Servitut behaupten; oder, der Eigentümer kann sich über die Anmaßung einer Servitut beschweren . . .

§ 906 German Civil Code:

    I The owner of a piece of land cannot prohibit the introduction of gases, vapors, odors, smoke, soot, heat, noise, trembling, and similar things that arise from another's land in so far as the effects do not impair the use of his land, or do so only trivially. . . .

    II The same applies insofar as an actual impairment is created by use of the other land in a manner that is customary in the locale and that cannot be prevented by means that are economically feasible for users of this kind. If the owner has to tolerate an effect of this kind, he can obtain from the user of the other land a commensurate compensation in money, if the effect of use of his land that is customary in the locale, or its output, causes an impairment that is beyond the reasonable amount.

    III The introduction [of such things] through a special route is impermissible.[39]

§ 1004 BGB

    I If ownership is interfered with in some way other than by dispossession or the withholding of possession, then the owner can demand relief from the interference from the person causing the disturbance. If there is a concern about continuing interference, the owner can sue for prohibition.

    II The complaint is not allowable if the owner is obligated to tolerate [the interference].[40]

Literature:

    Watson, Alan. *The Law of Property in the Later Roman Republic*. Oxford: Clarendon Press, 1968, 177ff.

    Rainer, J. Michael. "Die Immissionen: Zur Entstehungsgeschichte des § 906 BGB, in *Vestigia iuris Romani : Festschrift für Gunter Wesener zum 60. Geburtstag am 3. Juni 1992*, Georg von Klingenberg, ed. Graz, 1992, 358 ff.

---

[39] **§ 906 BGB:**

    I Der Eigentümer eines Grundstücks kann die Zuführung von Gasen, Dämpfen, Gerüchen, Rauch, Ruß, Wärme, Geräusch, Erschütterungen und ähnliche von einem anderen Grundstück ausgehende Einwirkungen insoweit nicht verbieten, als die Einwirkung die Benutzung seines Grundstücks nicht oder nur unwesentlich beeinträchtigt . . .

    II Das gleiche gilt insoweit, als eine wesentliche Beeinträchtigung durch eine ortsübliche Benutzung des anderen Grundstücks herbeigeführt wird und nicht durch Maßnahmen verhindert werden kann, die Benutzern dieser Art wirschaftlich zumutbar sind. Hat der Eigentümer hiernach eine Einwirkung zu dulden, so kann er von dem Benutzer des anderen Grundstücks einen angemessenen Ausgleich in Geld verlangen, wenn die Einwirkung eine ortsübliche Benutzung seines Grunstücks oder dessen Ertrag über das zumutbare Maß hinaus beeinträchtigt.

    III Die Zuführung durch eine besondere Leitung ist unzulässig.

[40] **§ 1004 BGB:**

    I Wird das Eigentum in anderer Weise als durch Entziehung oder Vorenthaltung des Besitzes beeinträchtigt, so kann der Eigentümer von dem Störer die Beseitigung der Beeinträchtigung verlangen. Sind weitere Beeinträchtigungen zu besorgen, so kann der Eigentümer auf Unterlassung klagen.

    II Der Anspruch ist ausgeschlossen, wenn der Eigentümer zur Duldung verpflichtet ist.

CASE 135

D 8.5.17.2 (Alfenus libro secundo digestorum)

Secundum cuius parietem vicinus sterculinum fecerat, ex quo paries madescebat, consulebatur, quemadmodum posset vicinum cogere, ut sterculinum tolleret. respondi, si in loco publico id fecisset, per interdictum cogi posses, sed si in privato, de servitute agere oportere: si damni infecti stipulatus esset, possit per eam stipulationem, si quid ex ea re sibi damni datum esset, servare.

Translation: (Alfenus in the second book of his *Digesta*)[41]

Someone against whose wall a neighbor had placed a dung-heap, and the wall had become damp, asked how the neighbor could be compelled to remove the dung-heap. I replied: if the neighbor has placed the dung-heap on public land, he could be compelled by interdict; if on private land, then one would have to proceed by means of suit on a servitude. If the neighbor had given a *stipulatio damni infecti* ["guarantee that no damage will be caused"], then compensation could be obtained from this *stipulatio*, to the degree that any damage had been caused by the matter.

Discussion Questions:

The text is found in Title D 8.5 *si servitus vindicetur vel ad alium pertinere negetur* ("If a servitude is the subject of a *rei vindicatio* or that it belongs to another is contested"). Write an exegesis of this text.

Literature:

Watson (Case 134) 177 ff.
Rainer, J. Michael. *Bau- und nachbarrechtliche Bestimmungen im klassischen römischen Recht.* Graz: Leykam, 1987, 105 ff.
Rainer (Case 134) 365 ff.
Rainer, J. Michael. "Zum Typenzwang der Servituten: Vom römischen Recht zum BGB," in *Collatio ivris Romani : études dédiées à Hans Ankum à l'occasion de son 65e anniversaire*, Hans Ankum and Robert Feenstra, eds. Amsterdam: J. C. Gieben, 1995, 417.

---

[41] On author and work, see Case 7 (D 18.6.15.1).

D. The *Interdictum quod vi aut clam* (Interpretation of the Edict)

This interdict is the most comprehensive legal remedy available for asserting rights against a neighbor. It serves to defend a wide range of disturbances to possession, and it can be invoked not only by the owner but by anyone who can establish a valid claim of legal interest. The following examples of the exposition of the *interdictum quod vi aut clam* by the Roman jurists should provide an overview of the relationship between jurisprudence and the praetorian edict.

The interdict reads as follows:

quod vi aut clam factum est, qua de re agitur, id, si non plus quam annus est, cum experiendi potestas est, restituas.

Translation:

What by force or stealth has been done, concerning the matter at issue in this action, you must restore, if not more than one year has passed from the time when the possibility of suing occurred.

To "restore" here means putting the plaintiff in the position that he would be in if his possession had not been disturbed. The *exceptio annua* [defense of one-year limitation] in the interdict also appears in the *interdictum unde vi*, among other places, and it demonstrates the penal character of the remedy (temporal limitation of the "revenge," non-inheritability of the claim, reckoning damages as of the time of the act).

CASE 136

D 43.24.2.5-6 (Ulpianus libro septuagensimo primo ad edictum)

> (5) *Quid sit vi factum vel clam factum, videamus. vi factum videri Quintus Mucius scripsit, si quis contra quam prohiberetur fecerit: et mihi videtur plena esse Quinti Mucii definitio.*
>
> (6) *Sed et si quis iactu vel minimi lapilli prohibitus facere perseveravit facere, hunc quoque vi fecisse videri Pedius et Pomponius scribunt, eoque iure utimur.*

D 43.24.20.1 (Paulus libro tertio decimo ad Sabinum)

Prohibitus autem intellegitur quolibet prohibentis actu, id est vel dicentis se prohibere vel manum opponentis lapillumve iactantis prohibendi gratia.

Translation: (Ulpian in the 71st book of his *Commentary on the Praetor's Edict*)[42]

> (5) Let us examine what *vi factum* ["done by force"] or *clam factum* ["done by stealth"] means. Quintus Mucius wrote that it counts as *vi factum* if someone has acted in a way that he has been forbidden to act. I consider this opinion of Quintus Mucius to be comprehensive (very broadly expressed).
>
> (6) But also if someone, who has been forbidden by the throw of even a pebble, goes ahead and acts, Paul and Pedius write that he too has acted *vi* [with force"], and that is valid law.

(Paul in the 13th book of his *Commentary on the* Ius Civile *of Sabinus*)

Any act of the person prohibiting—e.g., a verbal instruction forbidding something, or the lifting of the hand, or the throwing a stone—counts as a prohibition.

Notes on the Text:

The *iactus lapilli* ["throwing of a stone"] was customarily employed especially as an *operis novi (de)nuntiatio* (a formal objection to the construction of new work, employed by a neighbor who feels he will be harmed by the unauthorized completion of the construction). On *mihi videri* ["I consider"] and *intellegitur* ["counts as"] see on Case 72; on *eo iure utimur* ["that is valid law"] see under Case 156.

---

[42] On Ulpian, see Case 11 (D 18.6.1.2); on Paul, see Case 1 (D 41.2.3.1); Q. Mucius Scaevola (Pontifex, son of the Augur of the same name), consul 95 BCE, is the most important jurist of the pre-classical period. According to Pomponius (D 1.2.2.41), he was the first to represent the *ius civile "generatim"* (i.e., organized by topical genera and species). His 18 books on the *ius civile* were the subject of a commentary by Pomponius in the second century CE. On Pedius, see Case 123 (D 6.1.7); on Pomponius, see Case 29 (D 41.1.21 pr.).

Discussion Questions:

1) To what might Ulpian's qualification *sed et* ["but also if . . ."] (D 3.24.1.6) refer?

2) Does the pronouncement of Quintus Mucius recognize a development of the concept of *vis* ["force/violence"]?

3) Is it a case of *vis*, if someone digs a pit on another's land and, when the owner appears, runs off before the owner can issue a prohibition, but he later returns and resumes digging?

CASE 137

D 43.24.3.7 (Ulpianus libro septuagensimo primo ad edictum)

Clam facere videri Cassius scribit eum, qui celavit adversarium neque ei denuntiavit, si modo timuit eius controversiam aut debuit timere.

Translation: (Ulpian in the 71st book of his *Commentary on the Praetor's Edict*)[43]

Cassius writes that anyone will be considered as acting *clam* ("by stealth"), if he conceals his action from his opponent and does not inform him, because he fears opposition or ought to fear it.

Note on the Text:

On *videri* ["will be considered"] see on Case 72.

Discussion Questions:

1) What might have motivated the Roman jurists to develop broad definitions of *vi* ["with force"] and *clam* ["with stealth"]?
2) Does someone act *clam*, if he drives his flock of sheep across his neighbor's land in an openly visible manner but without prior notice?
3) Imagine some examples of actions on a neighbor's land that are neither *vi* nor *clam*.

---

[43] On author and work, see Case 11 (D 18.6.1.2); on Cassius, see Case 19 (D 41.2.21.3).

CASE 138

D 43.24.7.5-7 (Ulpianus libro septuagensimo primo ad edictum)

(5) *Notavimus supra, quod, quamvis verba interdicti late pateant, tamen ad ea sola opera pertinere interdictum placere, quaecumque fiant in solo. eum enim, qui fructum tangit, non teneri interdicto quod vi aut clam: nullum enim opus in solo facit . . .*

(6) *Si quis acervum stercoris circa agrum pinguem disiecerit, cum eo 'quod vi aut clam factum est' agi potest: et hoc verum est, quia solo vitium adhibitum sit.*

(7) *Plane si quid agri colendi causa factum sit, interdictum quod vi aut clam locum non habet, si melior causa facta sit agri, quamvis prohibitus quis vi vel clam fecerit.*

Translation: (Ulpian in the 71st book of his *Commentary on the Praetor's Edict*)[44]

(5) We have remarked above that according to established doctrine, despite the admittedly broad interpretation of the words of the interdict, the interdict applies only to those works that involve the ground. So, someone who handles the fruit is not liable under the interdict *quod vi aut clam*, because he has done nothing involving the ground.

(6) If someone has spread a dung-heap onto fertile land, one can proceed against him with the interdict "what was done by force or stealth." And that is correct, since harm has been done to the ground.

(7) Obviously if something is done for the cultivation of the land, the *interdictum quod vi aut clam* is not available, assuming the condition of the land is improved thereby, even though the actor has acted *vi aut clam*, despite having been prohibited to do so.

Discussion Questions:

1) Is the definition of *vis* by Quintus Mucius in D 43.24.1.5 (Case 136) limited by these decisions of Ulpian?

2) What legal remedies are available to the landowner who finds in his vegetable garden an outsider who immediately:

— intends to pluck an apple?
— lifts an apple from the ground?

---

[44] On author and work, see Case 11 (D 18.6.1.2).

CASE 139

D 43.24.22.1 (Venuleius libro secundo interdictorum)

Si quis vi aut clam araverit, puto eum teneri hoc interdicto perinde atque si fossam fecisset: non enim ex qualitate operis huic interdicto locus est, sed ex opere facto, quod cohaeret solo.

Translation: (Venuleius in the second book of his *On the Interdicts*)[45]

If someone has plowed *vi* or *clam*, I think that he is liable under this interdict, just as if he had made a ditch. The applicability of the interdict does not depend on the character of the work, but simply on the fact that the work is connected with the ground.

Discussion Questions:

Explain the relationship of this decision with Ulp. D 43.24.7.7 (Case 138) and of both decisions with the language of the edict (above, preceding Case 136).

---

[45] Venuleius Saturninus worked at the time of Antoninus Pius and the *divi fratres*, Marcus Aurelius and Lucius Verus, in the second half of the second century CE. His chief works were comprehensive treatments of *de interdictis* (6 books), *de actionibus* (10 books), and *de stipulationibus* (19 books).

CASE 140

D 43.24.22.3 (Venuleius libro secundo interdictorum)

Si stercus per fundum meum tuleris, cum id te facere vetuissem, quamquam nihil damni feceris mihi nec fundi mei mutaveris, tamen teneri te quod vi aut clam Trebatius ait. Labeo contra, ne etiam is, qui dumtaxat iter per fundum meum fecerit aut ovem egerit venatusve fuerit sine ullo opere, hoc interdicto teneatur.

Translation: (Venuleius in the second book of his *On the Interdicts*)[46]

If you have carried manure over my land after I forbade you to do so, Trebatius says that you are liable under the interdict *quod vi aut clam*, even if you have caused me no harm and have made no alteration to my land. Labeo is of the contrary view: that someone would have no liability under the interdict, even if he merely went over my land, or drove his sheep, or hunted, without building or doing anything [else].

Discussion Questions:

1) Is the interpretation of Trebatius covered by the language of the interdict? (See the introduction to Cases 136 ff.)
2) Evaluate the weight of the Labeo's *argumentum ad absurdum* (see Case 34 on this).
3) What is the purpose of the interdict according to Trebatius? What purpose according to Labeo?
4) How would Venuleius have probably decided [on the facts of this case]?

---

[46] On author and work, see Case 139 (D 43.24.22.1); on Trebatius, see Case 8 (D 41.5.1); on Labeo, see Case 10 (D 41.2.51).

CASE 141

D 43.24.11 pr. (Ulpianus libro septuagensimo primo ad edictum)

Is qui in puteum vicini aliquid effuderit, ut hoc facto aquam corrumperet, ait Labeo inter-dicto quod vi aut clam eum teneri: portio enim agri videtur aqua viva, quemadmodum si quid operis in aqua fecisset.

Translation: (Ulpian in the 71st book of his *Commentary on the Praetor's Edict*)[47]

According to Labeo, someone who has poured something into his neighbor's well in order to foul the water thereby is liable under the interdict *quod vi aut clam*, for spring water counts as part of the land, whatever the nature of the work he did to the water.

Discussion Questions:

Analyze this opinion of Labeo with reference to the Labeo citation in D 43.24.22.3 (Case 140).

---

[47] On author and work, see Case 11 (D 18.6.1.2); on Labeo, see Case 10 (D 41.2.51).

Servitudes

Introduction

Servitutes or servitudes are limited rights to the use of another's property. The holder of a servitude can legally exercise a limited degree of control over the property—i.e., even against the wishes of the owner and any third party.

The late classical jurist Marcian distinguishes in D 8.1.1 "personal servitudes" (like *usus* ["use"] and *usufructus* ["usufruct"]) from "real servitudes." The latter are also called "praedial servitudes" (*iura praediorum*) and are divided into "rustic" and "urban" servitudes: i.e., servitudes affecting land and buildings, respectively.

The purpose of a praedial servitude is to facilitate or make possible an owner's use of his land by means of a right of entry onto a neighboring piece of land. The oldest and, in terms of agricultural economy, most necessary praedial servitudes are footpaths and roadways (*iter, via*), the right to drive cattle across (*actus*), and the right to draw water across (*aquae ductus*). The owner of the burdened property is essentially obligated to put up with (*pati*) or to refrain from stopping (*non facere*) the activity, but he does not have any obligation to do something (*facere*): *servitus in faciendo consistere nequit* ["there can be no servitude requiring someone to do something"]. An exception is the *servitus oneris ferendi* ["servitude of bearing the load"], a servitude that obliges the owner of the servient property to keep up a wall that may be used by the dominant property.

While the exercise of praedial servitudes is always oriented to the needs of a certain piece of land, personal servitudes serve the interests of defined persons by conferring rights of use and benefit, not only in land but also in other kinds of property.

"Usufruct" (*usufructus*) is a right to the use or the fruits of another's property on condition of protecting the substance of the property. The right is highly personal—i.e., it is extinguished on the death of the person who has it, but its exercise can be alienated or leased out. The usufructuary must exercise his right according to the standard of a *vir bonus* ["an honest and upright man"], a standard that is widely documented in the casuistic sources [i.e., discussions of individual cases].

"Use" (*usus*) is in the first place a general right of use that carries no benefit of the fruits. Yet certain difficulties are presented in defining the use of fruit-bearing properties (e.g., a house with a garden, a forest, a flock of sheep).

The jurists ultimately developed a concept of *usus* in which the taking of certain fruits for one's own use was included.

Literature:

A. Praedial servitudes

Watson, A. *The Law of Property in the Later Roman Republic.* Oxford: Clarendon Press, 1968, 176 ff.

Rainer, J. M. "Zum Typenzwang der Servituten: Vom römischen Recht zum BGB," in *Collatio ivris Romani: études dédiées à Hans Ankum à l'occasion de son 65e anniversaire,* H. Ankum and R. Feenstra, eds. Amsterdam: Gieben, 1995, 415 ff.

B. Personal Servitudes

Watson, A. *The Law of Property in the Later Roman Republic.* Oxford: Clarendon Press, 1968, 203 ff.

Watson, A. "The Acquisition of Young in the usufructus gregis." *Iura* 12 (1961) 210–221.

Hammerstein, Jürgen. *Die Herde im römischen Recht: Grex als rechtliche Sachgesamtheit und Wirtschaftseinheit.* Göttingen: Musterschmidt, 1975, 65 ff.

Kaser M. "Partus ancillae," *ZRG* 75 (1958) 156–200, at 156 ff.

Thomas J. A. C. "Locare usumfructum," *IJ* 6 (1971) 367–371, at 367 ff.

A. Praedial Servitudes

CASE 142

D 8.5.6.2 (Ulpianus libro septimo decimo ad edictum)

Etiam de servitute, quae oneris ferendi causa imposita erit, actio nobis competit, ut et onera ferat et aedificia reficiat ad eum modum, qui servitute imposita comprehensus est. et Gallus putat non posse ita servitutem imponi, ut quis facere aliquid cogeretur, sed ne me facere prohiberet: nam in omnibus servitutibus refectio ad eum pertinet, qui sibi servitutem adserit, non ad eum cuius res servit. sed evaluit Servi sententia, in proposita specie, ut possit quis defendere ius sibi esse cogere adversarium reficere parietem ad onera sua sustinenda. Labeo autem hanc servitutem non hominem debere, sed rem, denique licere domino rem derelinquere scribit.

Translation: (Ulpian in the 17th book of his *Commentary on the Praetor's Edict*)[1]

Concerning the servitude which is imposed for the purpose of bearing a load [*oneris ferendi causa*], we also have a suit that he (i.e., the neighbor) both support the load and restore the building to the condition it was in when the servitude was imposed. And Gallus thinks that a servitude compelling someone to do something cannot be imposed, but only one that prohibits me from doing something. For with all servitudes maintenance [of the property] is an obligation of the party who claims the servitude for himself, not of the owner of the servient property. But in the case here proposed, the opinion of Servius is valid, namely, that someone can sue on a claim that he has a right to compel his opponent to maintain a wall for bearing his load. Labeo, however, writes that this obligation is on the property, not the person, and the owner may abandon the property [if he wishes to avoid the obligation].

Discussion Questions:

1) Aquilius Gallus relies on the general principle *servitus in faciendo consistere nequit* ("there can be no servitude requiring someone to do something"). What considerations of legal policy underlie this principle?

2) What arguments could Servius advance for an exception in the case of the *servitus oneris ferendi* ["servitude of bearing the load"]?

3) Which of the two opinions will sooner lead to the result that repairs are completed and buildings maintained?

4) Explain Labeo's point of view.

---

[1] On Ulpian, see Case 11 (D 18.6.1.2). C. Aquilius Gallus (praetor 66 BCE, the same year as Cicero) was the most important pupil of Q. Mucius Scaevola and a teacher in his own day of the prominent and multi-talented Servius Sulpicius Rufus (consul 51BCE). On Labeo, see Case 10 (D 41.2.51).

Compare with this Case:

§ 482 Austrian Civil Code:

All servitudes are alike in that the possessor of the servient property is not normally obligated to do something; but only to permit another to use his right, or to refrain from doing what he as owner would otherwise be entitled to do.[2]

§ 483 Austrian Civil Code:

Therefore the expense for maintenance or restoration of the property that is designated for the servitude must normally be borne by the person entitled to its use. If, however, this property is also used by the person obligated, he must share proportionately in the expense. . . .[3]

§ 487 Austrian Civil Code:

. . . The person who, therefore, has to tolerate the support of a neighboring building, the insertion of another's beam into his wall, or the drawing of another's smoke through his chimney must contribute proportionately to the maintenance of the relevant wall, column, partition, or chimney. It cannot be expected of him, however, that he improve the dominant property or repair his neighbor's chimney.[4]

§ 12 Austrian Land Registry Law (1955):

With servitudes and charges on land the content and scope of the invasive right must be defined with the greatest possible specificity; a specification of monetary value is not required.

If servitudes are limited to certain physical boundaries, these must be precisely specified.[5]

---

[2] **§ 482 ABGB:** Alle Servituten kommen darin überein, daß der Besitzer der dienstbaren Sache in der Regel nicht verbunden ist, etwas zu tun; sondern nur einem andern die Ausübung eines Rechtes zu gestatten, oder das zu unterlassen, was er als Eigentümer sonst zu tun berechtigt wäre.

[3] **§ 483 ABGB:** Daher muß auch der Aufwand zur Erhaltung und Herstellung der Sache, welche zur Dienstbarkeit bestimmt ist, in der Regel von dem Berechtigten getragen werden. Wenn aber diese Sache auch von dem Verpflichteten benützt wird; so muß er verhältnissmäßig zu dem Aufwande beitragen . . .

[4] **§ 487 ABGB:** . . . Wer also die Last des benachtbarten Gebäudes zu tragen; die Einfügung des fremden Balkens an seiner Wand; oder, den Durchzug des fremden Rauches in seinem Schornsteine zu dulden hat; der muß verhältnissmäßig zur Erhaltung der dazu bestimmten Mauer, Säule, Wand oder des Schornsteines beitragen. Es kann ihm aber nicht zugemutet werden, daß er das herrschende Gut unterstützen oder den Schornstein des Nachbars ausbessern lasse.

[5] **§ 12 Grundbuchgesetz (1955):**
Bei Dienstbarkeiten und Reallasten muß Inhalt und Umfang des einzutragenden Rechtes möglichst bestimmt angegeben werden; einer Angabe des Geldwertes bedarf es nicht.
Sollen Dienstbarkeiten auf bestimmte räumliche Grenzen beschränkt sein, so müssen diese genau bezeichnet werden.

§ 1018 German Civil Code:

A piece of land can be burdened to the benefit of the current owner of another piece of land in such a way that the latter may make use of the land in various ways, or that certain uses of the land may not be undertaken, or that the exercise of a right that exists in the ownership of the burdened land relative to the other land is barred (land servitude).[6]

§ 1105 German Civil Code:

A piece of land can be burdened in such a way that to the person in whose favor the burden runs, future benefits from the land are to be paid (charge on land). . . . [7]

Literature:

Watson (Case 134) 198 ff.

---

[6] **§ 1018 BGB:** Ein Grundstück kann zugunsten des jeweiligen Eigentümers eines anderen Grundstücks in der Weise belastet werden, daß dieser das Grundstück in einzelnen Beziehungen benutzen darf oder daß auf dem Grundstücke gewisse Handlungen nicht vorgenommen werden dürfen oder daß die Ausübung eines Rechtes ausgeschlossen ist, das sich aus dem Eigentum an dem belasteten Grundstücke dem anderen Grundstücke gegenüber ergibt (Grunddienstbarkeit).

[7] **§ 1105 BGB:** Ein Grundstück kann in der Weise belastet werden, daß an denjenigen, zu dessen Gunsten die Belastung erfolgt, wiederkehrende Leistungen aus dem Grundstücke zu entrichten sind (Reallast). . .

CASE 143

D 8.3.5.1 (Ulpianus libro septimo decimo ad edictum)

Neratius libris ex Plautio ait nec haustum nec appulsum pecoris nec cretae eximendae calcisque coquendae ius posse in alieno esse, nisi fundum vicinum habeat: et hoc Proculum et Atilicinum existimasse ait, sed ipse dicit, ut maxime calcis coquendae et cretae eximendae servitus constitui possit, non ultra posse, quam quatenus ad eum ipsum fundum opus sit.

Translation: (Ulpian in the 17th book of his *Commentary on the Praetor's Edict*)[8]

Neratius in his *Commentary on Plautius* says that one may not draw water, nor bring animals to drink, nor mine clay, nor burn limestone on another's land, unless one is the owner of a neighboring piece of land. And he says that Proculus and Atilicinus held this opinion. But he himself adds that especially the servitude for burning limestone and mining clay can be established only to the degree it is required for that (i.e., the dominant) property.

Discussion Questions:

1) Formulate the qualifications of Neratius as an abstract legal principle.
2) The owner of a servitude mines clay on his neighbor's land and makes amphorae out of it on his own land. In the amphorae he keeps his oil and sells his wine. Has he, according to Neratius, overstepped the permissible use of his servitude?
3) Can Titius grant a valid property right to his neighbor Seius, by the terms of which the latter may mine Titius' land for sand to whatever extent he wishes, and may sell what he mines?

Compare with this Text:

§ 484 Austrian Civil Code:

While the possessor of a dominant property can exercise his right in a manner to his own liking, servitudes may not be expanded; they must instead be limited to the scope that their nature and purpose of creation establishes.[9]

---

[8] On Ulpian, see Case 11 (D 18.6.1.2); on Neratius, see Case 73 (D 41.3.41); on Plautius, see Case 130 (D 21.3.2); on Proculus, see Case 9 (D 41.1.55). Atilicinus was a contemporary, perhaps a pupil, of Proculus.

[9] § 484 ABGB: Der Besitzer des herrschenden Gutes kann zwar sein Recht auf die ihm gefällige Art ausüben, doch dürfen Servituten nicht erweitert, sie müssen vielmehr, insoweit es ihre Natur und der Zweck der Bestellung gestattet, eingeschränkt werden.

§ 1019 German Civil Code:

A servitude in land can only involve a burden that benefits the use of the land of the person with the right. Beyond the limit established by this [principle] the content of a servitude cannot be extended.[10]

§ 1020 BGB

In exercising a servitude the person with the right to do so must take care for the interests of the owner of the burdened property as far as possible. . . .[11]

Literature:

Rainer, "Typenzwang" (Case 135) 419.

---

[10] **§ 1019 BGB:** Eine Grunddienstbarkeit kann nur in einer Belastung bestehen, die für die Benutzung des Grundstücks des Berechtigten Vorteil bietet. Über das sich hieraus ergebende Maß hinaus kann der Inhalt der Dienstbarkeit nicht erstreckt werden.

[11] **§ 1020 BGB:** Bei der Ausübung einer Grunddienstbarkeit hat der Berechtigte das Interesse des Eigentümers des belasteten Grundstücks tunlichst zu schonen . . .

CASE 144

D 43.20.1.18 (Ulpianus libro septuagensimo ad edictum)

Trebatius, cum amplior numerus pecoris ad aquam appelletur, quam debet appelli, posse universum pecus impune prohiberi, quia iunctum pecus ei pecori, cui adpulsus debeatur, totum corrumpat pecoris adpulsum. Marcellus autem ait, si quis ius habens pecoris ad aquam appellendi plura pecora adpulserit, non in omnibus pecoribus eum prohibendum: quod est verum, quia pecora separari possunt.

Translation: (Ulpian in the 70th book of his *Commentary on the Praetor's Edict*)[12]

Trebatius thinks, if a larger number of cattle are driven to water than is permitted, one can with impunity prohibit the entire herd from the water, because the addition of the cattle to the herd that has the right to the water, has abused the whole right of driving cattle to water. Marcellus, however, says if someone who has the right to drive a herd to water should drive more cattle [than permitted], he cannot be prohibited with respect to all his cattle. And that is right, because the herds can be separated.

Discussion Questions:

1) The servitude for driving cattle to water (*servitus pecoris ad aquam appellendi*) can be enforced by an *interdictum de fonte* ["interdict concerning the water-source"], by which the Praetor forbids the land owner from using force against the person with the drinking right. How should the owner act if the herd of the right-holder exceeds the permitted size?

2) Servitudes in land are extinguished by non-use (*non usus*) for a period of two years. Can one claim non-use if the contractually established modes of using the servitude are violated: e.g., different vehicles are used, or heavier loads transported, or a greater number of cattle are driven over the land, than is permitted under the servitude?

3) Produce arguments for the opposing viewpoints of Trebatius and Marcellus.

---

[12] On Ulpian, see Case 11 (D 18.6.1.2); on Trebatius, see Case 8 (D 41.1.5.1); on Marcellus, see Case 18 (D 41.2.19 pr.).

CASE 145

D 8.1.8 pr. (Paulus libro quinto decimo ad Plautium)

Ut pomum decerpere liceat et ut spatiari et ut cenare in alieno possimus, servitus imponi non potest.

Translation: (Paulus in the 15th book of his *Commentary on Plautius*)[13]

A servitude cannot be established to the effect that we may pluck fruit or walk around or dine upon another's land.

Discussion Question:

Justify the opinion of Paul.
1) Does Paulus rule out the possibility that the named activities can be granted as property rights?

Literature:

Rainer, "Typenzwang" (Case 135) 421.

---

[13] On Paul, see Case 1 (D 41.2.3.1); on his books *ad Plautium*, see Case 130 (D 21.3.2).

CASE 146

D 8.3.11 (Celsus libro vicensimo septimo digestorum)

Per fundum, qui plurium est, ius mihi esse eundi agendi potest separatim cedi. ergo suptili ratione non aliter meum fiet ius, quam si omnes cedant et novissima demum cessione superiores omnes confirmabuntur: benignius tamen dicetur et antequam novissimus cesserit, eos, qui antea cesserunt, vetare uti cesso iure non posse.

Translation: (Celsus in the 27th book of his *Digesta*)[14]

The right to travel over and drive cattle over a piece of land can be granted to me separately by multiple owners of the land. Therefore by strict reasoning the right will not become mine unless all the owners grant it and all the previous grants will be confirmed by the final grant. A fairer decision, however, will be that even before the last grant of permission, those who previously granted it cannot prevent me from using the right they granted.

Note on the Text:

Celsus decides according to the legal principle that no one should be permitted to take a legal position contrary to his own conduct: *venire contra factum proprium* [*non licet*]; cf. Ulp. D 1.7.25 pr. See also Cases 68 and 71.

Discussion Questions:

1) Co-owners Smith and Jones have granted a right of passage over land that also has other co-owners. Co-owner Brown has still not made any act of transfer (*in iure cessio*). Green goes over the land. Jones wants to sue Green to cause him to refrain on the grounds that there is no valid servitude until Brown consents. How will the Praetor decide? On the contrast between *subtilitas* and *benignitas*, see Case 68.

2) Will the Praetor decide differently if Brown brings the suit?

Literature:

Hausmaninger (Case 68) 64 ff.

---

[14] On author and work, see Case 2 (D 41.2.18.2).

CASE 147

D 8.2.6 (Gaius libro septimo ad edictum provinciale)

Haec autem iura similiter ut rusticorum quoque praediorum certo tempore non utendo pereunt: nisi quod haec dissimilitudo est, quod non omnimodo pereunt non utendo, sed ita, si vicinus simul libertatem usucapiat. veluti si aedes tuae aedibus serviant, ne altius tollantur, ne luminibus mearum aedium officiatur, et ego per statutum tempus fenestras meas praefixas habuero vel obstruxero, ita demum ius meum amitto, si tu per hoc tempus aedes tuas altius sublatas habueris: alioquin si nihil novi feceris, retineo servitutem. item si tigni immissi aedes tuae servitutem debent et ego exemero tignum, ita demum amitto ius meum, si tu foramen, unde exemptum est tignum, obtruraveris et per constitutum tempus ita habueris alioquin si nihil novi feceris, integrum ius suum permanet.

Translation: (Gaius in the seventh book of his *Commentary on the Provincial Edict*)[15]

These servitudes [i.e., urban servitudes] are extinguished in the same way as the rustic servitudes, through non-use for a certain period of time. Nevertheless there is a difference in that they are not extinguished by non-use alone, but only if the neighbor at the same time usucapts the free ownership. For example, if your building is burdened with a servitude in favor of my building, such that it cannot be built higher or it cannot interfere with the passage of light to my house, and I, for the legally requisite period, cover over my windows or wall them up, then I have lost my right, if you have raised your building higher during the same time. If, however, you have made no alterations to your building, then I retain the servitude. Likewise if your building is burdened with a servitude that allows me to place a supporting beam in it, and I have removed the supporting beam, I lose the right only if you wall up the hole left by the removal of the beam, and keep it walled up during the legally requisite period of time. If, however, you have undertaken no alterations to your building, then the servitude remains intact.

Discussion Question:

Why should the conditions required to extinguish urban servitudes be different from those required for the extinguishing of rustic servitudes?

Compare with this Text:

§ 1488 Austrian Civil Code:

The right of a servitude expires by limitation by non-use, if the obligated party blocks use of the servitude and the right-holder has not made his right effective over a period of three consecutive years.[16]

---

[15] On Gaius, see Case 6 (D 41.1.9.6); on his *libri ad edictum provinciale*, see Case 64 (D 41.2.9).

[16] § 1488 ABGB: Das Recht der Dienstbarkeit wird durch den Nichtgebrauch verjährt, wenn sich der verpflichtete Teil der Ausübung der Servitut widersetzt, und der Berechtigte durch drei aufeinanderfolgende Jahre sein Recht nicht geltend gemacht hat.

CASE 148

D 8.2.7 (Pomponius libro vicesimo sexto ad Quintum Mucium)

Quod autem aedificio meo me posse consequi, ut libertatem usucaperem, dicitur, idem me non consecuturum, si arborem eodem loco sitam habuissem, Mucius ait, et recte, quia non ita in suo statu et loco maneret arbor quemadmodum paries, propter motum naturalem arboris.

Translation: (Pomponius in the 26th book of his *Commentary on the Ius Civile of Quintus Mucius*)[17]

However, concerning what it is said I can accomplish with my building so as to usucapt the freedom of ownership, Mucius says that I would not accomplish, if I had placed a tree in the same place—and correctly, because a tree would not remain in its condition and place in the same way as a wall, because of the natural movement of a tree.

Discussion Questions:

1) Of what servitude is Q. Mucius speaking?
2) Does Q. Mucius think that the planting of a tree does not constitute an act that is contrary to the servitude?

Literature:

Watson (Case 134) 181 ff.

---

[17] On Pomponius, see Case 29 (D 41.1.21 pr.); on Quintus Mucius, see Case 136 (D 43.24.1.5).

B.   Personal Servitudes

a. *Usufructus*

CASE 149

D 7.1.68 pr.-2 (Ulpianus libro septimo decimo ad Sabinum)

(pr.) *Vetus fuit quaestio an partus ad fructuarium pertineret: sed Bruti sententia opti-
nuit fructuarium in eo locum non habere: neque enim in fructu hominis homo
esse potest. hac ratione nec usum fructum in eo fructuarius habebit. quid tamen
si fuerit etiam partus usus fructus relictus, an habeat in eo usum fructum? et cum
possit partus legari, poterit et usus fructus eius.*

(1) *Fetus tamen pecorum Sabinus et Cassius opinati sunt ad fructuarium pertinere.*
(2) *Plane si gregis vel armenti sit usus fructus legatus, debebit ex adgnatis gregem
supplere, id est in locum capitum defunctorum*

D 7.1.69 (Pomponius libro quinto ad Sabinum)

vel inutilium alia summittere . . .

Translation: (Ulpian in the 17th book of his *Commentary on the* Ius Civile *of Sabinus*)[18]

(pr.) It was an old controversy whether offspring [of a slave] belonged to a usufructuary. But the opinion of Brutus prevailed, that the usufructuary has no
place in it: nor can a human be among the fruits of a human. By this reasoning a usufructuary will [also] have no usufruct in it [i.e., the offspring]. But
what if a usufruct in offspring is bequeathed, should he [i.e., the recipient
of the bequest] have a usufruct in it? Since offspring can be bequeathed, a
usufruct in it can also be.

(1) The offspring of animals, however, belong to the usufructuary, according
to the opinion of Sabinus and Cassius.
(2) Clearly if the usufruct of a herd or ox is bequeathed, he [i.e., the legatee]
will be obliged to make up the herd from the other offspring: i.e., in place
of those that have died,

(Pomponius in the fifth book *ad Sabinum*)[19]
or to provide others in place of useless animals.

---

[18] On Ulpian and Sabinus, see Case 11 (D 18.6.1.2); on Brutus, see Case 100 (D 41.2.3.3); on
Cassius, see Case 19 (D 41.2.21.3).
[19] On author and work, see Case 29 (D 41.1.21 pr.).

Discussion Questions:

1) How might the opponents of Brutus (according to Cicero *de Finibus* 1.4.12 these were P. Scaevola and M'. Manilius) have argued?

2) Do you think Ulpian endorses the proposition he brings forward: that the fruit can belong to a category different from that of the bearer? Or will the offspring of a slave not be treated as fruit because only the typical produce of the main property falls within the concept of fruit? Or is it the nature of humans that resists treating them as fruit?

3) What economic considerations might underlie this controversy?

4) What content can the usufruct of a slave's offspring involve?

5) The usufructuary of a herd must substitute for individual animals that have died, but not for the accidental destruction of the entire herd (say through epidemic). How can this difference be explained?

6) Titius has the usufruct of the cow of Maevius. The cow dies. Must he replace it? Explain.

7) Is the usufructuary of a vegetable garden obliged to replace fruit trees with new plantings?

Compare with this Text:

D 7.1.1 (Paulus libro tertio ad Vitellium)

Usus fructus est ius alienis rebus utendi fruendi salva rerum substantia.

Translation: (Paul in the third book of his *Commentary on Vitellius*)[20]

The *usus fructus* is the right to use another's property and to take the fruits of it, while keeping the substance intact.

§ 509 Austrian Civil Code:

The usufruct is the right to enjoy another's property without limitation, but with care of the substance.[21]

§ 1030 I German Civil Code:

A piece of property can be burdened in such a way that the person to whose benefit the burden runs is entitled to products of it (usufruct).[22]

---

[20] The jurist Vitellius was probably active during the reign of Augustus. His work was the subject of commentaries by Sabinus and Paul. On Paul, see Case 1 (D 41.2.3.1).

[21] § 509 ABGB: Die Fruchtnießung is das Recht, eine fremde Sache, mit Schonung der Sustanz, ohne alle Einschränkung zu genießen.

[22] § 1030 I BGB: Eine Sache kann in der Weise belastet werden, daß derjenige, zu dessen Gunsten die Belastung erfolgt, gerechtigt ist, die Nutzungen der Sache zu ziehen (Nießbrauch).

Literature:

Kaser M. "Partus ancillae." *ZRG* 75 (1958) 156–200, at 156 ff.

Hammerstein, J. *Die Herde im römischen Recht. Grex als rechtliche Sachgesamtheit und Wirtschaftseinheit.* Göttingen, 1975, 66 ff., 101 ff.

Birks Peter. "An Unacceptable Face of Human Property," in *New Perspectives in the Roman Law of Property. Essays for Barry Nicholas*, Peter Birks ed. Oxford: Clarendon Press, 1989, 61 ff.

Filip-Fröschel (Case 104) 99 ff.

Herrmann-Otto, Elisabeth. *Ex ancilla natus: Untersuchungen zu den "hausgeborenen" Sklaven und Sklavinnen im Westen des römischen Kaiserreiches.* Stuttgart: F. Steiner, 1994, 268 ff.

Daubermann, Erich A. *Die Sachgesamtheit als Gegenstand des klassischen römischen Rechts: vornehmlich unter dem Blickwinkel von Veränderungen in ihrer Zusammensetzung.* New York: P. Lang, 1993, 55 ff., 62 ff.

Watson, A. "The Acquisition of Young in the usufructus gregis." *Iura* 12 (1961) 210–221, reprinted in *Studies in Roman Private Law.* Rio Grande, OH: Hambledon Press, 1991, 131 ff.

Rodger, A. "A Very Good Reason for Buying a Slave Woman" *LQR* 123 (2007) 446–454.

CASE 150

D 7.1.12.2 (Ulpianus libro septimo decimo ad Sabinum)

Usufructuarius vel ipse frui ea re vel alii fruendam concedere vel locare vel vendere potest: nam et qui locat utitur, et qui vendit utitur. sed et si alii precario concedat vel donet, puto eum uti atque ideo retinere usum fructum, et hoc Cassius et Pegasus responderunt et Pomponius libro quinto ex Sabino probat . . .

Translation: (Ulpian in the 17th book of his *Commentary on the* Ius Civile *of Sabinus*)[23]

The usufructuary can either enjoy the usufruct himself or allow another to enjoy it, or let it or sell it; for even he who lets it is using it, and he who sells it is using it. But if he lends it to another gratuitously, or gives it away, I think that he is using it and therefore retains it. Such was the response given by Cassius and Pegasus, and Pomponius approves it in the fifth book *on Sabinus*. . . .

Discussion Questions:

1) What is the effect of the death of the usufructuary on the legal position of the purchaser or lessee?
2) Is the *usus fructus* extinguished through non-use?
3) Might it be argued that only a usufructuary's grant of use to another for monetary compensation should be considered, not a grant without compensation?

---

[23] On Ulpian, see Case 11 (D 18.6.1.2); on Cassius, see Case 19 (D 41.2.21.3); on Pegasus, see Case 114 (D 41.1.27.2); on Pomponius, see Case 29 (D 41.1.21 pr.).

CASE 151

D 7.1.15.4 (Ulpianus libro octavo decimo ad Sabinum)

Et si vestimentorum usus fructus legatus sit non sic, ut quantitatis usus fructus legetur, dicendum est ita uti eum debere, ne abutatur: nec tamen locaturum, quia vir bonus ita non uteretur.

Translation: (Ulpian in the 18th book of his *Commentary on the* Ius Civile *of Sabinus*)[24]

If the use of clothing has not been bequeathed in such a way that the legacy specifies usufruct of a quantity, then it must be said that the usufructuary must use it so as not to use it up: nevertheless, he cannot rent it out, because a *vir bonus* would not use it in that way.

Note on the Text:

On the meaning of *vir bonus,* see on Case 107.

Discussion Questions:

1) Explain the difference between the two bequests referenced here and their different legal consequences.
2) May a usufructuary make alterations to a house of which he owns the usufruct?
3) May a usufructuary of land open it up to mining?
4) May a slave that is the object of a usufruct be employed in work for which the owner did not use him?

---

[24] On author and work, see Case 11 (D 18.6.1.2).

b. *Usus*

CASE 152

D 7.8.2.1 (Ulpianus libro septimo decimo ad Sabinum)

Domus usus relictus est aut marito aut mulieri: si marito, potest illic habitare non solus, verum cum familia quoque sua. an et cum libertis, fuit quaestionis. et Celsus scripsit et cum libertis: posse hospitem quoque recipere, nam ita libro octavo decimo digestorum scripsit, quam sententiam et Tubero probat. sed an etiam inquilinum recipere possit, apud Labeonem memini tractatum libro posteriorum. et ait Labeo eum, qui ipse habitat, inquilinum posse recipere . . .

D 7.8.4.1 (Ulpianus libro septimo decimo ad Sabinum)

Mulieri autem si usus relictus sit, posse eam et cum marito habitare Quintus Mucius primus admisit, ne ei matrimonio carendum foret, cum uti vult domo. nam per contrarium quin uxor cum marito possit habitare, nec fuit dubitatum. quid ergo si viduae legatus sit, an nuptiis contractis post constitutum usum mulier habitare cum marito possit? et est verum, ut et Pomponius libro quinto et Papinianus libro nono decimo quaestionum probat, posse eam cum viro et postea nubentem habitare . . .

Translation: (Ulpian in the 17th book of his *Commentary on the* Ius Civile *of Sabinus*)[25]

The use of a house has been left to either a husband or a wife. In the case of a husband, he can live there not only by himself but also with his slaves. There was a question whether he could do so also with his freedmen. And Celsus wrote, also with the freedmen and he could also receive a guest. For he wrote this in the 18th book of his *Digesta*, and the opinion met with the approval of Tubero. But whether he can even take in a tenant is a question I remember is treated by Labeo in a book of his posthumous writings. And Labeo says that the man who lives there can also take a tenant. . . .

(Ulpian *ibidem*)

If a wife is left the use, Quintus Mucius was the first to allow that she could live there also with her husband, so that she did not have to give up her marriage if she wished to use the house. For on the contrary there was no doubt that the wife could live with her husband. But what if the use is left to a widow? Can the woman, if she marries after the use is established, live there with her husband? And what Pomponius in the 15th book and Papinian in the 19th book of his *Legal Questions* approved is correct: that she can live there with her husband even in the case of a later marriage. . . .

---

[25] On Ulpian, see Case 11 (D 18.6.1.2); on Celsus, see Case 2 (D 41.2.18.2); Q. Aelius Tubero was a pupil of Ofilius (contemporary of Cicero); on Labeo, see Case 10 (D 41.2.1); on Q. Mucius, see Case 136 (D 43.24.1.5); on Pomponius, see Case 29 (D 41.1.21 pr.).

Discussion Questions:

1) How might the jurists prior to Q. Mucius have explained their decision against wives?
2) Why should the taking of a tenant be permissible only if the user himself dwells in the house?

Compare with this Text:

§ 505 Austrian Civil Code:

He who has the right to use property may make use of it, without regard to his other property, in a manner appropriate to his position, his occupation, and his household.[26]

§ 506 Austrian Civil Code:

The need is determined at the time of the grant of use. Subsequent changes in the position or occupation of the user gives no grounds for a claim of entitlement to more extended use.[27]

§ 1090 I German Civil Code:

A piece of land can be burdened in such a way that the person to whose benefit the burden runs is entitled to use the land in various ways, or that he has a special license which can constitute the subject of a servitude in land (limited personal servitude).[28]

Literature:

Wieling, Hans Josef. *Testamentsauslegung im römischen Recht.* München: Beck, 1972, 18 ff.

---

[26] **§ 505 ABGB:** Wer also das Gebrauchsrecht an einer Sache hat, der darf, ohne Rücksicht auf sein übriges Vermögen, den seinem Stande, seinem Gewerbe, und seinem Hauswesen angemessenen Nutzen davon ziehen.

[27] **§ 506 ABGB:** Das Bedürfniss ist nach dem Zeitpunkt der Bewilligung des Gebrauches zu bestimmen. Nachfolgende Veränderungen in dem Stande oder Gewerbe des Berechtigten geben keinen Anspruch auf einen ausgedehnteren Gebrauch.

[28] **§ 1090 I BGB:** Ein Grundstück kann in der Weise belastet werden, daß derjenige, zu dessen Gunsten die Belastung erfolgt, berechtigt ist, das Grundstück in einzelnen Beziehungen zu benutzen, oder daß ihm eine sonstige Befugnis zusteht, die den Inhalt einer Grunddiensbarkeit bilden kann (beschränkte persönliche Dienstbarkeit).

CASE 153

D 7.8.12.1–2 (Ulpianus libro septimo decimo ad Sabinum)

(1) *Praeter habitationem quam habet, cui usus datus est, deambulandi quoque et gestandi ius habebit. Sabinus et Cassius et lignis ad usum cottidianum et horto et pomis et holeribus et floribus et aqua usurum, non usque ad compendium, sed ad usum, scilicet non usque ad abusum: idem Nerva, et adicit stramentis et sarmentis etiam usurum, sed neque foliis neque oleo neque frumento neque frugibus usurum. sed Sabinus et Cassius et Labeo et Proculus hoc amplius etiam ex his quae in fundo nascuntur, quod ad victum sibi suisque sufficiat sumpturum et ex his quae Nerva negavit . . .*

(2) *Sed si pecoris ei usus relictus est, puta gregis ovilis, ad stercorandum usurum dumtaxat Labeo ait, sed neque lana neque agnis neque lacte usurum: haec enim magis in fructu esse. hoc amplius etiam modico lacte usurum puto. neque enim tam stricte interpretandae sunt voluntates defunctorum.*

Translation: (Ulpian in the 17th book of his *Commentary on the* Ius Civile *of Sabinus*)[29]

(1) The usuary will, in addition to habitation, have the right of walking around and riding on the property. Sabinus and Cassius think he may also use firewood for his daily needs and the garden and fruit and vegetables and flowers and water, not for the purpose of making a profit, but for his (own) use, but not to the point of using it up. Nerva says the same, and he adds that the usuary may also use the straw and brushwood, but not leaves, oil, grain, or crops. But Sabinus and Cassius, like Labeo and Proculus, more than this, allow him to take from whatever grows on the land, as much as is sufficient for himself and his dependents to support life, and also from the crops that Nerva excludes. . . .

(2) If the use of a herd has been left to him, say of a flock of sheep, Labeo says he may use it only for manure, and not take either wool or lambs or milk for himself. For these are much more a matter of fruits. I, more than this, think he may take a modest amount of milk. For the intentions of the deceased ought not to be interpreted so narrowly.

Discussion Questions:

1) Do you think Ulpian allows the usuary to take fruit for the entertainment of guests?
2) Must the usuary consume the fruit on the farm, or may he take it with him into the town?

---

[29] On Ulpian and Sabinus, see Case 11 (D 18.6.1.2); on Cassius, see Case 19 (D 41.2.21.3); on Nerva, see Case 13 (D 12.1.9.9); on Labeo, see Case 10 (D 41.2.51); on Proculus, see Case 9 (D 41.1.55).

3) Explain the distinction that Nerva draws.
4) The statement "But Sabinus and Cassius, like Labeo and Proculus, . . . " is often considered a Justinianic interpolation. What arguments can be got from the text in support of this opinion?
5) What does Ulpian's opinion in § 2 have to do with the intentions of the deceased?

CASE 154

D 7.8.22 pr. (Pomponius libro quinto ad Quintum Mucium)

Divus Hadrianus, cum quibusdam usus silvae legatus esset, statuit fructum quoque eis legatum videri, quia nisi liceret legatariis caedere silvam et vendere, quemadmodum usufructuariis licet, nihil habituri essent ex eo legato.

Translation: (Pomponius in the fifth book of his *Commentary on the* Ius Civile *of Quintus Mucius*)[30]

The deified Hadrian decided, in a case in which the use of a forest had been bequeathed, that use of the fruits had also been effectively left to the legatees, because if the legatees were not permitted to cut and sell the wood in the same manner as usufructuaries, they would have nothing from this legacy.

Notes on the Text:

On *videri* ("effectively") see Case 72. On the *argumentum ad absurdum*, see Case 34.

Discussion Question:

Discuss Hadrian's decision in connection with Ulp. D 7.8.12.1 & 2 (Case 153).

---

[30] On Pomponius, see Case 29 (D 41.1.21 pr.).

Secured Interests

Introduction

A secured interest is a limited property right that is given to a creditor for securing his claim on the property of the debtor. If the debt is not satisfied, the creditor may satisfy it from the debtor's property with priority over other claimants.

An exhaustive presentation of the many-sided and often difficult problems of Roman security law would exceed the scope of this casebook. The texts that are selected here deal with some especially important issues: the origin and extinction of security interests and the legal relationships when there are multiple security interests in the same piece of property.

Drawing upon the concepts of contract law, the jurists developed interpretive viewpoints and doctrinal constructions, like *pignus tacitum* ("silent pledge") and "curing," that originally had no place in the law of secured interests in another's property. Step-by-step they made possible the creation of multiple security interests in a piece of property, and they developed rules regarding the priority relationships among different creditors based on contractual clauses and their interpretation, causes of action, and defenses. Imperial involvement made major changes in classical security law through the creation of statutory security rights and priorities.

Literature:

Schuller W. "Zum pignus tacitum." *Labeo* 15 (1969) 267–284.

Wagner, Herbert. *Voraussetzungen, Vorstufen und Anfänge der römischen Generalverpfändung*, Bd. 16, 151. Marburg: N. G. Elwert, 1968, 125 ff.

Kaser M. "In bonis esse." *ZRG* 78 (1961) 173–220, at 197 ff. (review of von Wubbe. *Res aliena pignori data*, 1960).

_____. *ZRG* 78 (1961) 462–465 (review of Tondo, Salvatore. *Convalida del pegno...e corso dei pegni successivi*, Milano: Giuffre [1959]) at 462 ff.; 469 ff. (review of Miquel, Juan. *El rango hipotecario*).

Schanbacher, Dietmar. *Die Konvaleszenz von Pfandrechten im klassischen römischen Recht.* Berlin: Duncker & Humblot, 1987.

Kaser M. "Über mehrfache Verpfändung im römischen Recht," in *Studi in onore di Giuseppe Grosso* I, Torino, 1968–1969), 27–76, at 29 ff. (reprinted in *Ausgewählte Schriften* II [1976], 169 ff.) .

Wagner, Herbert. *Die Entwicklung der Legalhypotheken am Schuldnervermögen im römischen Recht: bis zur Zeit Diokletians.* Wien: Böhlau, 1974, 76 ff, 180 ff.

Kaser, M. *Studien zum römischen Pfandrecht: Neudrucke mit Nachträgen.* Napoli: Jovene, 1982.

Wacke, Andreas. "Max Kasers Lehren zum Ursprung und Wesen des römischen Pfandrechts." *ZRG* 115 (1998) 168–202.

Ankum, Hans. *ZRG* 118 (2001) 442–462 (review of Potjewijd, G. H. *Beschikkingsbevoegdheid,* Bekrachtiging En Convalescentie, 1998).

A. Creation and Extinction of Secured Interests

a. *Pignus tacitum* ["silent pledge"]

CASE 155

D 20.2.7 pr. (Pomponius libro tertio decimo ex variis lectionibus)

In praediis rusticis fructus qui ibi nascuntur tacite intelleguntur pignori esse domino fundi locati, etiamsi nominatim id non convenerit.

Translation: (Pomponius in the 13th book of his *Florilegium*)[1]

With [leased] rural property the fruits that grow there count as silently pledged[2] to the landowner, even if this has not been expressly agreed to.

Note on the Text:

On *intelleguntur* ("count as"), see Case 72.

Discussion Questions:

1) By what route does the jurist come to the construction of a security interest without express agreement: is he working from interpretation, legal fiction, customary law, etc.?
2) Justify the economic and the juristic need for this construction.
3) Can one impute to the tenant that he wanted to pledge the fruits?
4) Do the fruits count as pledged, if the tenant clarifies by contractual clause that he does not want this?
5) At what point in time and in what manner can the lessor put himself in possession of the fruits?

---

[1] On Pomponius, see Case 29 (D 41.1.21 pr.). His *Florilegium* contained excerpts from the works of various jurists, accompanied by the annotations of Pomponius. The collection comprised at least 41 books and was probably the first version of the large commentaries of Pomponius.

[2] Translator's note: Property could be secured in various ways. The classical law distinguished between *pignus* ("pledge") and *hypotheca* ("hypothec"). The former involved transfer of possession of the pledged property (i.e., pawning); with the latter, the property remained in the possession of the debtor. In view of this difference, *hypotheca* was typically used to secure land. The legal distinction between the two forms of security was essentially abolished by the time of the composition of the Digest, although both methods of securing property continued in use. Still a third form of security was *pactum fiduciae* (a transfer of ownership subject to a contractual requirement to re-transfer upon satisfaction of the debt: i.e., an arrangement similar to the common law "mortgage").

CASE 156

D 20.2.4 pr. (Neratius libro primo membranarum)

Eo iure utimur, ut quae in praedia urbana inducta illata sunt pignori esse credantur, quasi id tacite convenerit: in rusticis praediis contra observatur.

Translation: (Neratius in the first book of his *Legal Notes*)[3]

We use the rule that movables which are brought onto an urban property count as pledged, just as if there had been a silent pledge to that effect. The opposite is understood in the case of rustic properties.

Note on the Text:

Eo iure utimur ("we use the rule that") indicates a firmly established legal doctrine, just like *constat* ("it is established that") and *receptum est* ("it is accepted that").

Discussion Question:

Analyze and explain this distinction in comparison with D 20.2.7 pr. (Case 155).

Compare with this Text:

§ 1101 Austrian Civil Code:

(1) As a guarantee for continuation of the rent-payment, the lessor of immovable property has a security interest in the furnishings and goods that have been brought in and belong to the lessee and his family members who dwell in the same household. . .

(3) To the lessor of land there belongs, to the same extent and effect, the security interest in livestock present on the property and in the industrial equipment and in the fruits that are still on the property.[4]

---

[3] On author and work, see Case 73 (D 41.3.41).

[4] **§ 1101 ABGB:**

(1) Zur Sicherstellung des Bestandzinses hat der Vermieter einer unbeweglichen Sache das Pfandrecht an den eingebrachten, dem Mieter oder seinen mit ihm in gemeinschaftlichem Haushalte lebenden Familienmitgliedern gehörigen Einrichtungsstücken und Fahrnissen . . .

(3) Dem Verpächter eines Grundstückes steht in gleichem Umfange und mit gleicher Wirkung das Pfandrecht an dem auf dem Pachtgute vorhandenen Vieh und den Wirtschaftsgerätschaften und den darauf noch befindlichen Früchten zu.

§ 562 German Civil Code:

The lessor of land has from the lease relationship a security interest in property of the tenant that is brought in there. . . . It does not extend to property that is immune to distraint.[5]

§ 592 German Civil Code:

The security interest of the lessor of agricultural land can be made applicable to the entire amount of the lease agreement. . . . It extends also to the fruits of the land as well as to property that according to **§ 811 Nr. 4** of the Civil Process Rules is not immune to distraint.[6]

Art 272 Swiss Law of Obligations:

The lessor of immovable property has, for rent that is in arrears for a year and a half, a right of distraint [**ZGB 895** ff.] on the movable property [**ZGB 713**] that is located on the premises and that pertains to their furnishings or use. . . .[7]

Art 274 Swiss Law of Obligations:

If the lessee wishes to remove or discard property located on the leased premises, the lessor can, on the basis of his right of distraint, with the help of a person from the appropriate office, withhold as much of the property . . . as is required for his security. . . .[8]

Literature:

Schuller W. "Zum pignus tacitum." *Labeo* 15 (1969) 267–284, at 272 ff.

---

[5] **§ 562 BGB:** Der Vermieter eines Grundstücks hat für seine Forderungen aus dem Mietverhältnis ein Pfandrecht an den eingebrachten Sachen des Mieters . . . Es erstreckt sich nicht auf die der Pfändung nicht unterworfenen Sachen.

[6] **§ 592 BGB:** Das Pfandrecht des Verpächters eines landwirtscaftlichen Grundstücks kann für den gesamten Pachtzins geltend gemacht werden . . . Es erstreckt sich auf die Früchte des Grundstücks sowie auf die nach **§ 811 Nr. 4** der Zivilprozeßordnung der Pfändung nicht unterworfenen Sachen.

[7] **Art 272 OR:** Der Vermieter einer unbeweglichen Sache hat für einen verfallenen Jahreszins und den laufenden Halbjahreszins ein Retentionsrecht [**ZGB 895** ff.] an den beweglichen Sachen [**ZGB 713**], die sich in den vermieteten Räumen befinden und zu deren Einrichtung oder Benutzung gehören . . .

[8] **Art 274 OR:** Der Vermieter kann, wenn der Mieter wegziehen oder die in den gemieteten Räumen befindlichen Sachen fortschaffen will, auf Grund seines Retentionsrechtes mit Hilfe der zuständigen Amtsstelle so viele Sachen zurückhalten . . . als zu seiner Deckung erforderlich sind . . .

CASE 157

D 20.2.3 (Ulpianus libro septuagesimo tertio ad edictum)

Si horreum fuit conductum vel devorsorium vel area, tacitam conventionem de invectis illatis etiam in his locum habere putat Neratius: quod verius est.

Translation: (Ulpian in the 73rd book of his *Commentary on the Praetor's Edict*)[9]

If a warehouse is taken in lease, or an inn or a building site, Neratius believes that also in these cases there is a tacit agreement concerning the property that is carried in or brought in; and this is the better view.

Discussion Questions:

Verius est ["this is the better view"] signals a controversy (see Case 8). Try to make an economic argument in favor of each juristic position.

Literature:

Schuller (Case 156) 275 ff.

---

[9] On author and work, see Case 11 (D 18.6.1.2).

CASE 158

D 20.2.2 (Marcianus libro singulari ad formulam hypothecariam)

Pomponius libro quadragesimo variarum lectionum scribit: non solum pro pensionibus, sed et si deteriorem habitationem fecerit culpa sua inquilinus, quo nomine ex locato cum eo erit actio, invecta et illata pignori erunt obligata.

Translation: (Marcian in his monograph *On the Action for Secured Property*)[10]

Pomponius writes in the 40th book of his *Florilegium*: not only for the payment of rent but also if the tenant damages the dwelling through his own fault, for which reason the lessor can bring suit against him on the basis of the lease agreement, the property that has been carried or brought onto the premises counts as pledged.

Discussion Questions:

1) The renter is in arrears with the rent shortly before expiration of the lease agreement, or he has wrongfully damaged the leased property. What steps can the lessor take?
2) The renter has paid for all damage. The lessor does not release the property that was brought in. What can the renter do?
3) During the lease relationship, the renter alienates one of the items he brought onto the premises. Is the transfer valid?

Compare with this Text:

§ 1101 (2) Austrian Civil Code:

If the lessee leaves or property is removed without payment of the rent or guarantee of payment, then the lessor can keep the property in his own custody, though he must within three days apply for a security designation or else surrender the property.[11]

---

[10] Aelius Marcianus, like Modestinus, belonged to the last generation of the classical period. His chief work was a comprehensive *Institutiones* [textbook] in 16 books. His treatment of the action for secured property was probably a lemmatized commentary on the parts of the formula and was important both for teaching and practice. On Pomponius, see Case 29 (D 41.1.21 pr.); on his *Florilegium*, see Case 155 (D 20.2.7 pr.).

[11] **§1101 (2) ABGB:** Zieht der Mieter aus oder werden Sachen verschleppt, ohne daß der Zins entrichtet oder sichergestellt ist, so kann der Vermieter die Sachen auf eigene Gefahr zurückbehalten, doch muß er binnen drei Tagen um die pfandweise Beschreibung ansuchen oder die Sachen herausgeben.

§ 562b I German Civil Code:

The lessor, so long as he has a right to make opposition, may hinder the removal of the property underlying his security interest, even without recourse to court, and, if the lessee departs, take the property into his own possession.[12]

Literature:

> Frier (Case 107) 135 ff.

---

[12] **§ 562b I BGB:** Der Vermieter darf die Entfernung der seinem Pfandrecht unterliegenden Sachen, soweit er ihr zu widersprechen berechtigt ist, auch ohne Anrufen des Gerichts verhindern und, wenn der Mieter auszieht, die Sachen in seinen Besitz nehmen.

CASE 159

D 43.32.1 pr. (Ulpianus libro septuagensimo tertio ad edictum)

Praetor ait: "Si is homo, quo de agitur, non est ex his rebus, de quibus inter te et actorem convenit, ut, quae in eam habitationem, qua de agitur, introducta importata ibi nata factave essent, ea pignori tibi pro mercede eius habitationis essent, sive ex his rebus est et ea merces tibi soluta eove nomine satisfactum est aut per te stat, quo minus solvatur: ita, quo minus ei, qui eum pignoris nomine induxit, inde abducere liceat, vim fieri veto"

Translation: (Ulpian in the 73rd book of his *Commentary on the Praetor's Edict*)[13]

The Praetor says: "If the slave that is the subject of this action does not belong to the property concerning which there was between you and the plaintiff an agreement that everything that was led into or carried onto the premises, or was born or made there, would be a pledge to you for his payment of rent for the dwelling, or if it was indeed part of that property, but payment has already been made to you, or security has already been given on that account, or it is because of you that it has not been paid, then I forbid force to be used to prevent the person, who brought the slave onto the premises as pledged property, from leading him [the slave] away."

Discussion Questions:

Ulpian refers to the text of the *interdictum de migrando* ["interdict concerning change or residence"]. Consider whether it is applicable to the following situations:

    a) Titius lives for free in the house of Seius and has caused damage to his dwelling. Because Seius believes that Titius will soon leave without payment of compensation, he confiscates some valuable furniture belonging to Titius, thinking that this counts as silently pledged.

    b) Seius erroneously confiscates not only the property of his tenant Titius, but also the luggage of Marius, who lives there as a guest of Titius.

Literature:

Kaser, M. *Studien zum römischen Pfandrecht: Neudrucke mit Nachträgen.* Napoli: Jovene, 1982, 138 ff.

Frier (Case 107) 105 ff.

---

[13] On author and work, see Case 11 (D 18.6.1.2).

b. General Hypothecs and Pledges of Entire Property

CASE 159a

D 20.1.6 (Ulpianus libro septuagesimo tertio ad edictum)

Obligatione generali rerum, quas quis habuit habiturusve sit, ea non continebuntur, quae verisimile est quemquam specialiter obligaturum non fuisse. ut puta supellex, item vestis relinquenda est debitori, et ex mancipiis quae in eo usus habebit, ut certum sit eum pignori daturum non fuisse. proinde de ministeriis eius perquam ei necessariis vel quae ad affectionem eius pertineant.

D 20.1.7 (Paulus libro sexagesimo octavo ad edictum)

vel quae in usum cottidianum habentur Serviana non competit.

Translation: (Ulpian in the 73rd book of his *Commentary on the Praetor's Edict*)[14]

With a general hypothec of all property that someone has or will have, there will not be included anything that it is probable he would not have hypothecated specifically: for example, his house furniture. Also the clothing must be left to the debtor; and from the slaves, any who are used in such a way that it would be certain he would not have pledged them: namely, those who are directly necessary for his personal service or to whom he is especially attached.

(Paul in the 68th book of his *Commentary on the Praetor's Edict*)[15]

nor does the *actio Serviana*[16] apply to the property that is kept for his daily use.

Discussion Questions:

1) When will the creditor not be satisfied with the pledge of individual objects, but require the pledge of an entire property?
2) When will the debtor agree to the pledge of his entire present and future property?
3) The debtor, who has pledged his entire present and future property, sold his cow. What claim is available to the secured creditor? Compare Cases 159b and 164.
4) Debtor sells his toga. Does the creditor have a security interest in the sale proceeds?

Literature:

Wagner, Herbert. *Voraussetzungen, Vorstufen und Anfänge der römischen Generalverpfändung*, Bd. 16, 151. Marburg: N. G. Elwert, 1968, 125 ff.

---

[14] On author and work, see Case 11 (D 18.6.1.2).

[15] On author and work, see Case 1 (D 41.2.3.1).

[16] Translator's note. The *actio Serviana* was an action available to a creditor who sought to seize hypothecated property in satisfaction of the debt.

CASE 159b

D 20.1.34 pr. & 2 (Scaevola libro vicesimo septimo digestorum)

(pr.) *Cum tabernam debitor creditori pignori dederit, quaesitum est, utrum eo facto nihil egerit, an tabernae appellatione merces, quae in ea erant, obligasse videatur? et si eas merces per tempora distraxerit et alias comparaverit easque in eam tabernam intulerit et decesserit, an omnia quae ibi deprehenduntur creditor hypothecaria actione petere possit, cum et mercium species mutatae sint et res aliae illatae? respondit: ea, quae mortis tempore debitoris in taberna inventa sunt, pignori obligata esse videntur.*

(2) *Creditor pignori accepit a debitore quidquid in bonis habet habiturusve esset: quaesitum est, an corpora pecuniae, quam idem debitor ab alio mutuam accepit, cum in bonis eius facta sint, obligata creditori pignoris esse coeperint. respondit coepisse.*

Translation: (Scaevola in the 27th book of his *Digesta*)[17]

(pr.) When a debtor had pledged his shop to his creditor, it was asked whether he had accomplished nothing thereby, or if under the designation "shop" all the wares on the premises counted as pledged. And if in the passage of time these wares are sold and others bought and brought into the shop and then he dies, can the creditor sue with an action on the hypothec to take possession of all the property on the premises, although the kinds of wares have changed and new property has been brought in? Scaevola responded: what is in the shop at the time of the debtor's death counts as pledged.

(2) A creditor has accepted from a debtor a pledge of "everything that he has or will have among his property." It was asked whether a sum of money, which the debtor received from another person as a loan, had been pledged to the creditor as soon as it came into the property of the debtor. Scaevola said it did.

Discussion Questions:

1) Evaluate Scaevola's interpretation of the word *taberna* ("shop")—its consequences and method.
2) When does the security interest arise in individual wares that are bought, processed, and alienated? When is it extinguished?
3) Does the money that comes in [from the sale of goods] also count as pledged?
4) Try to argue for and against Scaevola's decision with regard to the money on loan.

---

[17] On author and work, see Case 101 (D 6.1.67).

Literature:

Schlosser, Hans, Fritz Sturm, and Hermann Weber. *Die rechtsgeschichtliche Exegese: römisches Recht, deutsches Recht, Kirchenrecht*, 2., neubearbeitete Aufl., Heft 10, 166. München: Beck, 1993, 26 ff.

Wagner H. "Zur wirtschaftlichen und rechtlichen Bedeutung der Tabernen," in *Studi in onore di Arnaldo Biscardi*, III. Milano: Istituto editoriale Cisalpino, La Goliardica, 1982, 391–422, at 391 ff.

Daubermann (Case 149) 116 ff.

Löffelmann, Arnd. *Pfandrecht und Sicherungsübereignung an künftigen Sachen: Rechtsvergleich zwischen deutschem und römischem Recht*. Köln: Böhlau,1996, 172 ff.

c. *Res aliena pignori data* ["Property of Another Given in Pledge"]

CASE 160

D 20.1.22 (Modestinus libro septimo differentiarum)

Si Titio, qui rem meam ignorante me creditori suo pignori obligaverit, heres exstitero, ex postfacto pignus directo quidem non convalescit, sed utilis dabitur creditori.

Translation: (Modestinus in the seventh book of his *Distinctions*)[18]

If I become heir to Titius, who without my knowledge has pledged my property to his creditor, granted that the security interest is not directly cured after the fact, the creditor will nevertheless be given an *utilis actio pigneraticia* ["a policy action on the pledge"].

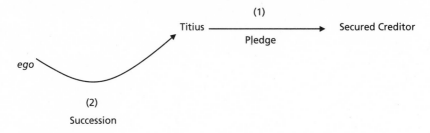

Discussion Questions:

1) What legal consequences ensue through the pledge of another's property?
2) What considerations lead the jurist to give the creditor a [policy action] (*actio pigneraticia utilis*) [rather than just an action on the pledge itself]?
3) Why does Modestinus refuse to recognize a "direct" curing of the security interest?

Compare with this Text:

Art. 884 Swiss Civil Code:

Movable goods, where the law does not make an exception, can be pledged only in a way that the possession of the pledged property is delivered to the secured creditor [992 ff.].

---

[18] On author and work, see Case 80 (D 50.16.109).

The good faith receiver of the pledged property acquires the security interest, to the extent that third parties do not have rights from earlier possession, even if the pledgor is not authorized to dispose of the property [933] . . .[19]

Literature:

Schanbacher, Dietmar. *Die Konvaleszenz von Pfandrechten im klassischen römischen Recht.* Berlin: Duncker & Humblot, 1987, 122 ff.

Wacke, Andreas. "Die Konvaleszenz von Pfandrecht nach römischem Recht." *ZRG* 115 (1998) 438–461, at 446 ff.

Ankum (Case 130) 455.

---

[19] **Art. 884 ZGB:**

Fahrnis kann, wo das Gesetz keine Ausnahme macht, nur dadurch verpfändet werden, daß dem Pfandgläubiger der Besitz an der Pfandsache übertragen wird [992 ff.].

Der gutgläubiger Empfänger der Pfandsache erhält das Pfandrecht, soweit nicht Dritten Rechte aus früherem Besitze zustehen, auch dann, wenn der Verpfänder nicht befugt war, über die Sache zu verfügen [933] . . .

CASE 161

D 13.7.41 (Paulus libro tertio quaestionum)

Rem alienam pignori dedisti, deinde dominus rei eius esse coepisti: datur utilis actio pign-eraticia creditori. non est idem dicendum, si ego Titio, qui rem meam obligaverat sine mea voluntate, heres extitero: hoc enim modo pignoris persecutio concedenda non est creditori, nec utique sufficit ad competendam utilem pigneraticiam actionem eundem esse dominum, qui etiam pecuniam debet . . .

Translation: (Paul in the third book of his *Legal Questions*)[20]

You have given the property of another for a pledge, then you became the owner of this property: the creditor gets the *actio pigneraticia utilis* ["a policy action on the pledge"]. This does not apply, however, if I become heir to Titius, who has pledged my property without my consent. In the latter case the creditor does not receive the right to act on the pledge, and the fact that the owner and debtor have become the same person is not sufficient for the *actio pigneraticia utilis*...

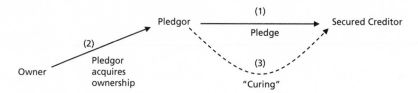

Discussion Questions:

1) Create some concrete examples of the curing of a security interest.
2) Why does the creditor acquire only an *actio utilis* in the first fact-situation?
3) Justify why Paul recognizes curing in one case but denies it in the other. Compare on this question Mod. 20.1.22 (Case 160).[21]

---

[20] On Paul see Case 1 (D 41.2.3.1). His *Quaestiones* are a collection of juristic problems (including practical cases, controversies, letters) in 26 books that follow the organizational scheme of the Digest.

[21] Translator's note: The contradiction between the second part of Case 161 and Case 160 may seem less stark if one keeps the relative chronology of the two passages in mind. Paul predates Modestinus, making Case 160 the later of the two cases. Modestinus concedes that technically there has been no curing under the facts presented, which is Paul's holding in Case 161 (second part), but he grants the remedy anyway. The rule of the first part of Case 161 was later confirmed in an imperial rescript, issued in the year 286 CE (Diocletian and Maximian C 8.15.5): *Cum res, quae necdum in bonis debitoris est, pignori data ab eo postea in bonis eius esse incipiat, ordinariam quidem actionem super pignore non competere manifestum est, sed tamen aequitatem facere, ut facile utilis persecutio exemplo pignoraticiae daretur.* "If property, which is not yet among the goods of the debtor, has been given in pledge *by him* and later begins to be among his goods, it is clear that

Literature:

Schanbacher (Case 160) 113 ff., 122 ff.
Wacke (Case 160) 445 ff.

---

the ordinary action on the pledge is not available; nevertheless, equity requires that an analogous action on the pledge should be granted without difficulty." Emphasis added.

CASE 161a

D 13.7.9 pr. & 4 (Ulpianus libro vicensimo octavo ad edictum)

(pr.) *Si rem alienam mihi debitor pignori dedit aut malitiose in pignore versatus sit, dicendum est locum habere contrarium iudicium.*

(4) *Is quoque, qui rem alienam pignori dedit, soluta pecunia potest pigneraticia experiri.*

Translation: (Ulpian in the 28th book of his *Commentary on the Praetor's Edict*)[22]

(pr.) If the debtor has pledged to me the property of another person, or he has conducted himself fraudulently with respect to the pledge, it must be said that there is a place for using the *actio contraria*.[23]

(4) Also the person who has given another person's property in pledge can use the *actio pigneraticia* after the money has been paid.

Discussion Questions:

1) What are examples of fraudulent conduct of the security-debtor?
2) What claims can the creditor validly make by means of the *actio contraria*?
3) What does the debtor seek with the *actio pigneraticia*?

Compare with this Text:

§ 456 Austrian Civil Code:

If another's movable property is pledged without the owner's consent, he [the owner] in general has the right to demand it back; but in those cases in which the ownership suit does not lie against a reasonable possessor (§ 367), he [the owner] is obliged either to hold the reasonable security-holder harmless, or to let the secured property go and be satisfied with his right of compensation against the pledgor.[24]

---

[22] On author and work, see Case 11 (D 18.6.1.2).

[23] Translator's note: While the *actio pigneraticia* was available to the pledgor against a pledgee for loss or damage to the security; the *actio pigneraticia contraria* was available to the pledgee against the pledgor for damage or loss caused by the *culpa* ("fault") of the latter.

[24] §456 ABGB: Wird eine fremde bewegliche Sache ohne Einwilligung des Eigentümers verpfändet, so hat dieser in der Regel zwar das Recht, sie zurückzufordern; aber in solchen Fällen, in welchen die Eigentumsklage gegen einen redlichen Besitzer nicht statt hat (§ 367), ist er verbunden, entweder den redlichen Pfandinhaber schadlos zu halten, oder das Pfand fahren zu lassen, und sich mit dem Ersatzrechte gegen den Verpfänder zu begnügen.

§ 458 Austrian Civil Code:

If the worth of the secured property through the fault of the security-debtor, or because of a defect of the property that just became visible, is no longer found sufficient to cover the debt, the creditor is entitled to demand another appropriate security from the security-debtor.[25]

Art. 890 Swiss Civil Code:

The creditor is liable for damage caused by the diminishment in the value of the secured property or for its loss, to the degree that he fails to show that it occurred without his fault [**Law of Obligations 97** ff.].

If the creditor alienates the secured property or pledges it to another, he is liable for all the damage that results therefrom.[26]

---

[25] **§ 458 ABGB:** Wenn der Wert eines Pfandes durch Verschulden der Pfandgebers, oder wegen eines erst offenbar gewordenen Mangels der Sache zur Bedeckung der Schuld nicht mehr zureichend gefunden wird; so is der Gläubiger berechtigt, von dem Pfandgeber ein anderes angemessenes Pfand zu fordern.

[26] **Art. 890 ZGB:**

Der Gläubiger haftet für den aus der Wertverminderung oder aus dem Untergang der verpfändeten Sache entstandenen Schaden, sofern er nicht nachweist, daß dieser ohne sein Verschulden eingetreten ist [OR 97 ff.].

Hat der Gläubiger das Pfand eigenmächtig veräußert oder weiterverpfändet, so haftet er für allen hieraus entstandenen Schaden.

d. Consensual Termination of a Security Interest

CASE 162

D 20.6.8.14 (Marcianus libro singulari ad formulam hypothecariam)

Quod si concesserit decem vendere, ille quinque vendiderit, dicendum est, non esse repellendum creditorem: in contrarium non erit quaerendum, quin recte vendit, si pluris vendiderit, quam concessit creditor.

Translation: (Marcian in his Monograph *On the Action for Secured Property*)[27]

But if the secured creditor has allowed the security-debtor to sell the property for 10 and the latter sold for five, it must be said that the creditor is not to be barred: conversely, there is no question that he sold validly if he sold for more than the creditor allowed.

Discussion Questions:

1) What reasons might cause the creditor to allow the debtor to sell the secured property?
2) How does granting permission [to dispose of the property] affect the security interest?
3) Is the sale for five valid?
4) What measures can the creditor take?
5) Why is the sale for a higher price valid?
6) How might the secured creditor assure himself, if he fears the security-debtor will not obey him in the sale?

---

[27] On author and work, see Case 158 (D 20.2.2).

CASE 163

D 20.6.8.15 (Marcianus libro singulari ad formulam hypothecariam)

Non videtur autem consensisse creditor, si sciente eo debitor rem vendiderit, cum ideo passus est veniri, quod sciebat ubique pignus sibi durare. sed si subscripserit forte in tabulis emptionis, consensisse videtur. nisi manifeste appareat deceptum esse. quod observari oportet et si sine scriptis consenserit.

Translation: (Marcian in his Monograph *On the Action for Secured Property*)[28]

The creditor is not understood to have agreed, if the debtor sold the property with the creditor's knowledge, provided the creditor allowed the sale to be made because he knew the security interest would endure anyway. But if he happens to have signed the sales contract, he is deemed to have agreed—unless it is obvious that he was deceived, which ought to be noted even if he agreed without a writing.

Note on the Text:

On *videtur* ("is understood"), see on Case 72.

Discussion Questions:

What legal effects are brought about by the sale of the pledged property under the following fact-situations (cf. on this Paul. D 47.2.67 pr. [Case 164]).

a) The creditor allows the sale with a reservation of his security interest.
b) The creditor does not know about the sale. Later he finds out and keeps silent, or agrees, or expresses his disapproval.
c) The creditor forbids the sale, but the debtor sells the property anyway.

Literature:

Wacke, Andreas. "Zur Lehre vom pactum tacitum und zur Aushilfsfunktion der exceptio doli. Stillschweigender Verzicht und Verwirkung nach klassischem Recht, II." *ZRG* 91 (1974) 251–284, at 264 ff.

Wacke, A. "Max Kasers Lehren zum Ursprung und Wesen des römischen Pfandrechts." *ZRG* 115 (1998) 168–202, at 197 ff.

---

[28] On author and work, see Case 158 (D 20.2.2).

CASE 164

D 47.2.67 (66) pr. (Paulus libro septimo ad Plautium)

Si is, qui rem pignori dedit, vendiderit eam: quamvis dominus sit, furtum facit, sive eam tradiderat creditori sive speciali pactione tantum obligaverat: idque et Iulianus putat.

Translation: (Paul in the seventh book of his *Commentary on Plautius*)[29]

If someone who has given property for a pledge sells it, even though he is the owner, he has committed theft, whether he delivered the property to the creditor or only pledged it without possession under a special agreement. And Julian thinks the same.

Discussion Questions:

1) Is the sale by the debtor valid?
2) What claims can the secured creditor make effective against the debtor? What claims against the buyer?
3) The expression *speciali pactione* ("special agreement") refers to the pledge of a specific item. Do you think that the same legal consequences would follow in the case of a general pledge (cf. on this Ulp. D 49.14.28, under Case 185).

Literature:

Kaser (Case 150) 204 ff.

---

[29] On Paul, see Case 1 (D 41.2.3.1); on his books *ad Plautium,* see Case 130 (D 21.3.2). On Julian, see Case 70 (D 41.1.36).

CASE 165

D 13.7.3 (Pomponius libro octavo decimo ad Sabinum)

Si quasi recepturus a debitore tuo comminus pecuniam reddidisti ei pignus isque per fenestra id misit excepturo, quem de industria ad id posuerit, Labeo ait furti te agere cum debitore posse et ad exhibendum: et, si agente te contraria pigneraticia excipiat debitor de pignore sibi reddito, replicabitur de dolo et fraude, per quam nec redditum, sed per fallaciam ablatum id intellegitur.

Translation: (Pomponius in the 18th book of his *Commentary on the* Ius Civile *of Sabinus*)[30]

If you, expecting to receive the money from your debtor in his presence, returned the security to him, and he threw the security out the window to someone whom he placed there deliberately, Labeo says that you can proceed against him with an *actio furti* ["action for theft"] and an *actio ad exhibendum* ["action for production of the property"]. And if, when you bring an *actio contraria pigneraticia* ["reverse action on the pledge"], the debtor raises the defense that the security was returned, you have a *replicatio* ["reply"] for *dolus* ["deceit"] and *fraus* ["fraud"], according to which it was not returned, but is deemed to have been carried off by deception.[31]

Discussion Questions:

1) What rights can the creditor assert with the *actio furti* and the *actio ad exhibendum*?
2) Could he also proceed against the debtor with the *actio Serviana* or the *interdictum utrubi*?
3) What does the creditor achieve with the *actio pigneraticia contraria*?
4) Explain the *exceptio de pignore sibi reddito* ["affirmative defense that the security was returned"] of the debtor.
5) Could the creditor proceed against a third party with the *actio Serviana*?

Literature:

Kaser (Case 159) 91 ff.
Wesener (Case 131) 124.

---

[30] On author and work, see Case 29 (D 41.1.21 pr.); on Labeo, see Case 10 (D 41.2.51).

[31] Translator's note. Although the facts of this case may seem rather comical and absurd, one can readily imagine similar interests and issues arising under less cartoonish circumstances.

e. Repayment of the Debt

CASE 166

D 20.1.19 (Ulpianus libro vicesimo primo ad edictum)

Qui pignori plures res accepit, non cogitur unam liberare nisi accepto universo quantum debetur.

Translation: (Ulpian in the 21st book of his *Commentary on the Praetor's Edict*)[32]

The person who has accepted multiple things as security is not required to release one of them unless the entire amount of the debt has been received.

Note on the Text:

Up until complete repayment of the debt the entire property or all the pledged items remain subject to the security interest. Partial repayment does not free individual parts or pieces of the property from the security interest: *pignoris causa indivisa est* ("the security interest is indivisible"). cf. Pap. D 21.2.65.

Discussion Question:

Justify Ulpian's opinion. What are the arguments for and against the indivisibility of the security-lien?

Compare with this Text:

§ 469 Austrian Civil Code:

The security interest ends by payment of the debt. . . .[33]

§ 1252 German Civil Code:

The security interest expires with the claim for which it exists.[34]

Art. 889 Swiss Civil Code:

If the security interest is extinguished as a consequence of payment of the claim or on other grounds, the creditor is to return the secured property to the person entitled to it. Before his complete satisfaction he is not required to return the security entirely or in part.[35]

Literature:
Wacke, A. "Ungeteilte Pfandhaltung." *Index* 3 (1972) 454–502, at 456 ff.

---

[32] On author and work, see Case 11 (D 18.6.1.2).

[33] **§ 469 ABGB:** Durch Tilgung der Schuld hört das Pfandrecht auf . . .

[34] **§ 1252 BGB:** Das Pfandrecht erlischt mit der Forderung, für die es besteht.

[35] **Art. 889 ZGB:** Ist das Pfandrecht infolge der Tilgung der Forderung oder aus anderem Grunde untergegangen, so hat der Gläubiger die Pfandsache an den Berechtigten herauszugeben. Vor seiner vollen Befriedigung ist er nicht verpflichtet, das Pfand ganz oder zum Teil herauszugeben.

f. Disposition of Security

CASE 167

D 20.5.8 (Modestinus libro quarto regularum)

Creditoris arbitrio permittitur ex pignoribus sibi obligatis quibus velit distractis ad suum commodum pervenire.

Translation: (Modestinus in the fourth book of his *Rules*)[36]

It is left to the creditor's judgment which of the pledged goods he wishes to sell in order to receive satisfaction of the debt.

Discussion Questions:

1) May the creditor, upon non-payment of the debt, sell the entirety of the pledged property?
2) May the creditor, if only a small amount of the claim is still outstanding, sell the most valuable piece of the pledged property?
3) Must the creditor take special effort to get the best possible sale price?

Compare with this Text:

§ 1230 German Civil Code:

When there are several pieces of secured property, the secured creditor, to the extent something else is not specified, may select those which should be sold. He can bring to sale only as many of the secured items as are required for his satisfaction.[37]

Literature:

Wacke (Case 166) 457 ff.

---

[36] On author and work, see Case 80 (D 50.16.109).

[37] § 1230 BGB: Unter mehreren Pfändern kann der Pfandgläubiger, soweit nicht ein anderes bestimmt ist, diejenigen auswählen, welche verkauft werden sollen. Er kann nur so viele Pfänder zum Verkaufe bringen, als zu seiner Befriedigung erforderlich sind.

CASE 168

D 20.5.12 pr. (Tryphoninus libro octavo disputationum)

Rescriptum est ab imperatore libellos agente Papiniano creditorem a debitore pignus emere posse, quia in dominio manet debitoris.

D 20.1.16.9 (Marcianus libro singulari ad formulam hypothecariam)

Potest ita fieri pignoris datio hypothecaeve, ut, si intra certum tempus non sit soluta pecunia, iure emptoris possideat rem iusto pretio tunc aestimandam: hoc enim casu videtur quoddammodo condicionalis esse venditio. et ita divus Severus et Antoninus rescripserunt.

Translation: (Tryphoninus in the eighth book of his *Disputations*)[38]

When Papinian headed the office *a libellis*,[39] the emperor issued a rescript that the creditor could buy the security from the debtor, since it remained in the debtor's ownership.

(Marcian in his monograph *On the Action for Secured Property*)[40]

The giving of security can take place in a way that the creditor, if the money is not paid within a specified time, can lawfully possess the property with the right of a buyer, at a price that is a fair evaluation of its worth at that time. In this case there is a kind of conditional sale, and the emperors Severus and Antoninus so decided in rescripts.

Discussion Questions:

1) Explain the reasoning of *quia in dominio manet debitoris* ("since it remained in the debtor's ownership").
2) Why was there a need for an imperial rescript in order to allow purchase of the security by the creditor?
3) Is it permissible to set [in advance] the purchase price at which the creditor will purchase the property secured by the security contract?

Compare with this Text:

§ 461 Austrian Civil Code:

If the secured creditor after passage of the specified time is not satisfied, he is authorized to demand a judicial sale of the security. . . . [41]

---

[38] On Tryphoninus, see under Case 172 (D 20.4.20); on Papinian, see Case 5 (D 18.1.74).

[39] Translator's note: The office *a libellis* dealt with "written petitions" to the emperor, including legal appeals.

[40] On author and work, see Case 158 (D 20.2.2).

[41] § 461 ABGB: Wird der Pfandgläubiger nach Verlauf der bestimmten Zeit nicht befriedigt; so ist er befugt, die Feilbietung des Pfandes gerichtlich zu verlangen . . .

§ 463 Austrian Civil Code:

Debtors have no right, when there is an auction of the property they have pledged, to take part in bidding.[42]

§ 1371 Austrian Civil Code:

All terms that are contrary to the nature of contracts for security and loans and all side contracts are invalid. Among these are agreements that after expiration of the time for payment of the debt the secured property will pass to the creditor; that he may alienate the property however he wishes or at a price that has already been previously specified, or that he can keep it for himself; that the debtor never redeem the security, or that he assign a piece of real property to no one else, or that the creditor, after the time of foreclosure, may not demand the alienation of the security.[43]

§ 1228 German Civil Code:

I   The satisfaction of the secured creditor from the security takes place through [its] sale.

II The secured creditor is entitled to the sale, as soon as the claim is due entirely or in part. . . . [44]

§ 1229 German Civil Code:

An agreement made prior to commencement of the right to sell, according to which the ownership of the property will pass or be transferred to the secured creditor, in case he is not satisfied or not timely satisfied, is a nullity.[45]

Art. 891 Swiss Civil Code:

In the case of non-satisfaction, the creditor has the right to pay himself from the proceeds of the security. . . . [46]

---

[42] § 463 ABGB: Schuldner haben kein Recht, bei Versteigerung einer von ihnen verpfändeten Sache mitzubieten.

[43] § 1371 ABGB: Alle der Natur des Pfand- und Darlehensvertrages entgegen stehende Bedingungen und Nebenverträge sind ungültig. Dahin gehören die Verabredungen: daß nach der Verfallzeit der Schuldforderung das Pfandstück dem Gläubiger zufalle; daß er es nach Willkür oder in einem schon im voraus bestimmten Preise veräußern, oder für sich behalten könne; daß der Schuldner das Pfand niemals einlösen, oder ein liegendes Gut keinem andern verschreiben, oder daß der Gläubiger nach der Verfallzeit die Veräußerung des Pfandes nicht verlangen dürfe.

[44] § 1228 BGB:
  I Die Befriedigung des Pfandgläubigers aus dem Pfande erfolgt durch Verkauf.
  II Der Pfandgläubiger ist zum Verkaufe berechtigt, sobald die Forderung ganz oder zum Teil fällig ist . . .

[45] § 1229 BGB: Eine vor dem Eintritte der Verkaufsberechtigung getroffene Vereinbarung, nach welcher dem Pfandgläubiger, falls er nicht oder nicht rechtzeitig befriedigt wird, das Eigentum an der Sache zufallen oder übertragen werden soll, ist nichtig.

[46] Art. 891 ZGB: Der Gläubiger hat im Falle der Nichtbefriedigung ein Recht darauf, sich aus dem Erlös des Pfandes bezahlt zu machen . . .

Art. 894 Swiss Civil Code:

Any agreement, according to which the secured property will become the property of the creditor, if he is not satisfied, is invalid.[47]

Literature:

Peters F. "Der Erwerb des Pfandes durch den Pfandgläubiger im klassischen und nach-klassischen Recht," in *Studien zum römischen Recht, Max Kaser zum 65. Geburtstag gewidmet von seinen Hamburgern Schülern,* D. von Medicus D. and H. H. Seiler eds., Berlin: Duncker und Humblot, 1973, 137–168, at 142 ff.

Kaser (Case 159) 20, 37.

Wacke, *Max Kasers Lehren* (Case 163) 187 ff.

---

[47] **Art. 894 ZGB:** Jede Abrede, wonach die Pfandsache dem Gläubiger, wenn er nicht befriedigt wird, als Eigentum zufallen soll, ist ungültig.

CASE 169

D 13.7.4 (Ulpianus libro quadragensimo primo ad Sabinum)

Si convenit de distrahendo pignore sive ab initio sive postea, non tantum venditio valet, verum incipit emptor dominium rei habere. sed etsi non convenerit de distrahendo pignore, hoc tamen iure utimur, ut liceat distrahere, si modo non convenit, ne liceat. ubi vero convenit, ne distraheretur, creditor, si distraxerit, furti obligatur, nisi et ter fuerit denuntiatum ut solvat et cessaverit.

Translation: (Ulpian in the 41st book of his *Commentary on the* Ius Civile *of Sabinus*)[48]

If an agreement has been made concerning the sale of the security, whether from the beginning or afterward, the sale is not only valid, but the buyer acquires ownership of the property. But even if there is not an agreement about sale of the security, we use the rule that it may be sold, unless there is an agreement that it may not be sold. When it has been agreed that it not be sold, the creditor, if he sells it, is liable for theft, unless demand for payment has been made to the debtor three times, and he [the debtor] has failed to make payment.

Discussion Question:

Write an analysis. Assume in doing so that the first sentence comes from Sabinus. For the expression *hoc iure utimur* ["we use the rule"], see on Case 156.

Literature:

> Kaser (Case 159) 72 ff.
> Wacke, *Max Kasers Lehren.* . . (Case 163) 182 ff.

---

[48] On author and work, see Case 11 (D 18.6.1.2).

g. Loss of Secured Property

CASE 170

D 20.1.29 (Paulus libro quinto responsorum)

Domus pignori data exusta est eamque aream emit Lucius Titius et exstruxit: quaesitum est de iure pignoris. Paulus respondit pignoris persecutionem perseverare et ideo ius soli superficiem secutam videri, id est cum iure pignoris: sed bona fide possessores non aliter cogendos creditoribus aedificium restituere, quam sumptus in exstructione erogatos, quatenus pretiosior res facta est, reciperet.

Translation: (Paul in the fifth book of his *Legal Opinions*)[49]

A house that had been given as security burned down. Lucius Titius then bought the plot and built on it. A question was asked about the security interest. Paul answered that the security interest remained in effect and the building followed with the right to the land: i.e., the security interest. However, the good faith possessor could only be forced to surrender the building to the creditor, if he received compensation for as much of his building costs as were covered by commensurate increase in the value of the property.

Notes on the Text:

With the loss of the property the security interest is extinguished: *re extincta pignus perit* (cf. Marcian D 20.6.8 pr.). The principle applies to all property rights.

Discussion Questions:

1) Did Lucius Titius acquire ownership of the land that was sold?
2) Does this opinion contradict the principle that with the loss of the secured property, the security interest is extinguished?
3) With what kind of action could the creditor claim the house? What defenses could a good faith possessor raise? Explain.
4) The value of the land alone is 50; with the originally pledged house it is 80; with the new house it is 90. How high is the limit on the compensation for costs that the good faith builder gets from the secured creditor?
5) Could the possessors also receive compensation for luxury additions (e.g., wall paintings)? On this question, cf. Case 107.
6) Could the possessors, after the loss of the land to the security creditor, make a valid claim against the seller?
7) The debtor has pledged a forest. Trees fall on it and a boat is made from then. Does the creditor have a security interest in the boat?

---

[49] On Paul, see Case 1 (D 41.2.3.1). His *Responsa* (in 23 *libri*) follow the usual plan: (1) facts of the case; (2) legal issue (*quaero* or *quaesitum est*); (3) decision of the jurist (introduced by *Paulus respondit*).

Literature:

Bürge (Case 107) 148 ff.

Meissel, Franz-Stefan. "Die Prüfungsexegese im römischen Recht. Dargestellt an D 20.1.29.2: Pfandrecht am abgebrannten Haus?" *JAP* 3 (1992/93) 198 ff.

CASE 170a

D 13.7.18.3 (Paulus libro vicensimo nono ad edictum)

Si quis caverit, ut silva sibi pignori esset, navem ex ea materia factam non esse pignori Cassius ait, quia aliud sit materia, aliud navis: et ideo nominatim in dando pignore adiciendum esse ait: "quaeque ex silva facta natave sint."

Translation: (Paul in the 29th book of his *Commentary on the Praetor's Edict*)[50]

If someone has made an agreement that a forest should be pledged to him, Cassius says that a ship made from the wood taken from the forest is not pledged, since the lumber is one thing and the ship another. Therefore, he says, one must expressly add in the security agreement: "and whatever is taken from or made from this forest."

Discussion Questions:

1) Do you think that Cassius would recognize a security interest in fallen trees?
2) Why does the ship not count as part of the security?
3) Does the person who built the ship come into the question? What suit does the security creditor have against him?
4) The debtor sells the lumber to a good faith shipbuilder, who does not know about either the pledge of the forest or about the special contract term. Does the creditor have a security interest in the ship?

Literature:

Schermaier (Cse 118) 458 ff.
Schermaier (Case 115) 224 ff.
Löffelmann, Arnd. *Pfandrecht und Sicherungsübereignung an künftigen Sachen: Rechtsvergleich zwischen deutschem und römischem Recht.* Köln: Böhlau, 1996, 158 ff.

---

[50] On author and work, see Case 1 (D 41.2.3.1); on Cassius, see Case 19 (D 41.2.21.3).

B. Multiple Pledges

a. *Prior tempore potior iure*

CASE 171

D 20.4.11.4 (Gaius libro singulari de formula hypothecaria)

Si paratus est posterior creditor priori creditori solvere quod ei debetur, videndum est, an competat ei hypothecaria actio nolente priore creditore pecuniam accipere. et dicimus priori creditori inutilem esse actionem, cum per eum fiat, ne ei pecunia solvatur.

Translation: (Gaius in his monograph *On the Action for Secured Property*)[51]

If the later creditor is ready to pay the earlier creditor what he is owed, we must consider whether the *actio hypothecaria* is available to [the later creditor], even if the earlier creditor does not want to receive the money. And we say that the *actio* is not available to the earlier creditor, if it is due to him that the money is not paid.

Note on the Text:

Especially with respect to acquiring property rights, the legal position of a party accords with the chronological sequence of events. The earlier in time has the better right: *prior tempore, potior iure* ("first in time is stronger in right"). For violations of this rule, see Cases 182 and 185.

Discussion Questions:

1) Why might a later secured creditor offer to satisfy the claim of an earlier creditor?
2) Can an earlier creditor be compelled to accept the offer?
3) The later creditor has satisfied the claim of the earlier creditor. Is the latter's right to claim against the debtor thereby extinguished? Has the later creditor acquired the earlier creditor's claim and/or his security interest?
4) The claim of the first creditor falls due before that of the second creditor. The first creditor sells the security. Does the second creditor have a claim against the buyer? Against the first creditor?
5) What risk attaches to the later creditor with his *ius offerendi* ["right of offering to pay the earlier creditor"]?

Literature:

Schanbacher (Case 160) 36.

---

[51] On Gaius, see Case 6 (D 41.1.9.6). Only a few fragments of his monograph on the *formula hypothecaria* are preserved.

CASE 172

D 20.4.20 (Tryphoninus libro octavo disputationum)

Quaerebatur, si post primum contractum tuum, antequam aliam pecuniam tu crederes, eidem debitori Seius credidisset quinquaginta et hyperocham huius rei, quae tibi pignori data esset, debitor obligasset, dehinc tu eidem debitori crederes forte quadraginta: quod plus est in pretio rei quam primo credidisti utrum Seio ob quinquaginta an tibi in quadraginta cederet pignoris hyperocha. finge Seium paratum esse offerre tibi summam primo ordine creditam. dixi consequens esse, ut Seius potior sit in eo quod amplius est in pignore, et oblata ab eo summa primo ordine credita usurarumque eius postponatur primus creditor in summam, quam postea eidem debitori credidit.

Translation: (Tryphoninus in the eighth book of his *Legal Controversies*)[52]

After your initial security contract and before you lent more money, Seius lent the debtor 50 and the debtor pledged to him the *hyperocha* ["excess"] of the property that he had earlier given to you in pledge. Then you gave the same debtor another loan of 40. Should the *hyperocha* (i.e., the surplus from the sale of the security after paying off your first loan) go to Seius for his claim of 50, or to you for your claim of 40? Assume that Seius is ready to repay you the sum of your initial loan. I replied that Seius properly has the better right to the surplus value that he gets in the security. After he has paid off the initial loan amount plus interest, he is placed in the position of first creditor over the whole amount that he subsequently lent to the same debtor.

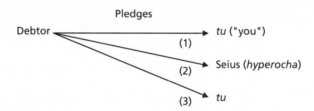

Discussion Question:

Write an analysis of the text. Examine especially the question of to what degree the decision of Tryphoninus rests on interpretation of the parties' agreements.

---

[52] Claudius Tryphoninus was a pupil of Cervidius Scaevola and wrote notes to the latter's work. With Papinian, he was a member of the *consilium* of Septimius Severus. His *disputationes* (in 21 books) contained discussion of cases from the *consilium* or from the law school.

Literature:

Kaser M. "Über mehrfache Verpfändung im römischen Recht," in *Studi in onore di Giuseppe Grosso* I.Torino: G. Giappichelli, 1968–1969, 27–76 (reprinted as *Ausgewählte Schriften* II [1976] 198 ff.)

Schanbacher, Dietmar. "Beobachtungen zum sog. 'pignus Gordianum.'" *ZRG* 114 (1997) 233–271, 248 ff.

CASE 173

D 20.1.15.2 (Gaius libro singulari de formula hypothecaria)

Qui res suas iam obligaverint et alii secundo obligant creditori, ut effugiant periculum, quod solent pati qui saepius easdem res obligant, praedicere solent alii nulli rem obligatam esse quam forte Lucio Titio, ut in id quod excedit priorem obligationem res sit obligata, ut sit pignori hypothecaeve id quod pluris est: aut solidum, cum primo debito liberata res fuerit. de quo videndum est, utrum hoc ita se habeat, si et conveniat, an et si simpliciter convenerit de eo quod excedit ut sit hypothecae? et solida res inesse conventioni videtur, cum a primo creditore fuerit liberata, an adhuc pars? sed illud magis est, quod prius diximus.

Translation: (Gaius in his monograph *On the Action for Secured Property*)[53]

Someone who has already pledged his property and wishes to pledge the same property to a second creditor, is obliged to make clear (in order to avoid the risk of penalty that is incurred by a person who pledges the same property more than once) that the property is pledged to no one else unless perhaps Lucius Titius, so that the property is pledged to the second creditor only to the extent that its value exceeds the amount of the first debt, so that the excess is pledged, or the whole value, once the first debt has been satisfied. The question arises whether the last point is valid only if it is expressly agreed to, or also if simply the pledge of the excess value is agreed to; and whether the whole property counts as included within the agreement, once it has been freed from the claim of the first creditor, or only part? But what we said earlier is much more the case.

Note on the Text:

On *videtur* ("counts as"), see on Case 72.

Discussion Questions [with model answers]:

1) What is the *periculum* ("risk of penalty") incurred by the pledgor, who does not notify the second creditor that the property has already been pledged?
2) What possibilities for multiple pledges of a piece of property does Gaius here consider?
3) What are the legal consequences for the second creditor, if the first creditor loses the property to a third party?
4) What is the legal position of the second creditor after satisfaction of the debt to the first creditor?
5) What is the legal position of the second creditor after his exercise of the *ius offerendi* ["right of offering to pay the prior creditor"]?

---

[53] On author, see Case 6 (D 41.1.9.6); on the work, Case 171 (D 20.4.11.4).

6) What is the legal position of the second creditor after disposal of the property by the first creditor?

7) Explain the problem that Gaius puts and his decision.

8) Find a justification for this decision.

Answers:

1) If he has acted with fraudulent intent, he commits the *crimen stellionatus* ("crime of deceitful conduct"). The maximum penalty for this was *opus metalli* (forced labor in the mines). Members of higher social classes were condemned to *motio ab ordine* (loss of social rank) or *relegatio ad tempus* (banishment for a specified period). Alternatively (or even in addition to criminal process), the pledgor can be sued with the *actio pigneraticia contraria*.

2) (a) Pledge of the property to the degree its value exceeds the amount of the first pledge; (b) conditional pledge of the entire property in the future.

3) "2(a)" gives the second creditor a security interest, pursuant to which he can demand the property from the third party. "2(b)" gives the second creditor only an expectancy interest until the condition is satisfied (extinction of the security interest of the first creditor). This interest cannot be made effective in the interim.

4) On the basis of "2(b)" the security interest of the second creditor now encompasses the entire property. He acquires the *ius vendendi* ["right of sale"].

5) As in the answer to question "3", the second creditor acquires a security interest in the entire property with respect to his own claim. With respect to the first claim, which he has satisfied, he has only a right based on the payment, not a security interest in the property (security interests are only accessory, they do not arise from the transfer of a claim.)

6) The security interest of the second creditor is extinguished. (The buyer of the secured property does not assume the obligation.)

7) The security contract with the second creditor contains only the first provision (pledge of the property to the degree its value exceeds the amount of the first claim). The first creditor is satisfied by the debtor. Does the second creditor thereby acquire a security interest in the whole property, although this was not expressly agreed to? Gaius says he does (interpretation in favor of the second creditor).

8) Existing practice in contracts allows the imputation of the parties' consent.

Literature:

Kaser (Case 172) 182 ff.

CASE 174

D 20.4.9.3 (Africanus libro octavo quaestionum)

Titia praedium alienum Titio pignori dedit, post Maevio: deinde domina eius pignoris facta marito suo in dotem aestimatum dedit. si Titio soluta sit pecunia, non ideo magis Maevii pignus convalescere <Iuliano> placebat. tunc enim priore dimisso sequentis confirmatur pignus, cum res in bonis debitoris inveniatur: in proposito autem maritus emptoris loco est: atque ideo, quia neque tunc cum Maevio obligaretur neque cum Titio solveretur in bonis mulieris fuerit, nullum tempus inveniri; quo pignus Maevii convalescere possit, haec tamen ita, si bona fide in dotem aestimatum praedium maritus accepit, id est si ignoravit Maevio obligatum esse.

Translation: (Africanus in the eighth book of his *Legal Questions*)[54]

Titia pledged first to Titius and then to Maevius a plot of land belonging to another. Later she became the owner of the secured land and gave it to her husband at an assessed value in the dowry. <Julian> decided: if the debt to Titius was paid, the security interest of Maevius was still not cured. After discharge of the first creditor, the security interest of the subsequent creditor would be confirmed only if the property was in the bonitary ownership[55] of the debtor. Under the proposed facts, however, the husband was in the position of a buyer. Since the land was in the wife's bonitary ownership neither at the time of the pledge nor at the time of the payment to Titius, there was no point in time when the security interest of Maevius could have been cured. This opinion, however, assumes that the husband obtained the assessed property in the dowry *bona fide*: i.e., if he did not know that it was pledged to Maevius.

---

[54] On author and work, see Case 90 (D 41.4.11).

[55] Translator's note: "bonitary ownership" (Lat. *in bonis esse*) is a form of ownership that is recognized and protected by the praetorian law, though technically defective under the strict civil law, typically because *res mancipi* is involved and the transfer was effected by *traditio* rather than *mancipatio* or *in iure cessio* (see Introduction to Chapter III). After the requisite period of prescription runs, bonitary ownership ripens into civil law ownership.

Note on the Text:

On <*Iuliano*> *placebat* ("Julian decided"), see under Case 90.

3a. Cure of security interest

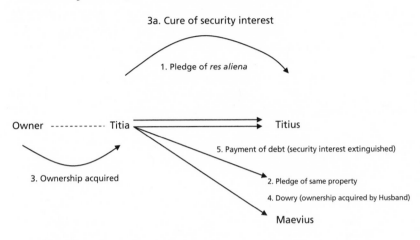

1. Pledge of *res aliena*

Owner - - - - - - - - - Titia ═══════════▶ Titius

5. Payment of debt (security interest extinguished)

3. Ownership acquired

2. Pledge of same property

4. Dowry (ownership acquired by Husband)

Maevius

Discussion Questions [with model answers]:

1) What is the legal position of Titius before Titia acquires ownership?
2) What legal position would Maevius have acquired under the contract of pledge, if Titia had been the owner from the beginning?
3) Was the security interest of Titius cured by the subsequent acquisition of ownership by Titia?
4) What would have been the effect on the legal position of Maevius, if Titia had paid Titius prior to establishing the dowry?
5) Why was the security interest of Maevius not cured?
6) What legal position did the husband attain? What would have been the effect of his *mala fides* on the legal position of Maevius?

Answers:

1) Titius has no security interest in a *res aliena pignori data* ["another's property given in pledge"]—*nemo plus iuris transferre potest* . . . ["No one can transfer a greater right than he himself possesses"]—but he does have claims arising from the contract of pledge (*actio pigneraticia contraria*, and possibly also an *actio de dolo* and *crimen stellionatus*).
2) A conditional security interest that becomes effective only when the first creditor is removed but otherwise creates no "anticipatory consequences" relating to the property (mere expectation interest).
3) Yes.

4) Emergence of an unconditional security interest senior to all others (curing and advancement), which can be enforced by means of the *actio pigneraticia utilis*.

5) Because at the time of the emergence of the (suspended, conditional) right of Maevius (i.e., when the first creditor's interest was extinguished) the property was not *in bonis* ["in the property"] of the woman who alienated it. During the period of Maevius' mere expectation interest, curing cannot take place.

6) The husband becomes the owner. The husband's bad faith, however, is no grounds for curing the security interest of Maevius. The latter could possibly proceed against the husband with an *actio de dolo*.

Literature:

Schanbacher (Case 160) 21 ff.

Wieling (co-editor) in Sturm, Fritz. *Römisches Recht*, WEX 12 (1977) 78 ff.

Ankum, Hans and Eric Pool. "*Rem in bonis esse* and *rem in bonis meam esse*: Traces of the Development of Roman Double Ownership," in *New Perspectives in the Roman Law of Property: Essays for Barry Nicholas*, P. Birks ed. Oxford: Oxford University Press, 1989, 5–42, at 19 ff.

Ankum (Case 130) 448, 453.

CASE 175

D 20.4.12 pr. (Marcianus libro singulari ad formulam hypothecariam)

Creditor qui prior hypothecam accepit sive possideat eam et alius vindicet hypothecaria actione, exceptio priori utilis est 'si non mihi ante pignori hypothecaeve nomine sit res obligata': sive alio possidente prior creditor vindicet hypothecaria actione et ille excipiat 'si non convenit, ut sibi res sit obligata,' hic in modum supra relatum replicabit. sed si cum alio possessore creditor secundus agat, recte aget et adiudicari ei poterit hypotheca, ut tamen prior cum eo agendo auferat ei rem.

Translation: (Marcian in his monograph *On the Action for Secured Property*)[56]

If the creditor, who has obtained an earlier security interest, possesses the property, and another person sues him with the *actio hypothecaria*, he can defend the suit with the defense "unless the property has been pledged to me earlier." If another person possesses the property and the senior creditor brings the *actio hypothecaria*, and if the defendant raises the defense "unless it was agreed that the property is pledged to me," the senior creditor will use a *replicatio* as related above. But if the second creditor sues a different possessor, he will sue rightfully, and the security will be awarded to him, subject, however, to the senior creditor's right to take the property in a suit with him.

Discussion Question:

Can the second creditor take the pledged property away from the debtor? Can he claim it from a third creditor? Can he get the property from another possessor?

Literature:

Wacke, A. "Prozeßformel und Beweislast im Pfandrechtsprätendentenstreit." *TR* 37 (1969) 395 ff.

---

[56] On author and work, see Case 158 (D 20.2.2).

CASE 176

D 20.1.10 (Ulpianus libro septuagesimo tertio ad edictum)

Si debitor res suas duobus simul pignori obligaverit ita, ut utrique in solidum obligatae essent, singuli in solidum adversus extraneos Serviana utentur: inter ipsos autem si quaestio moveatur, possidentis meliorem esse condicionem: dabitur enim possidenti haec exceptio: 'si non convenit, ut eadem res mihi quoque pignori esset.' si autem id actum fuerit, ut pro partibus res obligarentur, utilem actionem competere et inter ipsos et adversus extraneos, per quam dimidiam partis possessionem adprehendant singuli.

Translation: (Ulpian in the 73rd book of his *Commentary on the Praetor's Edict*)[57]

If the debtor has pledged his property to two creditors at the same time, such that the entirety of it is secured for each of them, each creditor may bring the *actio Serviana* against a third party for the whole property. If, however, a suit arises between the two creditors themselves, the position of the possessor is better, because the possessor will have the defense "unless it was agreed that the property is pledged to me." But if it was intended that the property be pledged proportionally, an *actio utilis* is available both between the creditors and against a third party, by which each creditor can obtain possession of half of it.

Note on the Text:

Roman pledge contracts note the applicable day and year, but not the time of day. "At the same time" therefore means "on the same day."

Discussion Question:

Analyze the decision. On the *melior condicio possidentis* ["the position of the possessor is better"], see Case 132 and Case 178a.

Literature:

Wacke (Case 175) 395 ff.
Schanbacher (Case 160) 64 ff.
Sirks, A.J.B. "La pluralité des créanciers hypothécaires sans rang en droit romain classique et Paul.5 ad Plaut. D.20.4.13." *Bulletino dell'Istituto di Diritto Romano* 89 (1986) 305–326.

---

[57] On author and work, see Case 11 (D 18.6.1.2).

CASE 177

D 20.4.9 pr. & 1 (Africanus libro octavo quaestionum)

(pr.) *Qui balneum ex calendis proximis conduxerat, pactus erat, ut homo Eros pignori locatori esset, donec mercedes solverentur: idem ante calendas Iulias eundem Erotem alii ob pecuniam creditam pignori dedit. consultus, an adversus hunc creditorem petentem Erotem locatorem praetor tueri deberet, respondit debere: licet enim eo tempore homo pignori datus esset, quo nondum quicquam pro conductione deberetur, quoniam tamen iam tunc in ea causa Eros esse coepisset, ut invito locatore ius pignoris in eo solvi non posset, potiorem eius causam habendam.*

(1) *Amplius etiam sub condicione creditorem tuendum putabat adversus eum, cui postea quicquam deberi coeperit, si modo non ea condicio sit, quae invito debitore impleri non possit.*

Translation: (Africanus in the eighth book of his *Legal Questions*)[58]

(pr.) Someone, who rented a bath from the start of the following month, agreed that the slave Eros would be pledged to the lessor until payment of the rent. The same man, before the beginning of July, pledged the same Eros to a third party for a loan. (Julian) was asked whether the Praetor should protect the lessor against the suit of the creditor, who was suing for Eros. He answered that the Praetor should protect him. For although the slave was given in pledge at a time when there was nothing yet owed on the rental contract, the legal position of the lessor was stronger, since Eros had already come into the matter such that the security interest in him could not be extinguished without the lessor's consent.

(1) Additionally, he thought that the creditor on the basis of his conditional claim, also must be protected against any later creditor, assuming the condition was not one that could not be fulfilled without the debtor's consent.

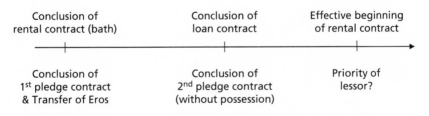

Conclusion of rental contract (bath)	Conclusion of loan contract	Effective beginning of rental contract
Conclusion of 1st pledge contract & Transfer of Eros	Conclusion of 2nd pledge contract (without possession)	Priority of lessor?

---

[58] On author and work, see Case 90 (D 41.4.11).

Discussion Question:

Do Julian and Africanus break the fundamental principle of the accessory nature of the security interest?

Literature:

> Schanbacher (Case 160) 56 ff.
> Wacke (Case 160) 456 ff.

CASE 178

D 20.4.11.2 (Gaius libro singulari de formula hypothecaria)

*Si colonus convenit, ut inducta in fundum illata ibi nata pignori essent, et antequam indu-
cat, alii rem hypothecae nomine obligaverit, tunc deinde eam in fundum induxerit, potior
erit, qui specialiter pure accepit, quia non ex conventione priori obligatur, sed ex eo quod
inducta res est, quod posterius factum est.*

Translation: (Gaius in his monograph *On the Action for Secured Property*)[59]

If a tenant has agreed that the property brought onto the farm and the fruits [of
that property] are given in security, and [then] he pledged one item to another
person before he brought it in, then the latter has the stronger right, the one who
obtained the property on the basis of an unconditional special pledge, since he
[the tenant] is obligated to the first creditor [regarding this property] not on the
basis of his agreement, but because of bringing it in, which is an action that took
place later.

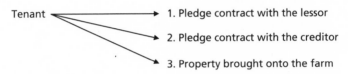

Tenant
1. Pledge contract with the lessor
2. Pledge contract with the creditor
3. Property brought onto the farm

Discussion Question:

Analyze the positions in connection with Afric. D 20.4.9. pr. and 1 (Case 177).

---

[59] On author, see Case 6 (D 41.1.9.6); on the work, see Case 171 (D 20.4.11.4).

CASE 178a

D 20.4.14 (Paulus libro quarto decimo ad Plautium)

Si non dominus duobus eandem rem diversis temporibus pigneraverit, prior potior est, quamvis, si a diversis non dominis pignus accipiamus, possessor melior sit.

Translation: (Paul in the 14th book of his *Commentary on Plautius*)[60]

If a non-owner at different times pledges the same property to two creditors, the first has the stronger position; but if we assume the pledges to be from different non-owners, then the possessor is in the better position.

Discussion Question:

Clarify the distinction Paul is making. In doing so refer back to Ulpian D 6.2.9.4 (Case 132) and Neratius D 19.1.31.2 (Case 133). For application of the rule *in pari causa melior est condicio possidentis* ["in a case of equal claims the position of the possessor is better"] also see Case 176.

Literature:

> Schanbacher (Case 160) 150 ff.
> Apathy (Case 130) 174 ff.
> Ankum/Pool (Case 174) 23.

---

[60] On Paul, see Case 1 (D 41.2.3.1); on his *libri ad Plautium*, see Case 130 (D 21.3.2).

b. Substitution

CASE 179

D 20.3.3 (Paulus libro tertio quaestionum)

Aristo Neratio Prisco scripsit: etiamsi ita contractum sit, ut antecedens dimitteretur, non aliter in ius pignoris succedet, nisi convenerit, ut sibi eadem res esset obligata: neque enim in ius primi succedere debet, qui ipse nihil convenit de pignore: quo casu emptoris causa melior efficietur. denique si antiquior creditor de pignore vendendo cum debitore pactum interposuit, posterior autem creditor de distrahendo omisit non per oblivionem, sed cum hoc ageretur, ne posset vendere, videamus, an dici possit huc usque transire ad eum ius prioris, ut distrahere pignus huic liceat. quod admittendum existimo: saepe enim quod quis ex sua persona non habet, hoc per extraneum habere potest.

Translation: (Paul in the third book of his *Legal Questions*)[61]

Aristo wrote [as follows] to Neratius Priscus: if it has been contractually agreed that the temporally earlier creditor is satisfied, the new creditor succeeds to his security interest only if it was agreed that the same property would be pledged to him. A person who has not himself concluded a security agreement cannot succeed to the right of the first creditor, which is why the buyer's position will be stronger.

If the earlier creditor had made an agreement with the debtor concerning sale of the security, but the later creditor omitted a term concerning sale, not through forgetfulness, but because it was foreseen that he could not sell, we must examine whether it can be said that the right of the earlier passes to the later creditor to the degree that he is authorized to sell. I think that must be recognized. For frequently it happens that one acquires from another a right that he does not have in his own person.

The Facts:

Debtor and new creditor agree to pay off the old creditor. The new creditor advances credit expressly to make this possible, but he omits from the agreement that he succeeds to the security interest of the satisfied prior creditor.

Discussion Questions [with model answers]:

1) How does one frame the legal issue?
2) Is the issue about the *ius offerendi* ["right of offering to pay the earlier creditor"]?
3) Try to justify Aristo's decision.
4) What is meant by *emptoris causa melior efficietur* ["the buyer's position will be stronger"]?

---

[61] On Paul, see Case 1 (D 41.2.3.1); on his *quaestiones*, see Case 161 (D 13.7.41); on Aristo, see Case 134 (D 8.5.8.5); on Neratius, see Case 73 (D 41.3.41).

5) Is it permissible to have a contract for a security interest that excludes the *ius vendendi* ["right of sale"]?
6) How would the jurist have decided if the *ius vendendi* had been forgotten in the security agreement?
7) What possibilities of satisfaction might a secured creditor have without the *ius vendendi*?

Answers:

1) Does the [subsequent] creditor acquire the security interest [of the former creditor]?
2) No, since that does not require the consent of the debtor.
3) Without a security agreement there is no security interest. The construction of *pignus tacitum* is an exception that is based on special justification.
4) If the debtor sells the property, the buyer acquires it without having to fear that he can be evicted by the secured creditor using the *actio Serviana* (Gai. D 20.6.7 pr.: *Si consenserit venditioni creditor, liberatur hypotheca* ["If the creditor consents to the sale, the security interest is removed"]).
5) Yes.
6) In the same way (i.e., permissibility of selling the security). Justification: *tacita conventio* ["tacit agreement"].
7) Forfeiture of the security; agreement to take the fruits; agreement that the debtor will sell the security. The so-called "protective" or "custodial" security confers no possibility of satisfaction.

Literature:

Kaser (Case 172) 174 ff.

CASE 180

D 20.4.12.9 (Marcianus libro singulari ad formulam hypothecariam)

Si tertius creditor pignora sua distrahi permittit ad hoc, ut priori pecunia soluta in aliud pignus priori succedat, successurum eum Papinianus libro undecimo responsorum scripsit. et omnino secundus creditor nihil aliud iuris habet, nisi ut solvat priori et loco eius succedat.

Translation: (Marcian in his monograph *On the Action for Secured Property*)[62]

If a creditor in the third rank agrees to the sale of his security in order for the first creditor to be paid off so that he [the third creditor] can succeed him [the first creditor] in another security agreement, he will succeed him, Papinian writes in the twelfth book of his *Legal Opinions*. And the creditor in the second rank will only have the right of satisfying the creditor in the first rank and succeeding to his place.

The Facts:

The owner pledges a piece of property to *Primus*, then to *Secundus*, and finally to *Tertius*, who already has other secured property from the same debtor. *Tertius* allows the owner to sell his security and to satisfy *Primus* with the proceeds, if he himself can succeed to the security rank of Primus.

Discussion Questions [with model answers]:

1) Why might the debtor be interested in this transaction?
2) How is the bar against advancement of the second creditor justified?
3) Assess the risk and the possible interest of *Tertius* in this transfer of secured debt.
4) Is it assumed that the claims of *Primus* and *Tertius* are equally high?
5) According to PS 2.13.8 [= *Pauli Sententiae* 2.13.8] the senior creditor can also exercise the *ius offerendi* against the junior creditor. What considerations might lead a first creditor to take this step?

Answers:

1) Consolidation of his debts; especially getting a more favorable loan from *Tertius* than *Primus* and *Secundus* gave; higher return than could be got from disposal of the secured property. (Secured creditors for the most part reserve the right to alienate the security by sale without a "guarantee of good title"—*pactum de non praestanda evictione*, which drives the price down considerably.)

---

[62] On author and work, see Case 158 (D 20.2.2); on Papinian, see Case 5 (D 18.1.74).

2) The possibility of transferring the debt should not be taken from the debtor. The rights of the junior pledgee seem to be sufficiently protected by the *ius offerendi*.

3) The risks are high: the creditor gives up his own security interest in the property to be sold and must count on the debtor actually using the proceeds for satisfaction of the first creditor. Possible motives of the creditor: concentration of his own security interest in a more valuable and more easily transferable security; act of friendship.

4) No, although the secured interest of *Tertius* is limited to the amount of the secured claim of *Primus*.

5) Perhaps he himself has a further junior interest, e.g., in the third rank, and he pays off the creditor in the second rank in order to avoid his exercise of the *ius offerendi*; investment loan; right of use; right of possession (in place of security without possession up to this point).

Literature:

Kaser (Case 172) 205 ff.

CASE 181

D 20.4.12.8 (Marcianus libro singulari ad formulam hypothecariam)

A Titio mutuatus pactus est cum illo, ut ei praedium suum pignori hypothecaeve esset: deinde mutuatus est pecuniam a Maevio et pactus est cum eo, ut, si Titio desierit prae-dium teneri, ei teneatur: tertius deinde aliquis dat mutuam pecuniam tibi, ut Titio sol-veres, et paciscitur tecum, ut idem praedium ei pignori hypothecaeve sit et locum eius subeat: num hic medius tertio potior est, qui pactus est, ut Titio soluta pecunia impleatur condicio, et tertius de sua neglegentia queri debeat? sed tamen et hic tertius creditor secundo praeferendus est.

Translation: (Marcian in his monograph *On the Action for Secured Property*)[63]

Someone who received a loan from Titius agreed that his land would be pledged to him. Thereafter he obtained a loan from Maevius and agreed with [Maevius] that the land would be security for his claim if it ceased to be secured in favor of Titius. Finally a third person gives you [i.e., the same debtor] a loan of money with which you satisfy Titius and agree that the same land should be pledged to [the third creditor] and that he should take the place of Titius. In this case is the middle creditor, who agreed that the condition [of his security interest] would be fulfilled if Titius were paid his money, in a better position than the third, and the third creditor has only his own negligence to complain about? But here too the third creditor is to be preferred over the second.

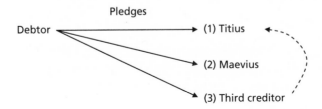

Discussion Question:

Write an analysis of this case, taking into account Marcian D 20.4.12.9 (Case 180).

Literature:

Kaser (Case 172) 204.

[63] On author and work, see Case 158 (D 20.2.2).

c. Statutory Security Rights and Priority Privileges

CASE 182

D 20.4.5 (Ulpianus libro tertio disputationum)

Interdum posterior potior est priori, ut puta si in rem istam conservandam impensum est quod sequens credidit: veluti si navis fuit obligata et ad armandam eam vel reficiendam ego credidero.

Translation: (Ulpian in the third book of his *Disputations*)[64]

Sometimes the later secured creditor is in a better position than the earlier: e.g., if the loan of the later creditor is used for preservation of the property, say, if a ship has been pledged and I obtain a loan for its arming or refitting.

Discussion Questions:

1) For this privilege of priority should the contracted purpose of the loan be decisive, or its actual use?
2) What is the justification for this privilege?
3) What are the dangers for the legal and economic order of breaking the temporal priority (on the rule *prior tempore potior iure,* see Case 171)?

---

[64] On Ulpian, see Case 11 (D 18.6.1.2); on his *Disputations,* see Case 44 (D 41.2.34 pr.).

CASE 183

D 27.9.3 pr. (Ulpianus libro trigesimo quinto ad edictum)

Sed si pecunia alterius pupilli alteri pupillo fundus sit comparatus isque pupillo vel minori traditus, an pignoris obligationem possit habere is, cuius pecunia fundus sit emptus? et magis est, ut salvum sit ius pignoris secundum constitutionem imperatoris nostri et divi patris eius ei pupillo, cuius pecunia comparatus est fundus.

Translation: (Ulpian in the 35th book of his *Commentary on the Praetor's Edict*)[65]

If with the money of one *pupillus* ["ward"] a piece of land is purchased for another *pupillus* and is transferred to the [latter] *pupillus* or *minor*, can the one whose money purchased the property have a security interest? And rather it must be decided, on the basis of a constitution of our emperor and his deified father, that the security interest of the *pupillus* whose money purchased the property is safe.

C 7.8.6 Imp. Alexander Augustus Auctori.

Si tutor tuus de pecunia tua servos emptos manumisit, quoniam huiusmodi servi sicut ceterae res pupillaribus pecuniis emptae iure pignoris ex constitutione divorum parentium meorum obligati sunt favore pupillorum, liberi facti non sunt.

Translation: (Caesar Alexander to Auctor)[66]

If your *tutor* ["guardian"] manumits slaves that were purchased with your money, they are not free, since slaves of this kind, just like other property that is purchased with a ward's money, are subject to a security interest in favor of the ward, pursuant to a constitution of my deified parents.

Discussion Questions:

1) Is the *tutor* the owner of the slaves that he wishes to manumit?
2) Try to formulate a precise rule based on the decision of Severus and Caracalla [i.e., "the deified parents"] and also a justification for it.
3) Why does Ulpian hesitate to use the decision of the two emperors in his case?
4) The security interest of the *pupillus* enjoys a privilege of priority. Make up a fact-situation that would serve as an example.

Literature:

Wagner, Herbert. *Die Entwicklung der Legalhypotheken am Schuldnervermögen im römischen Recht: bis zur Zeit Diokletians.* Wien: Böhlau, 1974, 74 ff.

---

[65] On author and work, see Case 11 (D 18.6.1.2).

[66] More than 400 constitutions of the Emperor Alexander Severus are preserved in the *Codex Iustinianus*. During his reign the jurists Ulpian (Case 1) and Paul (Case 11) held the office of Praetorian Prefect.

CASE 184

C 8.14.2 Imp. Antoninus A. Proculo

Certum est eius qui cum fisco contraxit bona veluti pignoris titulo obligari, quamvis specialiter id non exprimitur.

Translation: (Emperor Antoninus to A. Proculus, 214 CE)[67]

It is certain that the property of the person who has contracted with the fisc is subject to an obligation like a security interest, even if this has not been specifically expressed.

Note on the Text:

On *certum est* ("it is certain"), see on Case 27.

Discussion Question:

Referring also to Ulp. D 49.14.28 (Case 185), try to clarify the justification, type, and rank of the security interest in favor of the fisc.

Literature:

Wagner (Case 183) 76 ff.
Wieling Hans-Josef. "Privilegium fisci, praediatura und Protopraxie." *ZRG* 106 (1989) 404–433, at 417 ff.

---

[67] Two hundred constitutions of the Emperor Caracalla (211–217 CE) are preserved in the *Codex Iustinianus*. Possibly the jurist Callistratus (see Case 35) was at the head of his chancellery for rescripts as *magister libellorum* ["Master of Petitions"].

CASE 185

D 49.14.28 (Ulpianus libro tertio disputationum)

Si qui mihi obligaverat quae habet habiturusque esset cum fisco contraxerit, sciendum est in re postea adquisita fiscum potiorem esse debere Papinianum respondisse: quod et constitutum est. praevenit enim causam pignoris fiscus.

Translation: (Ulpian in the third book of his *Disputations*)[68]

If someone, who has pledged to me "what he has and will have in the future," contracts with the fisc, one must recognize that Papinian has issued an opinion that the fisc should have the stronger right in property acquired thereafter. That is also established by imperial constitution. For the fisc takes precedence in the establishment of security.

Discussion Questions:

1) At what point in time does the general pledge of present and future property create a secured interest in the property of the goods of the debtor that are still not acquired? See on this question Case 159b.
2) Is the principle *prior tempore* ["first in time is stronger in right"] violated by Papinian's decision? Cf. on this question C 8.14.2 (Case 184).
3) Does a general pledge block the alienation of individual items by the debtor without the creditor's consent? Cf. Paul D 47.2.67 pr. (Case 164).

Literature:

Wagner (Case 183) 180 ff.
Wieling (Case 184) 426 ff.

---

[68] On Ulpian, see Case 11 (D 18.6.1.2). On his *Disputations,* see Case 44 (D 41.2.34 pr.). On Papinian, see Case 5 (D 18.2.74).

APPENDIX

Case Analysis of D 41.1.5.1 (Case 8)

(limited to the issue of acquiring possession)

I. Facts:

A hunter has so wounded a wild animal that it can be caught, and he begins to pursue the animal.

II. Legal Issue:

Has the hunter already acquired possession (and therewith also ownership) of the animal by wounding and following it?

III. Discussion:

The treatment of the legal question is a subject of juristic controversy: Trebatius decides for immediate possession and ownership. Gaius maintains the opposite view, which he believes is consistent with established doctrine (*plerique . . . putaverunt*). He considers it more correct (*verius est*) that the acquisition first happens with the grasping or catching of the animal.

I. Concerning the Opinion of Trebatius

Trebatius supports the interpretation that the wounding of the animal, such that it becomes possible to catch it, constitutes a sufficient physical relationship for the acquisition of possession. By following the animal, this physical relationship creates a legal right.

Trebatius gives no explicit reasoning for his decision. From the text it is clear that he had before him a case in which a hunter was on the point of a seemingly certain successful chase, when another person took the wounded animal for himself, before the hunter could grab it. Trebatius might have argued that touching or grasping the property is not required for acquiring possession if, according to established doctrine, the property is already in the acquirer's sphere of control, or if there is no essential hindrance in the way of his getting control. The animal is so wounded that it can be caught: i.e., it is so weakened and limited in its freedom of movement that it cannot escape the hunter by its own power. In the ordinary course of events the acquirer will grasp it within a short time. Since the capture is for practical purposes unavoidable, the hunter has already acquired possession by means of the wounding and pursuit.

If one tries to find support for the interpretation of Trebatius in other Roman jurists, s/he should try to refer to a series of case decisions in which Roman jurists acknowledge possession without the need for touching (or grasping) the property.

So, for example, Celsus in D 41.2.18.2 (Case 2) is on point: i.e., the transferor can deliver possession of a neighboring plot of land by pointing it out from a tower belonging to the transferee, without the transferee having to step on the land. Another example of this kind of acquisition of possession is in the statement of Javolenus that the creditor takes possession of money which the debtor sets down before his eyes and at his command (Case 3: D 46.3.7.9). The jurist defines this event as *traditio longa manu* ["delivery with a long hand"]. Finally, Paul in D 41.2.1.21 (Case 4) makes a general formulation that agreement in the presence of the property is sufficient for transferring possession; touching or grasping the property is not necessary. Here, however, one must note that in these cases derivative possession is involved, not original possession, as in D 41.1.5.1 [Case 8]. With derivative possession the previous possessor is transferring an established condition of possession. With the original possession of the hunter, however, there is a situation in which legitimate claimants stand in a rival relationship with the property. The criterion that one must consider in the case of a rival claimant will be to focus on determining the necessary degree of physical relationship. For original possession of a wild animal, therefore, a stricter measure will be used, one that cannot be drawn from cases of derivative possession.

The case that is closest in facts and decision to the present case is that of the boar, decided by Proculus at D 41.1.55 (Case 9). In that case, a wild boar has been caught in a snare that was set out. Proculus lets the person who set the snare, according to the circumstances, obtain possession of the boar even before actually grasping it. For his decision it is crucial whether one can infer that the boar had come into the *potestas* (sphere of control) of the person who laid the snare. This will be the situation, if the boar is firmly caught and cannot free itself from the snare, and if the snare in addition has been put in a place where the interference of another person is not to be expected.

Still, it remains questionable whether Proculus would have decided that the wounded animal was in the *potestas* of the pursuing hunter, like the boar in the snare of the snare-setter.

II. Concerning the Opinion of Gaius

The expounders of the dominant doctrine (*plerique*), whom Gaius joins, set forth stricter requirements of physical relationship than does Trebatius. They feel that in the course of the hunter's pursuit much can happen (*multa accidere possunt*) that would block the capture. Therefore they do not grant the hunter possession through wounding and pursuit of the animal, until the animal is actually caught.

What might Gaius have understood with the reasoning: *quia multa accidere possunt* ["because much can happen"]? For one thing, the animal might possibly escape the grasp of the pursuer by fleeing into impassable terrain (a hole, thicket, etc.). For another, a different person might grab it before the pursuer reached it. Only when the animal has been caught or killed is it certain who actually controls it.

This interpretation can also be supported by the boar-case of Proculus: if the boar could free itself from the snare by more struggle, or the snare was placed where the intervention of another person is to be imagined, say on public land or on private land without the owner's consent, Proculus does not let the snare-setter acquire possession.

The Digest text at D 41.2.33 (Case 100) requires an especially close physical relationship for acquiring possession of buried treasure-trove. Paul there reproduces the opinion of Sabinus, who thinks a landowner cannot acquire possession of buried treasure-trove before he moves it; previously he does not have it in his control (*custodia*), even though it was buried on his land.

The decisional rationale of Gaius and the dominant doctrine (*quia multa accidere possunt*) can also be supported by the principle that Javolenus formulates at D 41.2.2.2 (Case 55): expectation of duration is a prerequisite for acquiring possession. The person who runs the risk that the property will soon be outside of his control will not be deemed a possessor.

III. Considerations of Legal Policy

When Trebatius recognizes possession and ownership for the hunter who has wounded an animal so that it can be caught, he is rewarding efforts undertaken to bring the goods of untamed nature to human consumption. Rival efforts from this time forward can be resisted as impermissible invasions of existing rights.

Gaius and the dominant doctrine hinder the premature segregation of goods, which are available for appropriation by anyone (*res nullius* ["property of no one"], like game and fish), by means of pursuits leading to consequences that are not unambiguously foreseeable. Only the ultimately successful inclusion of this property in a private sphere of control will bring an end to legitimate rivalry for their acquisition.

An issue that is important in itself is not expressly considered by the Roman jurists: namely, the recognizability of the award of the property to the first pursuer (hunter, snare-setter), something that properly should hinder the second pursuer from interfering with the claims of the first (publicity function of possession, assurance of the good faith of second pursuer).

The solution of Trebatius will essentially tend to prevent conflict, as will that of Gaius. For this purpose the most important aspect of any rule is its clarity. Gaius's conception allows easier formulation of an unambiguous rule than does that of Trebatius.

It could be argued that Gaius gives insufficient protection to the legal right of the hunter (and Proculus to the right of the snare-setter), because he puts too much weight on the chance actions of a third party, rather than preventing these actions by force of law, as soon as a clearly recognizable and fundamentally foreseeable acquisition of the pursued animal is before the hunter (*ita vulnerata . . . ut capi possit* ["so wounded . . . as to be able to be captured"]).

Case Analysis of D 41.2.13 pr. (Case 47)

I. The Facts:

Stones that sank in the Tiber after a shipwreck are raised again after the passage of some time.

II. Legal Issue:

Was possession and ownership of the stones lost when they sank?

III. Decision:

According to the interpretation of Ulpian, the possession is lost, but the ownership remains intact. The solution of Pomponius is missing: clearly it was removed by the compilers. The emphasis of Ulpian's formulation (*ego . . . puto*) allows the inference that he held a different opinion from Pomponius. If Ulpian's remark *nec est simile fugitivo* ["it is not like a fugitive slave"] refers to the argument of Pomponius, the latter would have held in favor of the retention of both possession and ownership of the stones (something like: "If one can retain valid possession in a *servus fugitivus*, then he can do the same of stones in the Tiber"). Less likely is the view that Pomponius would have argued for loss of both possession and ownership—on this question see the observations of Ulpian/Pomponius at D 41.1.44 (wolves steal swine: Case 96). In any event, if there were no prospect of recovery (depth of the Tiber, inadequate technology, etc.), the ownership could also be extinguished because of "total loss of the property."

IV. Reason for the Decision:

The criterion for retention and loss of possession in movables is fundamentally *custodia*, see Nerva in Paulus at D 41.2.3.13 (Case 46). Stones in the Tiber, in Ulpian's opinion, have been removed from this *custodia* (possessor's sphere of control); the possession of them is lost. By Ulpian's reckoning, in this case there is clearly no longer a sufficient physical relationship, although there is scarcely any need to consider the possible actions of other persons. The possession would, however, have remained intact, if the owner had placed a guard near the place of the accident.

Retention of possession *solo animo* ("by intent alone") in a fugitive slave, on the other hand, is, according to the prevailing doctrine, an exception: cf. Paul at D 41.2.1.14 (Case 31) and D 41.2.3.13 (Case 46). Ulpian emphasizes the exceptional character of this ruling, which he does not allow to extend to stones in the Tiber. In a fugitive slave, the possession must remain so that he cannot, as it were, "steal himself." Because of their intelligence, slaves can escape the control of their *dominus* more easily than other property. Therefore this [i.e., the master's control] seems to be in special need of protection. Slaves are especially valuable in economic terms. They can acquire possession [of other property] for their *dominus*.

Possession of the slave, however, is a precondition of possession through the slave (Case 31). In addition to legal policy considerations of this kind, Ulpian would also have been able to make use of an argument that was more strongly influenced by legal dogma: *custodia* is not a suitable criterion of possession for slaves. Slaves cannot be constantly watched, because they would otherwise fail to serve most of the purposes for which they are used.

From Ulpian's report it can be inferred that Pomponius used an *argumentum a maiore ad minus* ["argument from the greater to the lesser"]: "If possession of a fugitive slave remains intact, then possession of stones in the Tiber does so even more (stones certainly cannot run off, but only remain until they are raised again)." In any event, Pomponius could also have argued that the *custodia* of the stones in the Tiber had not ended, as long as no one else had raised them—cf. the decision of Papinian at D 41.2.44 pr. (Case 47a), who, in reference to money that someone had buried in (his own or another's) land, kept the possession intact.

Loss of ownership of the stones would be understood to have occurred, if the owner had no expectation of getting them back again. In such a case, just as with complete destruction, one might speak of the total loss of the property. So, for example, of wild animals that escape, or of a silver vase thrown into the deep ocean, ownership is lost along with possession (see Gaius D 41.1.5.1 [Case 8] and Proculus D 41.1.55 [Case 9]).

That the stones, as stated in the facts, were actually raised, does not *per se* exclude the possibility that ownership was lost. Probably the case was put to the jurists because someone else, not the owner, raised them and believed he had thereby acquired ownership of *res nullius*. The jurist could have looked to whether loss of the property was to be understood according to general practice. (Cf. on this question the observations of Pomponius and Ulpian in D 41.1.44 [Case 96].) If he found an affirmative answer to this question, he could consider the ownership to be extinguished. Then the possessor, who recovered them contrary to any expectation, thereby also acquired original ownership of them.

Ulpian (and probably Pomponius too) clearly proceeded from the assumption that the Tiber was so shallow that in normal circumstances the lost stones could be recovered. Therefore the ownership remained intact.

Index of Sources

I. Pre-Justinianic Sources

Gai Institutiones	Case	Pauli Sententiae	Case
2.73	106	5.2.2	33
2.78	111		
2.94	21		
2.95	32		

II. Justinianic Sources

Digesta	Case	Digesta	Case
4.3.31	66	8.1.8 pr.	145
5.3.40 pr.	127	8.2.6	147
6.1.3.2	116	8.2.7	148
6.1.5 pr.	115	8.3.5.1	143
6.1.5.1	118	8.3.11	146
6.1.7	123	8.5.6.2	142
6.1.9	121	8.5.8.5	134
6.1.15.3	127	8.5.17.2	135
6.1.16.1	126	12.1.9.9	13
6.1.17 pr.	128	12.1.18 pr.	71
6.1.23.3	112	13.7.3	165
6.1.23.5	113	13.7.4	169
6.1.27.1	122	13.7.9 pr.	161a
6.1.33	125	13.7.94	161a
6.1.37	129	13.7.18.3	170a
6.1.38	107	13.7.41	161
6.1.59	109	18.1.74	5
6.1.67	101	18.6.1.2	11
6.1.77	20	18.6.15(14).1	7
6.1.79	125	19.1.31.2	133
6.2.9.1	14	19.2.19.4	109
6.2.9.4	132	19.2.60.1	60
7.1.1	149	20.1.6	159a
7.1.12.2	150	20.1.7	159a
7.1.15.4	151	20.1.10	176
7.1.68 pr.	149	20.1.15.2	173
7.1.68.1	149	20.1.16.9	168
7.1.68.2	149	20.1.19	166

(Continued)

(Continued)

II. Justinianic Sources (Continued)

Digesta	Case	Digesta	Case
43.24.7.5	138	47.2.43.8	98
43.24.7.6	138	47.2.43.9	98
43.24.7.7	138	47.2.67(66) pr.	164
43.24.11 pr.	141	49.14.28	185
43.24.20.1	136	50.16.109	80
43.24.22.1	139	50.17.54	67
43.24.22.3	140	50.17.131	128
43.32.1 pr.	159	*Codex*	
44.2.17	124	7.8.6	183
44.4.4.32	131	8.14.2	184
46.3.78	119	*Institutiones*	
46.3.79	3	2.1.34	112
47.2.14.17	38	2.9.5	36

III. Modern Statutes

ABGB (Austrian Civil Code)

Section	Case	Section	Case
§ 151 (3)	22	§ 366	131
§ 297	106	§ 367	67
§ 309	1	§ 369	121
§ 310	22	§ 370	119
§ 312	1	§ 371	119
§ 319	17	§ 372	132
§ 326	80	§ 374	132
§ 330	102	§ 375	121
§ 331	107	§ 376	123
§ 332	107	§ 377	123
§ 339	56	§ 378	123
§ 344	57	§ 380	69
§ 345	56	§ 381	94
§ 346	56	§ 384	94
§ 349	39	§ 386	97
§ 364	134	§ 390	98
§ 391	98	§ 463	168

(Continued)

III. Modern Statutes (Continued)

ABGB (Austrian Civil Code)

BGB (German Civil Code)

BGB (German Civil Code) (Continued)

Section	Case	Section	Case
§ 965 I	98	§ 1090 I	152
§ 973 I	98	§ 1105 I	142
§ 984	100	§ 1228	168
§ 985	121	§ 1229	168
§ 1004	134	§ 1230	167
§ 1018	142	§ 1252	166
§ 1019	143		

ZGB (Swiss Civil Code)

Section	Case	Section	Case
Art. 718	94	Art. 727	110
Art. 719	94	Art. 884	160
Art. 720/1	98	Art. 889	166
Art. 722/1 and 2	98	Art. 890	161a
Art. 723	100	Art. 891/1	168
Art. 724	100	Art. 894	168
Art. 726	120		

OR (Swiss Law of Obligations)

Section	Case	Section	Case
Art. 272/1	156	Art. 7274/1	156

Code Civil (French Civil Code)

Section	Case
Art. 1138	69

IV. Roman Legal Maxims

	Case		Case
Accessio cedit principali	110	Nemo plus iuris transferre potest quam ipse habet	67
Actori incumbit probatio	132	Nemo sibi ipse causam possessionis mutare potest	15–17
Casum sentit dominus	127	Numquam nuda traditio transfert dominium	69

(Continued)

IV. Roman Legal Maxims (Continued)

V. Argumentational Principles and Strategies in Roman Jurists

Translator's Glossary of Latin Terms and Phrases

Latin terms and phrases used in this casebook have normally been translated wherever first encountered. If re-used, however, the same terms are not always re-translated. This glossary provides definitions of all words and phrases that (1) occur more than once in the casebook, and (2) have been left undefined in one or more of those occurrences. A word of caution: Legal terms and phrases may have multiple meanings that vary by context or that are nuanced in ways that cannot be fully explained in a brief definition. Fuller definitions of the Roman legal concepts expressed by Latin terms of art may be found in Adolf Berger, *Encyclopedic Dictionary of Roman Law*, Philadelphia: American Philosophical Society, 1953 (1980), on which many of the glosses in the following entries have relied.

Accessio cedit principali. "[The] accession yields to [the] principal"—i.e., where two pieces of property are combined into one, the combined property retains the identity of the more important component while the identity of the accessory element is extinguished.

Accipiendum est; acceptum est. "It must be accepted"; "it has been accepted."

Actio. "Action"; "lawsuit."

Actio ad exhibendum. "Action to compel production [of property]"; an *in personam* action to compel the defendant to produce in court property of contested ownership that is in his possession.

Actio communi dividundo. "Action for dividing common property"—i.e., an *in rem* partition action for property that is co-owned.

Actio contraria pigneraticia (or actio pigneraticia contraria). "Reverse action on the pledge"; an *in rem* or *in personam* action by a creditor for recovery of possession of property held by a debtor, or for damages to the property caused by the fault of the debtor.

Actio de dolo. "Action concerning deceit." An *in personam* action seeking damages for fraudulent conduct by the defendant. Also called *actio doli*.

Actio de tigno iuncto. "Action concerning the joining of timber"; an *in personam* action for recovery of twice the value of building materials that have been fraudulently appropriated into another's structure.

Actio furti. "Action for theft"; an *in personam* private law action, somewhat comparable to the common law tort of conversion, although carrying a penalty of twice (or even four times, if "manifest") the value of the stolen property.

Actio hypothecaria. "Action on a hypothec"; an *in rem* action by a creditor for possession of property secured by hypothec and currently in the possession of the debtor. Cf. *actio Serviana*.

Actio in factum. "Action [based] on what was done"; an *in personam* action based on facts that, if proven, would give rise to recovery, as opposed to an action based on a statutory definition. See fn. under Case 9.

Actio in personam. "Action against a person"; an action for money damages or specific performance based on an obligation incurred by the defendant. Also called an *actio personalis*. Cf. *actio in rem*.

Actio in rem. "Action against property"; an action to recover the possession or use of property currently in the possession of the defendant. Cf. *actio in personam.*

Actio negatoria. "Action to deny"; an *in rem* action for a judicial declaration denying the defendant's interest in a servitude (including the personal servitudes of use and usufruct).

Actio pigneraticia. "Action on a pledge"; an *in rem* or *in personam* action brought by a debtor for recovery of possession of secured property held by a creditor, or for damage or loss of the property due to the fault of the creditor. Cf. *actio contraria pigneraticia.*

Actio pigneraticia utilis. "Policy action on the pledge"; see *actio utilis.*

Actio Publiciana. "Publician Action"; an action that was first granted by the Praetor Publicius and retained his name thereafter. It was an action *in rem* for recovery of property by a dispossessed plaintiff who would have usucapted the property but for the dispossession. It was analogous to a *vindicatio,* except that the plaintiff was not yet technically the legal (as opposed to bonitary) owner of the property in dispute.

Actio Serviana. "Servian action"; an *in rem* action originally based on a lessor's security interest that had been created by a lessee's tacit pledge of movables that had been and would be brought onto the leased premises. The same action was later made available to any secured creditor with respect to hypothecated property. Cf. the *actio hypothecaria.*

Actio utilis. Lit. "useful action"; an action arising from facts that are different from but similar to those normally covered by an otherwise recognized cause of action. The action is termed "useful," because judicial recognition of it is motivated by considerations of practical utility (*utilitas*). In English translation the *actio utilis* is sometimes called a "policy action" (i.e., justified by public policy) or an "analogous action" (i.e., analogous to an otherwise recognized cause of action).

Actori incumbit probatio. "The [burden of] proof rests with the Plaintiff."

Actus. "Driving" or "right of driving" [animals or vehicles over the land of another]; one of the right of use that might be included within a servitude. The word *actus* also means simply an "act."

Adsessor. "Legal advisor" (or one of a panel of legal advisors) who assists a judicial magistrate in the conduct of trials and other legal process.

Aequitas; aequum esse. "Fairness; to be fair."

Animo enim coepit possidere. "For s/he has begun to possess with intent."

Animo nostro corpore alieno. "With our intent [but] another's body."

Animus possidendi. "Intention of possessing."

Animus/animo. "Intent/with intent."

Apiscimur possessionem corpore et animo, neque per se animo aut per se corpore. "We acquire possession with body and intent, not with intent by itself or with body by itself."

Aquae ductus. "Transport" or "drawing of water"; aqueduct.

Argumentum ad absurdum. "Argument [that leads] to absurdity."

Auctor. "Approver, person who authorizes."

Auctoritas tutoris. "Authorization given by the guardian."

Benignitas. "Good will, benevolence"; an equitable factor that can be taken into account in judicial decisionmaking, where strict application of the law is deemed to be too harsh.

Bona fide serviens. [Mistakenly] "serving as a slave" to someone who believes "in good faith" that the person serving is a slave.

Bona fides. "Good faith."

Bona inducta et illata . . . invecta. "Goods led in and brought in . . . carried in"; typically referring to the movable property of a lessee. When brought onto the leased premises, such property becomes security for the lessee's rental payments to the lessor.

Bona; in bonis. "Goods/property"; "among [one's] goods". The phrase *in bonis* is used to refer to "bonitary ownership" as opposed to *in dominio*, which means in civil law ownership. Bonitary ownership is technically defective until it ripens into civil law ownership by usucapion.

Bonus vir; bonus iudex; bonus pater familias. "Good man"; "good judge"; "good head of the family"; refers to an objective behavioral standard associated with such individuals.

Casum sentit dominus. "The owner feels the loss."

Causa. "Cause, case, reason, legal basis."

Causa detentionis. "Cause/reason for holding [property]."

Causa possessionis. "Cause of possession"; legal grounds for possession.

Causa traditionis. "Cause of delivery"; legal grounds for delivery.

Cautio damni infecti. An enforceable guarantee that no damage will be caused.

Certum est. "It is certain."

Clam; clam factum. "Secretly", "secretly done."

Clausula arbitraria. "Clause pertaining to a factual issue requiring determination"; part of a trial formula that refers to a contingent issue of fact that may need to be resolved.

Colonus. "Tenant farmer."

Commodatum. A gratuitous loan of movable property that transfers neither possession nor ownership.

Condictio. An *in personam* action for damages or specific performance. Cf. *actio in personam*.

Confusio. "Intermingling"; as used in property law it refers to the combination of like movables belonging to two different owners into an undifferentiated whole that is owned by both.

Consilium; consilia. "Advice or council; advisory councils."

Constat. "It is established that, there is agreement that . . . ."

Constitutum possessorium. "Possessory agreement."

Corpore et animo. Lit. "with body and with mind"; physically and with intent.

Corpus; corpore. "body, with body"; physical form/physically.

Corpus Juris Civilis. "Body of Civil Law"; the post-antique label that refers collectively to the Justinianic legislation comprised of the *Institutes*, *Digest*, *Codex*, and *Novels*.

Crimen stellionatus. "Crime of cheating/fraud/deception." Cf. the private *actio de dolo*.

Culpa. "Fault."

Curator. Person charged with administering the affairs of a minor over the age of puberty or of someone otherwise deemed to be legally incompetent. The term is also used more generally in various non-legal contexts.

Custodia. "Custody, safekeeping"; sphere of control.

Depositum. "Deposit" of property with someone other than the owner; the contract regulating such a deposit. *Depositum* is similar to common law "bailment."

Detentor. "Holder" of property. Someone who has physical control but not legal possession of the property. Also called a *naturalis possessor*.

Dolus/dolus malus. "Fraud, deceit."

Dominium. "Ownership."

Dominus. "Owner."

Eo iure utimur. "We use this rule"; referring to a well established rule of law.

Error facti. "Error of fact."

Error iuris. "Error of law."

Exceptio (pl. exceptiones). Lit. an "exception" to a rule that is otherwise applicable—the portion of a formula that recognizes applicable elements of an affirmative defense; the affirmative defense itself.

Exceptio doli. Affirmative defense based on fraudulent conduct of the Plaintiff.

Exceptio (iusti) dominii. "Affirmative defense of (legitimate) ownership."

Exceptio in factum. Affirmative defense based on the conduct of the Plaintiff under the facts assumed.

Exceptio rei iudicatae vel in iudicium deductae. Affirmative defense of *res judicata* or *lis pendens*.

Exceptio rei venditae et traditae. "Affirmative defense that the property was sold and delivered."

Exceptio vitiosae possessionis. "Affirmative defense of defective possession."

Familia. "Family," including slaves.

Favor negotii. A judicial policy that is sensitive to the interests of commercial activity.

Fictus possessor. "Fictive possessor."

Filius. "Son."

Fraus. "Fraud."

Fructus percepti. "Fruits" that have been "separated, gathered."

Fructus percipiendi. "Gathering" (or separation) of fruits."

Fundus. "Farm, farmstead."

Furiosus. "Insane person."

Homo liber bona fide serviens. "Free man [mistakenly] serving as a slave" to someone who believes "in good faith" that the person serving is a slave.

Hyperocha. Surplus from sale of secured property after the debt has been satisfied from the sale proceeds. Also called *superfluum*.

Hypotheca. "Hypothec"; a security interest in property that is to remain in the possession of the debtor. Cf. *pignus*.

Implantatio. "Planting."

Impubes. "A youth [between the ages of 7 and 14]." See chart at Case 86.

Inducta et illata. See *bona inducta et illata*.

In bonis. See *bona*.

In conspectu. "In view."

In factum. See *actio in factum*.

In iure cessio. "Surrender in law"; a formal procedure by which transfer of ownership to property, or other change of legal condition, was effected in the court of a competent magistrate.

In maiore minus inest. "The lesser is included in the greater."

In personam. See *actio in personam*.

In potestate. "In [the] power [of another]." See *potestas*.

In rem. See *actio in rem*.

Infans. Lit. "infant"; a minor below the age of 7. See chart at case 86.

Intellegi. "To be understood as . . ."

Intentio. "Charge." The portion of a formula that summarizes the factual issue underlying the cause of action.

Interdictum. A standardized judicial order issued by a competent magistrate in response to a petitioner's request. Interdicts forbid or require the performance of some action by the party so ordered.

Interdictum de migrando. "Interdict concerning a change of abode"; a judicial order requiring a landlord to return possession of movables that have been distrained under the pretext of non-payment of rent.

Interdictum de vi armata. "Interdict concerning armed force"; a judicial order granting re-possession of immovable property from which the petitioner has been ousted by armed force. Cf. *interdictum unde vi*.

Interdictum quod vi aut clam. "Interdict [of the form] 'what by force or stealth'"; a judicial order compelling restitution for some invasion of the petitioner's interest in immovable property.

Interdictum unde vi. "Interdict [of the form] 'whence by force'"—a judicial order compelling the restoration of possession of immovable property from which the petitioner has been ousted by force. Cf. *interdictum de vi armata*.

Interdictum uti possidetis. "Interdict [of the form] 'since you possess'"—a judicial order forbidding the use of force to dispossess the party who is deemed to be the last fault-free possessor.

Interdictum utrubi. "Interdict [of the form] 'with whichever of the two parties'"; a judicial order protecting the possession of movable property by whichever of the two litigants held it for the longer period within the previous 12 months.

Invecta et illata. See *bona inducta et illata*.

Iter. Lit. "way, path"; an easement appurtenant to a dominant tenement, consisting of the right to walk or ride across a portion of the servient tenement. The easement did not include the right of other uses, such as driving animals across the servient tenement. Cf. *via*.

Iudex. Lit. "judge"; in private law, typically referring to an individual selected by the parties and appointed by a magistrate to try the facts of a case.

Ius civile. "Civil law"; commonly used to refer collectively to Roman civil law arising from sources other than the edicts of magistrates. The *ius civile* consists primarily of substantive private law. Cf. *ius honorarium*.

Ius gentium. "Law of nations/peoples"; a notional term referring to rules or doctrines that are presumptively recognized by all peoples' legal systems.

Ius honorarium. "Honorary law"; refers generically to the primarily procedural law developed by competent magistrates (the magistracies being collectively called "honors") and promulgated through their edicts. The most important source of honorary law was the edict of the magistrate called the "Urban Praetor," which itself is called *ius praetorianum*.

Ius offerendi (et succedendi). "Right of offering (and succeeding to)"; the right of (typically) a junior secured creditor to pay off a senior creditor secured by the same property and thereby promote the junior creditor's security interest.

Ius respondendi. "Right of giving [legal] responses"; a license granted by an emperor to issue presumptively authoritative opinions on issues of law.

Ius tollendi. "Right of removal"; typically in reference to building materials.

Ius vendendi. "Right of sale."

Ius. "Right, law."

Ius commune. Lit. "common law"; the continental European tradition of Roman-based civil law; not to be confused with the English "common law."

Iusta causa. "Just cause"; legitimate reason.

Iusta possessio. "Legitimate/valid possession."

Leges. "Statutes."

Lex Atinia. "Atinian Statute"; a statute that was promulgated by a certain Atinius and retained his name in the title. The statute established that stolen property could not be usucapted unless it had first returned to the control of the owner.

Litis aestimatio. A judicial determination of the money value of contested property.

Litis contestatio. "Joinder of issue."

Longa manu. See *traditio longa manu*.

Mala fides; mala fide. "Bad faith, with bad faith."

Mancipatio. "Mancipation"; a formalized procedure that transfers ownership of *res mancipi*.

Mancipium. An archaic form of ownership that applied to certain kinds of property. See *res mancipi*.

Mandatum. Lit. "mandate"; a gratuitous contract of agency obliging the agent ("mandatary") to perform a specified task for his principal ("mandator").

Mandatarius. "Mandatary"; a kind of agent. See *mandatum*.

Materia. "Material"; typically in reference to building materials.

Media sententia. "Middle opinion."

Melius est. "It is better."

Minor. Lit. "minor"; a person between the ages of 14 and 25. See Case 86.

Mutuum, mutua. "Loan, loans" of money or other fungible property. *Mutuum* transfers ownership of the property to the recipient. Cf. *commodatum*.

Naturalis possessio. "Natural possession"; actual holding, detention. Also called *detentio*.

Naturalis possessor. "Natural possessor"; holder, detentor.

Ne bis in idem. "Not twice on the same matter."

Nemo plus iuris transferre potest quam ipse habet. "No one can transfer more right than he himself has."

Nemo sibi ipse causam possessionis mutare potest. "No one can [unilaterally] change to his own benefit the legal basis of his possession."

Occupatio. "Occupation"; taking possession and ownership of ownerless property.

Oculis et affectu. "With [one's] eyes and expression."

Opus in solo factum. "Work done on the soil/ground."

Pactum de distrahendo. "Agreement about withdrawal/sale [of the security]."

Pater familias. "Father of the family"; legal head of the household.

Peculium. A sum of money or other property that is granted to a son-in-power or to a slave for the recipient's more-or-less discretionary use and management, though with the notional purpose of benefiting the father or master. Although technically still owned by the latter, *peculium* constitutes a separate property and is subject to different legal treatment.

Per extraneam personam nobis adquiri non posse. "[Possession] cannot be acquired through another person."

Periculum est emptoris. "The buyer has the risk [of loss]."

Periculum. "Risk [of loss]."

Persona. "Person."

Pignoris causa indivisa est. "The security interest is indivisible."

Pignus. "Pledge"; a security interest in property that is to be placed in the possession of the creditor; the pledged property itself. Cf. *hypotheca*.

Pignus tacitum. "Silent pledge"; an implied (constructive) security interest.

Plerique. "Many [jurists], most [jurists]."

Plus est in re quam in existimatione. "There is more [significance] in the [objective] fact than in the [subjective] opinion."

Possessio. "Possession" as a legal concept.

Potestas. "[Legitimate] power/[legal] control"; typically in reference to the *potestas* of the *pater familias* over the persons and property belonging to the family.

Precario. "By request."

Prior tempore potior iure. "Prior in time is greater in right."

Pro donato. *Iusta causa* for good faith possession of property acquired by a putative donee.

Pro dote. *Iusta causa* for good faith possession of property acquired by the putative recipient of a dowry

Pro emptore. *Iusta causa* for good faith possession of property acquired by a putative buyer.

Pro herede. *Iusta causa* for good faith possession of property acquired by a putative heir.

Pro legato. *Iusta causa* for good faith possession of property acquired by a putative legatee.

Pro suo. *Iusta causa* for good faith possession of property held by a putative owner.

Pro tradita erit accipienda. "[The property] will be deemed to have been delivered."

Procurator. "Procurator"; a kind of agent, typically with broad discretion and general power to manage the affairs of his principal. The agency is created by *mandatum*.

Prodigus. "Spendthrift, prodigal"; a person who has been legally so deemed.

Pupillus. "Ward."

Quaesitum est. "The question has been asked . . ."

Quasi procurator. "As if a procurator."

Receptum est. "It has been received that . . . ; the traditional rule is that . . . "

Rectius. "Better, more correct."

Rei vindicatio. "Vindication of property"; the legal proceeding by which an owner seeks to recover possession of his property that is currently in another's possession. See section "A" of Chapter IV.

Replicatio (pl. **replicationes**). "Reply" to an affirmative defense.

Replicatio rei venditae et traditae. "Reply that the property was sold and delivered."

Res. "Property; subject matter."

Res aliena. "Property of another."

Res aliena pignori data. "Property of another given in pledge."

Res cottidianae. "Everyday [legal] matters"; the title of a work ascribed to the jurist Gaius.

Res derelictae. "Abandoned property."

Res furtivae. "Stolen property."

Res judicata. "Matter that has already been adjudicated."

Res mancipi. Property of a kind that requires the formal procedure of *mancipatio* or *in iure cessio* in order for the civil law ownership to be validly transferred. *Res mancipi* included "buildings and land on Italian soil, rustic (not urban) servitudes connected with such land, slaves, and farm animals of draft and burden" (Berger, translating Gaius, Inst. 1.120). See *mancipium*.

Res nec mancipi. "Property that is not of the kind *res mancipi*."

Res nullius. Lit. "property of no one"; ownerless property.

Responsum. "Response"; typically of a jurist's opinion regarding a legal question that has been posed.

Reversio. "Return."

Reversio ad dominum. "Return to the owner."

Reversio in potestatem. "Return to the power/control [of the master or owner]."

Ridiculum. "Ridiculous."

Saltus. "Place of pasturage, pasture, grove(s)."

Senatusconsulta. "Resolutions of the Senate."

Servus furiosus. "Slave who is mad/insane."

Servitus. "Servitude."

Servitus oneris ferendi. An urban servitude that requires the servient property to "support the load" (typically a wall) on the adjacent dominant property.

Servus fugitivus. "Fugitive slave."

Servus impubes. "Slave [who is an] *impubes*."

Signum; signare. "Sign, mark, signature; to sign or mark."

Solo animo. "By means of intent alone."

Stipulatio. An enforceable promise in the form of an oral contract.

Subtilitas. "Subtlety"; in reference to a captious insistence on legal technicalities.

Superficies solo cedit. "The surface goes with the ground"; a specific instance of the more general principle defined under *accessio cedit principali*.

Superfluum. "Surplus" from the sale of secured property after the debt has been satisfied from the sale proceeds. Also called *hyperocha*.

Taberna. "Shop."

The(n)saurus. "Treasure"; in a legal context, "treasure-trove."

Tignum iunctum. "Joined timber." See *actio de tigno iuncto*.

Traditio. "Delivery."

Traditio brevi manu. "Delivery by means of a short hand"; referring to constructive delivery when the property is already held by the designated possessor.

Traditio ex iusta causa. "Delivery based on a legitimate reason."

Traditio longa manu. "Delivery by means of a long hand"; referring to a form of delivery that is effective even though there is no physical contact with the property by the transferor or his agent at the time of the transfer.

Tutor. "Guardian"; typically for minors under the age of puberty; also often for adult women in connection with legal transactions.

Usuarius. "Usuary"; a person who has the right to use another's property as the beneficiary of the personal servitude of *usus*.

Usucapio. "Usucapion, usucaption"; acquisition of ownership by prescription.

Usucapio libertatis. "Usucapion of the liberty [of ownership]"; referring to the extinguishment of an urban servitude by the servient tenant's acting in a manner inconsistent with the servitude's existence during a limitations period of non-use by the dominant tenant.

Usufructuarius. "Usufructuary"; a person who has the right to use and take the fruits of another's property as the beneficiary of the personal servitude of *usu(s)fructus*.

Usu(s)fructus. "Usufruct"; a personal servitude conferring a right to the exclusive use and fruits of another's property.

Usus. "Use"; a personal servitude conferring the right to use another's property".

Utilis. "Useful"; typically in reference to public policy or to the benefit of private litigants in specified circumstances.

Utilitas. "Utility"; typically in reference to public policy or to the benefit of private litigants in specified circumstances.

Utilitatis causa [iure singulari] receptum. "Accepted [by special rule] for the sake of *utilitas.*"

Vacua possessio. Lit. "empty possession"; referring to unencumbered or unimpeded possession.

Venire contra factum proprium non licet. "It is not permitted to come [into court] complaining of [the consequences of] one's own act."

Verius est. "It is more correct."

Veteres. "The old [jurists]"; in reference to those of the notionally pre-classical period.

Vis/vi, vi factum. "Force/by force, done with force."

Via. Lit. "Road, way"; an easement appurtenant to a dominant tenement, consisting of the right to travel over and to drive animals over a portion of the servient tenement. Cf. *iter.*

Vicinitas. "Vicinity"; in reference to the principle that praedial servitudes can only benefit properties adjacent to the servient property.

Vim vi repellere licet. "One may repel force with force."

Vir bonus. See *bonus vir.*

Vis armata. "Armed force."

Vulgo dictum, vulgo dicitur, vulgo traditum. "It is commonly said that; it is traditionally held that."